THE A-
CAREERS A

THE A–Z *of* CAREERS AND JOBS

EIGHTH EDITION

EDITED BY

Diane Burston

Acknowledgements
The editor would like to thank everyone who has helped in the compilation of this book and in particular Vivien Donald, Jean Joss, Jacqueline Murray and Pat Sheldon for their assistance with the first edition.

First published in 1984
Eighth edition 1997

Kogan Page Limited
120 Pentonville Road
London N1 9JN

British Library Cataloguing in Publication Data

A CIP record for this book is available from the British Library.

ISBN 0 7494 2431 1

Typeset by Kogan Page Ltd
Printed and bound by Clays Ltd, St Ives plc

Introduction

This book is aimed primarily at young people still at school; its intention is to give brief information about careers or jobs in which they are already interested and to suggest others that they may not have considered. It is hoped that careers officers will also find it a source of ready reference.

The information given provides a starting point. At a glance, students can see whether they have the necessary qualifications for a particular job or career and, if they wish, then take the matter further; over 330 different occupations have been included in an attempt to be comprehensive.

As far as possible, the occupations in this book are distinct and recognisable. Occupations that do not differ significantly from each other apart from place of work, such as sweet manufacture and toy manufacture, are not included. These jobs would appear under the guise of factory work.

National Vocational Qualifications (NVQs), mentioned under 'Qualifications and Training' for some occupations, are based on national standards of occupational competence and are designed to ensure that possession of a qualification is proof that the holder is capable of carrying out work to an agreed national standard.

The information is arranged alphabetically and there is also an index, providing easy access to subheadings. Some useful addresses are to be found on page 375.

Unless otherwise stated or highly unlikely, the male pronoun is intended to include the female, and vice versa.

In many cases, no formal educational qualifications are required for a job. However, it should be pointed out that in times of an over-supply of jobseekers, those with qualifications may be preferred to those without.

The starting salaries given apply at the time of writing, are generally the minimum for 1997 and, unless stated, do not include bonuses, London weighting or other allowances. In many cases people will earn more than the figure given. Salaries quoted are annual, unless stated otherwise.

National telephone dialling codes are given but local codes may differ.

An attempt has been made to include as many careers and jobs as possible; however, if there are important omissions the editor would be pleased to be informed. Information on changes in qualifications and addresses would also be welcomed.

Diane Burston, 1997

Abbreviations

A level	Advanced level (GCE)
AS level	Advanced Special level (GCE)
BTEC	Business and Technology Education Council
CAM	Communication, Advertising and Marketing Foundation
CCETSW	Central Council for Education and Training in Social Work
CQSW	Certificate of Qualification in Social Work
GCE	General Certificate of Education
GCSE	General Certificate of Secondary Education
GNVQ	General National Vocational Qualification
GSVQ	General Scottish Vocational Qualification
H grade	Higher grade (SCE)
HNC/HND	Higher National Certificate/Higher National Diploma
HTC	Higher Technical Certificate
NC/ND	National Certificate/National Diploma
NCVQ	National Council for Vocational Qualifications
NVQ	National Vocational Qualification
O level	Ordinary level (GCE)
SCE	Scottish Certificate of Education
SCOTVEC	Scottish Vocational Education Council
SNC/SND	Scottish National Certificate/Scottish National Diploma
SVQ	Scottish Vocational Qualification

Note: The Scottish equivalent of the GCSE is known by its full name – Standard grade (SCE).

Accountant

Accountants are trained to examine, interpret and plan all types of financial transaction. Those who work in accountancy firms deal with such matters as auditing, analysing, verifying and interpreting clients' accounts, advising on taxation, executorship and trusteeship, and liquidations. Accountants employed in industry and commerce or by local authorities are concerned rather with financial planning and the allocation of funds. Some accountants, after qualifying, specialise in such areas as taxation, auditing or management consultancy. They may also specialise in clients from a particular field, eg music or the theatre.

Qualifications and Training

Accountants must obtain membership of one of the many professional bodies. Minimum educational requirements are five GCSE/SCE passes to include English language and maths, two at A level or an advanced GNVQ plus at least three GCSEs or, in Scotland, three at H grade and three ordinary grades. For the Institute of Chartered Accountants in England and Wales, these must be followed by a degree in any subject or an Accountancy Foundation course. For the Institute of Chartered Accountants of Scotland all entrants must hold a degree. It is generally compulsory for students to undertake a period of practical training – of three to four years' duration – in addition to taking professional examinations before being admitted as a professional member of an Institute.

Personal Qualities

Numeracy, careful attention to detail, and a logical and analytical mind are all required, but more important are good interpersonal skills and management potential.

Starting Salary

Unqualified trainees £12,500 depending on age, educational qualifications, employer and region; newly qualified accountants £15,000–£16,000.

Further Information

The Association of Cost and Executive Accountants, 141–149 Fonthill Road, London N4 3HF; 0171 272 3925

The Chartered Association of Certified Accountants, Student Recruitment and Training, 29 Lincoln's Inn Fields, London WC2A 3EE; 0171 396 5800

The Chartered Institute of Management Accountants, 63 Portland Place, London W1N 4AB; 0171 637 2311

The Chartered Institute of Public Finance and Accountancy (CIPFA), 3 Robert Street, London WC2N 6BH; 0171 895 8823

The Institute of Chartered Accountants in England and Wales, PO Box 433, Chartered Accountants' Hall, Moorgate Place, London EC2P 2BJ; 0171 920 8100

The Institute of Chartered Accountants of Scotland, 27 Queen Street, Edinburgh EH2 1LA; 0131 225 5673

The Institute of Company Accountants, 80 Portland Place, London W1N 4DP and 40 Tyndalls Park Road, Bristol BS8 1PL; 0117 973 8261

Careers in Accountancy, Kogan Page

Account Executive*, see *Advertising

Accounting Technician

The purpose of this job is to work in support of professionally qualified accountants. Accounting technicians are involved in the day-to-day practical work of accountancy, including the preparation of information and accounts and the interpretation of computer information. Accounting technicians are widely employed in public finance, industry and commerce, and private practice. A growing number of accounting technicians provide a wide range of services direct to the public and manage their own practices.

Qualifications and Training

The Association of Accounting Technicians' (AAT) education and training scheme is open access, although candidates must demonstrate numeracy and literacy skills. The scheme, which usually takes three years part-time, is competence based and accredited at NVQ levels 2 to 4. Practical assessments are combined with relevant work experience during the training period. The three stages of the scheme are Foundation (NVQ level 2 in accounting), Intermediate (NVQ level 3 in accounting) and Technician (NVQ level 4 in accounting).

Personal Qualities
The job requires a methodical, systematic approach and the ability to work with figures. Computer skills are an advantage.

Starting Salary
With experience: £13,000 in London, £7500 to £12,500 elsewhere; fully qualified £18,000 in London, £13,000–£14,000 elsewhere.

Further Information
The Association of Accounting Technicians, 154 Clerkenwell Road, London ECIR 5AD; 0171 837 8600

'Qualifying as an Accounting Technician' (The Association of Accounting Technicians)

Actor *see Theatre*

Acting involves the interpretation of someone else's work and the communication of it to an audience. Actors and actresses are employed in the various types of theatre (commercial, subsidised, community and fringe theatre, theatre-in-education) and also in television, television and radio commercials, film and radio. Competition is keen, and because it is such a precarious profession, those entering must be prepared for long periods of unemployment.

Qualifications and Training
Most potential actors/actresses attend drama school. (The National Council for Drama Training should be consulted for information on accredited courses.) A good general education is important and some schools require GCSEs and/or A levels. Training courses at established schools usually last two or three years. Entrance is by audition and is competitive. Further experience may be gained from working in a repertory company or in fringe theatre and this may be an alternative way of entering the profession, although it is becoming increasingly difficult to enter solely by this method.

Personal Qualities

Acting requires a combination of intelligence, sensitivity and imagination, together with a good memory, determination and physical stamina.

Starting Salary

Comparatively low: minimum weekly salaries are set by theatre employers after negotiations with Equity (the actors' union) as £195 for subsidised repertory, provincial commercial £204, £225 for small-scale touring and £250 the West End. Equity have a number of different agreements for television and film work, all of which is more highly paid than stage work.

Further Information

British Actors Equity Association, Guild House, Upper St Martin's Lane, London WC2H 9EG; 0171 379 6000

National Council for Drama Training, 5 Tavistock Place, London WC1H 9SS; 0171 387 3650
(For list of accredited courses send sae.)

Careers in the Theatre, Kogan Page

Contacts (theatrical directory; The Spotlight Casting Directory, Charles House, 7 Leicester Place, London WC2H 7BP; 0171 437 7631)

Actuary

The work of an actuary largely concerns the application of mathematical probability theory, statistical techniques and the theory of compound interest to all kinds of practical problems. It is a small but influential profession, and there are good opportunities to go into management. The majority of actuaries still work in insurance but a large percentage also work as consultants, while some work in Government service, the Stock Exchange, industry or are academics. Prospects are good and there is a continuing demand for trained actuaries.

Qualifications and Training

Most trainees have a degree in maths, statistics or economics, although it is possible to enter with two A levels or three H grades in mathematical subjects, providing the grades are good. Proficiency in English, equivalent to GCSE grade C is also required. Training is on the job, often with an insurance company or firm of consultants, and is combined with part-time study for the examinations of the Institute or the Faculty of Actuaries. On average, it takes five to six years to complete all of the examinations and become a qualified actuary.

Personal Qualities

Prospective actuaries should have an aptitude for mathematics, a practical outlook and an analytical mind, as well as the ability to express themselves clearly and accurately.

Starting Salary

Actuarial students earn in the region of £13,000–£25,000, £30,000+ when qualified. London salaries are higher.

Further Information

England and Wales: Institute of Actuaries, Napier House, 4 Worcester Street, Oxford OX1 2AW; 01865 794144

Scotland: The Faculty of Actuaries, 17 Thistle Street, Edinburgh EH2 1DF; 0131 220 4555

A Head Start – Your Guide to Careers in the Actuarial Profession (available from either of the above addresses)

Acupuncturist

Acupuncture is a Chinese system of curing many symptoms and relieving pain by inserting fine needles into one or more points of the body. Acupuncture in China is also used to anaesthetise and operations are performed without use of further drugs.

Qualifications and Training

In order to apply to the British College of Acupuncture, applicants must be registered with one of the following professional bodies: General Medical Council, General Dental Council, Chartered Society of Physiotherapy, Royal College of Veterinary Surgeons, General Council and Register of Osteopaths, British Chiropractic Association, General Council and Register of Naturopaths, or be a state registered nurse, a registered general nurse, a radiographer or hold a similar qualification.

The course lasts for three years and applicants may take an advanced course lasting a further two years.

A Chinese herbal course is open to students who have graduated.

Personal Qualities

In addition to possessing the necessary medical knowledge, acupuncturists must be able to put patients at their ease and gain their confidence.

Starting Salary

Salaries vary depending on number of patients and amount charged. After qualifying, acupuncturists may practise on their own, or as they choose.

Further Information

British Acupuncture Association and Register Ltd, 34 Alderney Street, London SWIV 4EU

The British College of Acupuncture, 8 Hunter Street, London WC1N 1BN; 0171 833 8164

Working in Complementary and Alternative Medicine, Kogan Page

Administrative Management

Administrative management is about managing information through people. Information is central to all management processes. And people are the resources who use that information to add value. So administrative management is at least an element of all managers' and most professionals' jobs, whether they are employed in finance, personnel, the Arts, facilities management, purchasing, marketing or general administration. The ability of an organisation to manage its administrative operations effectively in this era dominated by information technology is often crucial to its success or even survival. This is a sector that offers potential for people to start in clerical and junior administrative jobs and to proceed to any level according to their capability and qualifications. Administrative management is a key process in all industries and throughout the public sector.

Qualifications and Training

The Institute of Administrative Management (IAM) offers a range of professional education qualifications including the certificate, diploma, advanced diploma and BA(Hons) in administrative management.

IAM qualifications are offered through colleges, universities and distance learning providers. The IAM has 12,000 members throughout the world in jobs ranging from administration officer to chief executive; 42% of members are senior executives or board directors.

Personal Qualities

Individuals who enjoy organising and who work cooperatively with other people will find satisfying opportunities in administrative management. They should be numerate and effective communicators – verbally and in writing. An aptitude for using computers will increase dramatically the number of opportunities for a career in this field.

Starting Salary

Salaries in this diverse field are very varied. Supervisory posts start at around £12,000–£15,000 per annum, depending on qualifications, experience and special expertise (eg high levels of skills in IT). Managerial grades start at around £18,000 per annum and the most senior IAM members and fellows are paid at company director levels.

Further Information

The Institute of Administrative Management, 40 Chatsworth Parade, Petts Wood, Orpington, Kent BR5 1RW; 01689 875555. Fax: 01689 870891

Advertising *see Artist*

Advertising is a very complex industry providing a wide range of openings, mostly with agencies that plan, organise and run advertising campaigns.

On behalf of their clients, advertising agencies study the product or service to be advertised and its market, then plan how it should be sold and distributed and how the media might be used to the best advantage.

Account Executive

He or she is responsible for a particular client or group of clients, interpreting the client's wishes; coordinates and supervises the work of the different creative groups within the agency, eg creatives, account planners, copy and script writers, seeks advice from other experts such as media executives, and then presents the ideas most likely to meet with the client's approval.

Account Planner

Some agencies employ full-time planners. On the marketing side they are involved in annual planning and in making longer-range plans for the future. They also may plan future campaigns for particular accounts and consider the long-term position regarding media advertising. Apart from knowledge of the activities being planned, account planners need imagination, common sense and an ability with figures.

Market Researcher

The function of market research is to provide information about the needs, likes and dislikes of the potential consumer and of the client, and to indicate how a particular product should be presented. Information is gathered by interviews, surveys and questionnaires involving considerable research and skill in the interpretation of statistics.

Media Executive
He or she provides expert advice on which medium will best suit the particular campaign – television, cinema, posters, newspapers, journals, and also negotiates for the most economical rates.

Copy and Script Writers
As their names suggest, they produce headings, text and jingles, copy for articles in journals and scripts for films and commercials. Copywriters often work closely with art editors/visualisers.

Artistic Editor/Executive
This position involves coordinating the work of the creative department, first by converting the client's original intentions into a visual form for his approval and upon which others, eg copy writers, may elaborate.

Artists
They prepare initial layouts of adverts, posters, displays and final artwork for printing. Some artists may produce their own typography, and others may work with specialists who are responsible for printing and type selection.

Qualifications and Training
There are courses in advertising and marketing that provide a useful background, but none of them is an automatic passport to a job in advertising. The Communication, Advertising and Marketing (CAM) Education Foundation runs certificate and diploma courses. The CAM certificate in communication studies takes an average of two years to complete and provides a background to the business, before specialisation is necessary, in such subjects as marketing, advertising, public relations etc. Minimum entry requirements for the certificate are passes in five GCSE/SCE subjects, two of which should be at A level or Scottish equivalent. As an alternative, BTEC/SCOTVEC national awards, ND/SND, NC/SNC in business studies or five GCSEs and at least one year's experience of full-time employment in communications are also acceptable. Business studies graduates and postgraduates or holders of diplomas in management or BTEC/SCOTVEC, HND/HNC business studies may be exempt from the certificate.

The diploma may be studied for in one year by candidates who hold the certificate; it covers international, industrial and consumer advertising and marketing. The Dorset Institute of Higher Education offers a BA degree in creative advertising.

Graduates in relevant subjects or those with BTEC/SCOTVEC

qualifications are preferred for market research positions and training is given mostly on the job, starting as a research assistant. The Market Research Society diploma is awarded to entrants with degrees and diplomas who have successfully completed courses of practical training. Creative staff who have attended a recognised college of art or have a degree in art and design are preferred.

Personal Qualities

Advertising account and media executives require the ability to lead and organise; they must be persuasive, critical, enthusiastic, confident and able to get on well with the public. They need boundless drive and stamina and considerable business acumen. Market researchers deal a lot with the public and a pleasant personality is therefore very important. They must be methodical, objective and unbiased. Creative staff require imagination and ingenuity in order to express ideas and concepts accurately and economically, emphasising the most important aspects of a product. Copy and script writers must have a flair for writing and communication.

Starting Salary

Trainees' salaries are £12,000+, but there are opportunities for experienced staff to earn very high salaries.

Further Information

Advertising Association, Abford House, 15 Wilton Road, London SW1V 1NJ; 0171 828 2771

CAM Foundation Ltd (*address as above*; 0171 828 7506)

Institute of Practitioners in Advertising, 44 Belgrave Square, London SWIX 8QS; 0171 235 7020

Careers in Marketing, Advertising and Public Relations, Kogan Page

Getting Into Advertising, The Advertising Association

How to Get On in Marketing, Kogan Page

Advocate,* see *Barrister

Aerial Erector

Aerial erectors fix aerials to roof structures along with the necessary cabling to feed equipment such as televisions, VCRs and radio receivers. With the extension of broadcasting methods and the growth of multi-channel viewing, many installers offer cable and satellite-dish installation alongside normal aerial installation. A number of businesses specialise in satellite installation as well as communication aerial installation.

Qualifications and Training

Formal qualifications are not necessary as training is often given on the job by experienced colleagues; however, formal training is given in all aspects of aerial and satellite installation through the CAI. The ability to drive is an advantage.

Personal Qualities

A head for heights plus the ability to work in a confined space are essential (aerials and the relevant cabling are sometimes installed in lofts), so too is good colour vision. As all the work takes place in customers' homes, it is necessary to be pleasant and polite.

Starting Salary

Low when training, varying according to experience and whether working in a firm. The majority of aerial installers are self-employed, sometimes working on a sub-contract basis to establish a steady income.

Further Information

Confederation of Aerial Industries Ltd (CAI), Fulton House Business Centre, Fulton Road, Wembley Park, Middlesex HA9 0TF; 0181 902 8998

Local Jobcentres and Careers Offices

Aeronautical Engineering*, see *Engineering

Agricultural Contractor

Agricultural contractors employ experienced workers and managers to provide specific help to farmers at certain times of the year. About 60 per cent of farms use contractors from time to time.

Qualifications and Training

While specific qualifications are not essential, NVQs are available in relevant subjects and these, together with certificates at national or advanced national level in agriculture or agricultural contracting, obtained at a college of agriculture, would considerably enhance chances of employment.

Personal Qualities

Agricultural contractors must have a genuine sympathy with farmers and an appreciation of their needs, combined with efficiency, reliability and a good business sense.

Starting Salary

Variable depending on whether or not the contractor is an employee or running his own concern, and the size of the operation.

Further Information

Careers, Education and Training in Agriculture and the Countryside, Warwickshire Careers Service, 10 Northgate Street, Warwick CV34 4SR

Agricultural Engineering,* see *Engineering

Agricultural Surveying,* see *Surveyor, Surveying Technician

Agriculture,* see *Farming

Ambulance Service

People employed in the ambulance service spend most of their time working with people – patients, hospital staff and members of other services. The work involves dealing with accidents and emergencies, conveying patients needing regular care to hospitals, and completing the necessary paperwork. All ambulance personnel are skilled in first aid. They work in pairs and must act as driver or attendant interchangeably.

Ambulance Care Assistants

They are mainly concerned with transporting elderly, infirm or handicapped people to hospitals or day centres. They may also do some work in hospital units.

Ambulance Technicians

They are involved with accidents and emergencies, including calls by GPs to take seriously ill people to hospital. They are able to use various types of life-saving equipment.

Ambulance Paramedics
They are technicians with additional training who are able to use more advanced forms of life-support equipment. For example, they may set up a drip or, in certain circumstances, administer drugs.

Control Room Assistants
They work in ambulance stations or central control units answering calls from GPs and the public; they keep in radio contact with ambulance crews.

Qualifications and Training

Formal educational qualifications are not required. It is necessary to hold a current British driving licence, and experience of driving heavier vehicles is useful. Physical fitness is important, since the job is physically demanding and involves heavy lifting. Recruits must complete a trial period as driver/attendant, involving non-emergency work driving minibuses, cleaning vehicles and helping out at the ambulance station. If considered suitable, they can then apply to train as fully qualified ambulance workers. Applicants must be 18 although in some areas cadet schemes are available at 16 and 17. Academic qualifications vary but four GCSEs grades A to C (SCE Standard grades 1 to 3) are an advantage.

Technicians have normally trained as care assistants first but in some cases with four GCSEs grades A to C (SCE Standard grades 1 to 3) and subjects including English, maths and a science, direct entry is possible.

Technicians take an eight-week residential course followed by 12 months' accident and emergency experience, leading to the National Ambulance Proficiency Certificate.

Paramedics must have a minimum of 12 months' experience in all aspects of ambulance work and may then qualify for a four-week intensive course.

The scope of training is being widened to increase life-saving skills.

Personal Qualities

For this work, tact and sympathy in dealing with people are needed and the ability to cope well in an emergency.

Starting Salary

At 18 or over ambulance persons (non-emergency) receive £10,648, ambulance persons (accident and emergency) £14,641, and control room assistants £9260–£10,752. London staff receive a London allowance of £1695.

Further Information

Local Department of Health
London: London Ambulance Service Headquarters, 220 Waterloo Road, London SE1 8SD; 0171 928 0333

Analyst

Analysts work in industry providing a service for research, development and production departments. They analyse the results of experiments and advise what a newly produced substance may be. An analyst may check the quality of raw materials bought in by his company and examine the quality of the company's own products.

Public analysts are employed by local authorities to examine, for example, the state of the water supply; the adequacy of the sewage treatment system; toxic and suspect materials and leachate from county landfill sites. They may also be asked to examine food from a suspect restaurant. Public analysts are frequently required to give witness on their findings in courts of law and should be familiar with the law relating to goods and services.

Qualifications and Training

A degree in chemistry, or in some instances an approved equivalent qualification, is necessary. To become a public analyst it is necessary to hold the Mastership in Chemical Analysis (MChemA), a qualification awarded by the Royal Society of Chemistry.

Personal Qualities

A meticulous care for detail and a sense of responsibility are essential.

Starting Salary

£13,000–£14,000.

Further Information

The Royal Society of Chemistry, Burlington House, Piccadilly, London W1V 0BN; 0171 437 8656
Careers with Chemistry, Royal Society of Chemistry

Ancient Monuments Inspector

These inspectors are employed by the Civil Service in the Department of the Environment to preserve ancient monuments and historic buildings. The work involves inspection generally, and particularly when conservation or restoration work is being carried out. Inspectors may also have to write reports and small guide books and occasionally attend courts of inquiry.

Qualifications and Training
A relevant degree is necessary – history or archaeology – or a non-relevant degree with a postgraduate qualification. All recruits start as assistant inspectors.

Personal Qualities
An ability to concentrate on details plus a sense of responsibility are required. A liking for being out of doors is also useful.

Starting Salary
£17,000–£25,000; more in London.

Further Information
Royal Commission for the Ancient Monuments of England, 55 Blandford Street, London W1H 3AF; 0171 208 8200

Animal Nursing Auxiliary*, see *Veterinary Nurse

Animal Technician

This is a job for people who like working with animals but are not just sentimental about them. It involves looking after the animals kept in laboratories for the purposes of medical research. By law, new medical and a wide variety of domestic and industrial products must be tested. It is the responsibility of the animal technicians, as well as observing the effects of experiments, to act as nurses to the animals, making sure that they are well cared for and that they do not suffer unnecessarily.

Qualifications and Training
Qualifications required are four GCSE passes, grades A to C (or Scottish equivalents). The subjects should include English, mathematics and biology, or two subjects in the sciences plus an interest in animal welfare. Training is in-house and trainees may work towards the diploma of the Institute of Animal Technicians. BTEC/SCOTVEC courses are available, and national and higher national certificates.

Personal Qualities
The job requires people who are good with animals and can handle them with confidence. An interest in scientific research is also an advantage. Since the job requires close observation of the animals, the ability to give careful attention to detail is important.

Starting Salary
First-year trainee, £7500–£8000.

Further Information
The Association of the British Pharmaceutical Industry, 12 Whitehall, London SW1A 2DY; 0171 930 3477

The Institute of Animal Technology, 5 South Parade, Summertown, Oxford OX2 7JL

Universities Federation for Animal Welfare (UFAW), 8 Hamilton Close, South Mimms, Potters Bar, Hertfordshire EN6 3QD; 01707 658202

Careers Working with Animals, Kogan Page

Anthropologist

Anthropologists study the development of human societies, making comparisons between different communities and cultures. This academic discipline is linked with the other social sciences and with biology. Much of the work still concerns non-industrial, 'primitive' or rural cultures, but changes brought about by contact with more sophisticated outside influences and pressures from 'modern' societies are an important aspect of study and many anthropologists undertake research in urban or industrial societies. This career involves a combination of research, teaching and finding out more about the people being studied by going to live with them over a period of time. Increasingly, anthropologists are finding employment as consultants, for instance in the development, health and humanitarian fields, and in such professions as journalism, human resource management and planning.

Qualifications and Training
A good degree in anthropology. Postgraduate study is usually required.

Personal Qualities
Those wishing to embark on this career must normally be committed to an academic way of life and be prepared to spend long spells abroad, often in basic conditions. Physical and mental stamina is

required, as well as independence and resourcefulness. Anthropologists must be prepared to work on their own for much of the time. Linguistic ability is useful.

Starting Salary
Salaries vary considerably, but £13,000–£14,000 is to be expected.

Further Information
Royal Anthropological Institute of Great Britain and Ireland, 50 Fitzroy Street, London W1P 5HS; 0171 387 0455

Antique Dealer

The buying and selling of antiques for profit entails expert knowledge of the field, combined with sound managerial and business sense. Comparatively few people make a living at this trade and many businesses are family concerns. Dealers frequently specialise in particular types of antiques and trade among themselves as well as with private buyers and sellers. Dealers may work for a large saleroom or in a small shop.

Qualifications and Training
No specific qualifications are required, although a broad artistic background may be useful. The accepted route into the business is via a job with an established antique dealer, which provides an opportunity for learning the trade.

Personal Qualities
A good memory for detail is necessary in order to acquire the expertise required, and good business acumen is also important.

Starting Salary
Salaries are generally low but may be more if secretarial skills are also offered.

Further Information
British Antique Dealers' Association, 20 Rutland Gate, London SW7 1BD; 0171 589 4128

Arboriculturist*, see *Horticulturist

Archaeological Surveying*, see *Surveyor/Surveying Technician

Archaeologist

Archaeology, building up a picture of the past, is both an art and a science; its modern practitioners use highly technical and scientific methods of discovery, analysis and identification to reconstruct and study men and women in the past from their material remains. The evidence is collected through field work, including excavations, where clues are sought in objects, their surroundings, the ground itself and remains of living things. The evidence is analysed, subjected to experiment, assessed, identified, catalogued, conserved and possibly exhibited. Archaeologists usually specialise in a particular period, technique or geographical area. Opportunities for full-time, permanent positions are limited, and competition is consequently fierce for the few jobs which are to be found in central and local government, museums and universities, independent units and trusts, as well as a variety of positions in commercial operations. Some work will take place abroad.

Qualifications and Training

A good honours degree in archaeology is necessary for a position as a qualified archaeologist. Archaeology is offered at universities both as a single and a combined course. Five GCSE/SCE passes and two A levels or three H grades are the minimum qualification for university entry (20 points). Practical experience of archaeological field work is advantageous.

A postgraduate qualification is highly recommended for work in some areas of archaeology; training in a variety of specialities is available.

The conservation of archaeological, historical and ethnographical artefacts requires a specialist training of its own. A certificate in conservation is offered by the Museums Association to people working in museums, and the Institute of Archaeology offers a diploma on a block, or day, release scheme. Degrees in conservation are also available.

Archaeological science also holds opportunities: bioarchaeology is the study of animal and plant remains – bones, teeth, grain – found on an archaeological site; materials science allows precise dating of artefacts; geoarchaeology is the study of sediments deposited on a site; forensic archaeology involves the use of archaeological techniques in police investigations.

Personal Qualities

Archaeologists need endless patience and must pay great attention to detail, have imagination and enquiring minds. They must be able to use computers, write reports, plan and administer, work as a team with other academic experts and get on well with their workforce. Languages are useful as is an ability to negotiate, and talent in drawing or photography. Archaeologists should be healthy and willing to work in all conditions, situations and environments.

Starting Salary
£11,000–£13,000 for salaried posts. Less for short contracts.

Further Information

Council for British Archaeology, Bowes Morrell House, 111 Walmgate, York YO1 2UA; 01904 671417

Institute of Archaeology, University College London, Gower Street, London WC1H 6BT; 0171 387 7050

The Museums Association, 42 Clerkenwell Close, London EC1R 0AT; 0171 608 2933

Architect

Architecture is a profession requiring the practical combination of imaginative design with scientific and technological principles, to produce plans for new buildings and for the extension, or renovation, of those already existing. In the first instance conceptual design is based on information supplied by the client as to the function of the building, the proposed budget and site. When the design is agreed, working drawings are produced for the builder which show dimensions and materials and how everything will be put together. On large jobs there will be a team of architects working with engineers and other specialists and it may take months to prepare all the drawings and schedules. Alternatively, very small jobs take only a few weeks. After the contract documents have been prepared and a builder selected, work begins on site. The architect visits frequently as the building goes up. This can involve tramping around in boots and a hard hat and climbing up and down ladders, as well as taking the chair at site meetings.

There are opportunities for employment in private practice, with local authorities, central government and in some industrial organisations.

Qualifications and Training
Candidates should have passes in at least two subjects at A level or one A level and two AS levels together with passes in at least five other subjects at GCSE level. Subjects should be drawn from academic fields of study and include: maths, English language and a separate science (physics or chemistry) or a double certification in science.

Training takes a minimum of seven years, but only five of those are spent at a school of architecture. After a three-year degree course, students spend a year in an architect's office. Students often work abroad during this year or work in other parts of the building industry. Another two years' further study to obtain a diploma or higher degree is followed by another year of working in an office, ending with a professional practice exam to become registered as an architect and a full member of the Royal Institute of British Architects (while studying it is possible to be a student member). Registration with the Architects' Registration Council of the United Kingdom is required in order to use the title architect in business. Part-time training is an alternative which is offered by a few schools for students already working in an architect's office on a day-release basis.

Personal Qualities

Architects must have artistic ability, be imaginative but at the same time able to understand and apply technical information; adopt a practical approach to their work and be able to communicate their ideas and instructions to a variety of people. Business acumen, a professional approach, discretion and willingness to conform to a strict code of practice and professional conduct are very important.

Starting Salary

While completing their two years' practical training architectural students may expect to earn between £10,000 and £15,000; when fully registered this will increase to about £16,000, and thereafter will be dependent upon position, experience and employer, £23,956 being the average.

Further Information

The Architects Registration Council of the United Kingdom, 73 Hallam Street, London W1N 6EE; 0171 580 5861

Royal Incorporation of Architects in Scotland, 15 Rutland Square, Edinburgh EH1 2BE; 0131 229 7545/7205

Royal Institute of British Architects, Public Information Line, 66 Portland Place, London W1N 4AD; 0891 234 400

Careers in Architecture, Kogan Page

Architectural Technologist

Architectural technologists work alongside architects and other professionals as an essential part of the building design and construction team. The architectural technologist is concerned primarily with the science of architecture and, as such, could be involved in: project management, design presentations, submissions and negotiations to gain statutory approvals, materials selection and specification, coordinating the work of other professionals, contract administration, inspection and certification of construction and application of CAD techniques.

Qualifications and Training

Four GCSEs to include maths, a science and a subject showing the use of English or a national certificate (diploma) in building studies, or GCE A levels or GNVQ advanced level in construction and the built environment, to study BTEC/SCOTVEC or university degree courses leading to associate membership of the British Institute of Architectural Technologists.

Personal Qualities

Architectural technologists should be able to work both as part of a team and on their own, unsupervised. Attention to detail is necessary and the ability to take account of other professionals' needs.

Starting Salary

Junior technicians at 18 with a national certificate, £7000–£9000; qualified technologists at 24 with three years' experience, £12,000–£13,500; senior technologists at 30 with appropriate educational qualifications and ten years' experience, £18,000.

Further Information

British Institute of Architectural Technologists (BIAT), 397 City Road, London EC1V 1NE; 0171 278 2206

Archivist

Archivists preserve the records of the past, in the form of all types of documents; contemporary records also include microfilm, tape recordings etc. They take charge of the documents in national or local collections, which may be publicly or privately owned. Some industrial and commercial concerns also employ archivists. Their job includes the study and selection of material, and it is the responsibility of the archivist to see that documents are handled correctly and preserved against decay. They also take charge of indexing and cataloguing and give help and advice to scholars and students using the collections.

Qualifications and Training
This is a small profession, requiring a strong academic background. Entrants should have a good degree, with an interest in history, and preferably some knowledge of Latin. The recognised qualification is a postgraduate diploma in archive studies or administration. This can be taken as a one-year full-time course or a two-year part-time course.

Personal Qualities
Meticulous attention to detail is very important; archivists should also possess practical ability, since the work requires such skills in the physical care of the records.

Starting Salary
£11,500+.

Further Information
Society of Archivists, Information House, 20–24 Old Street, London EC1V 9AP; 0171 253 5087

Army

The Army is the largest of the three armed forces and offers a wide range of opportunities to both men and women, both in the UK and abroad. Regiments and corps provide opportunities in the Armoured Corps, Royal Artillery, Royal Engineers, Royal Signals, Infantry, Army Air Corps, Royal Logistics Corps, Military Police, in Pay and Administration, teaching, catering and for qualified doctors, dentists, vets, lawyers and chaplains.

Qualifications and Training

Officers
There are two main types of commission: a regular commission (up to the age of 55) and a short service commission (three to eight years). The minimum entry qualification is five passes at GCSE (grade A, B or C) to include English and mathematics. Applicants for a regular commission must have two passes at A level.

Sponsorship
Cadetships and bursaries are available for those studying for a recognised first degree. All successful applicants complete 11 months' officer training at the Royal Military Academy, Sandhurst.

Soldiers and Servicewomen
Single entry from age 16 to 25; some apprentice vacancies are also available. Recruits enlist usually on an open engagement by which they agree to serve for 22 years, although it is possible to leave after a minimum of 3 years and 3 months' service over the age of 18, provided one year's notice is given.

Personal Qualities
Applicants must be British or Commonwealth citizens, born of British or Commonwealth parents and have been resident in the UK for the past five years. All candidates must be medically fit, intelligent, have the ability to work in a team and show dedication, courage, patriotism and a sense of responsibility.

Starting Salary
Soldiers: 16–17 £5720, 17–17½ £6939, 17½ and over £9180. Officers: £19,340.

Further Information
Officer entry: write for an information pack to:
Officer Entry, Freepost 4335, Department 0253, Bristol BS1 3YX
Local Army Career Information Offices.

Artist *see Advertising, Interior Decorator, Interior Designer*

Only the very few are able to earn a living solely by the sale to clients of original work. Many more artists work as designers in advertising, industry and publishing, the latter also offering opportunities for illustrators particularly for jackets and children's books, or teach art in a school or college. Design work includes graphic design concerned with display, lettering, packaging – all aspects of visual communication; fashion and textile design; environmental design – office and shop interiors as well as some museums and galleries; interior design; and product design – the appearance of equipment such as televisions, cars and also more scientific apparatus.

There are limited opportunities for work as a community artist, community arts officer (encouraging art in the community) and artist in residence.

Qualifications and Training
For the majority of artists academic qualifications are necessary, ranging from foundation courses for 16 year olds with some GCSEs or equivalents and lasting two years, to one-year courses for older

students with at least five GCSEs or equivalents and one A level, and degree courses requiring at least five GCSE passes with two A levels or three H grades. There are BTEC/SCOTVEC courses available too, providing both for general and specific qualifications (eg fashion design). Teachers in maintained schools require appropriate teaching qualifications.

Personal Qualities

Qualities vary according to the work undertaken. Creativity, talent and imagination are all important, as well as enthusiasm and, in some cases, the ability to work as part of a team and to meet deadlines.

Starting Salary

Designers £11,000–£12,000 and teachers a minimum of £13,350.

Further Information

Art and Design: ADAR Handbook, ADAR, Penn House, 9 Broad Street, Hereford HR4 9AP; 01432 266653

Careers in Art and Design, Kogan Page

Arts Administration

This is the administration and management of theatres, orchestras, opera houses, ballet companies and arts centres. The Arts Council, responsible for the promotion of art throughout the country, has its own administrative staff. The British Council, responsible for displaying British arts abroad, also employs a small number of staff.

Qualifications and Training

Experience is often more important than formal educational qualifications although a good general education is expected. This applies also to courses in administration sponsored by the Arts Council.

The examinations of the Institute of Chartered Secretaries and Administrators are at three levels. To enter the first level, the Foundation Programme, specific academic requirements are not necessary. This level must be completed before going on to the Pre-professional Programme and the Professional Programme. Graduates or equivalent have certain exemptions.

Personal Qualities

The ability to communicate and to get on with people is vital. Practical administrative and organisational skills are also required.

Starting Salary
£11,000+ as an assistant.

Further Information
The Arts Council, 14 Great Peter Street, London SW1P 3NQ; 0171 333 0100

Art Therapist

Art therapy is used as a treatment for psychological and emotional disorders. Drawing, painting, modelling and sculpture are among the creative activities employed. Most art therapists work in hospitals, some in special schools and child guidance clinics and some in prisons, detention centres and community homes. As most posts are part time, full-time therapists usually work for more than one institution within an area.

Qualifications and Training
A degree in art or design followed by a postgraduate course is the recommended training. The postgraduate qualification is usually a two-year full-time course, or a three-year part-time course.

Personal Qualities
Art therapists should have an interest in teaching and the ability to apply art in a practical way, together with a great deal of patience. A calm disposition is also an asset, as well as one year's relevant work experience.

Starting Salary
Salaries vary greatly according to the place of employment. Therapists employed by the National Health Service earn from approximately £13,900 to £20,550.

Further Information
The British Association of Art Therapists, 11a Richmond Road, Brighton, East Sussex BN2 3RL (*an information folder costs £5; please send sae for list*)
Careers in Art and Design, Kogan Page

Astronomer

Astronomers study the sun, planets, stars, galaxies and other objects in the sky analysing the radio, infrared, optical, ultraviolet, X- and γ-radiations they emit to find out how they work. Some of these radiations do not penetrate the earth's atmosphere and so observations by satellite are necessary as well as from the ground. Modern astronomical detectors are usually based on electronic methods and give results which can be analysed by computer.

Qualifications and Training

To become a research astronomer, a good degree in physics or mathematics is necessary (some universities offer such courses with astronomy or astrophysics) followed by a doctorate. Various grants are available to support students during their three-year doctoral courses.

Astronomy-related careers at an engineering or technical level are also open to those with skills in applied physics, electronics, computer hardware and software, optics and mechanical engineering. Direct entry with A level or Scottish highers is now unusual and recruits should expect to obtain their initial technical training, leading to an HNC, outside astronomy.

Personal Qualities

Astronomers need curiosity and imagination; they must be able to make logical deductions from the available observations. Working long and unusual hours and travelling to remote observatories may also be involved.

Starting Salary

Post-doctoral salaries start at around £13,000, technical salaries after training at around £11,500.

Further Information

Royal Astronomical Society, Burlington House, Piccadilly, London W1V 0NL; 0171 734 4582

Royal Greenwich Observatory, Madingley Road, Cambridge CB3 0EZ; 01223 374000

Auctioneer *see Estate Agent, Valuer*

The auctioneer's work involves the sale, by auction, of property of all kinds, including all types of buildings (eg houses, farms and estates), livestock, and goods such as furniture, antiques, paintings, glass, toys, carpets and china. The work also entails valuations for various purposes, including investment, insurance etc.

Qualifications and Training

Auctioneers' work involves the valuation of land and property, and for this reason surveying qualifications are necessary.

There are two components to qualifying as a chartered surveyor. First you must successfully complete a Royal Institution of Chartered Surveyors (RICS) accredited degree or diploma and second a period of practical training known as the Assessment of Professional Competence (APC).

Postgraduate conversion courses are also available; full-time one year and part-time two years.

Personal Qualities

The ability to pay attention to detail is an important quality for this job, together with a practical and astute mentality and an aptitude for figures. In fine art auctioneering, a certain flair and the ability to distinguish a fake from the genuine article are desirable.

Starting Salary

While qualifying, salaries are in the region of £10,000 for trainees with A levels to £13,000–£14,000 for graduates with a relevant degree. Once fully qualified, salaries can be very high, particularly in London.

Further Information

ISVA (The Incorporated Society of Valuers and Auctioneers), 3 Cadogan Gate, London SW1X 0AS; 0171 235 2282

The Institute of Revenues, Rating and Valuation, 41 Doughty Street, London WC1N 2LF; 0171 831 3505

The Royal Institution of Chartered Surveyors, 12 Great George Street, London SW1P 3AD; 0171 222 7000

Audio Assistant*, see *Broadcasting

Audiology Technician

They carry out tests to assess the presence, nature and extent of a hearing loss, using complex and advanced techniques. They take aural impressions for individual moulded ear inserts, fit and instruct the patients on how to use their hearing aids and review their progress.

Qualifications and Training

Four GCSEs of at least C grade or their equivalents are needed in English, mathematics, physics and another science. Training involves two years of combined theory and practice while in employment, leading to a BTEC qualification in medical physics and physiological measurement or NVQ equivalent.

Personal Qualities

Candidates must be patient, have clear speaking voices and have the ability to get on with people.

Starting Salary

Trainee £6693–£8179. Once qualified: depending on grade £9064–£25,908.

Further Information

British Society of Audiology, 80 Brighton Road, Reading RG6 1PS; 0118 966 0622

Society of Hearing Aid Audiologists, Bridle Croft, Burgh Heath Road, Epsom KT17 4LF; 01372 725348

Auditor*, see *Accountant

B

Bacteriologist

Some bacteriologists work in research; for example, the details of the structure and development of a bacterium may be used to develop new drugs, and the testing of the new drugs for cancer and other diseases may produce information about how cells work. Much of the work is likely to be routine examination of specimens and meticulous record keeping. There are also opportunities in the National Health Service, the Blood Transfusion Service and public health laboratories as well as in the pharmaceutical, food, brewing, wool, cotton, dairy and leather industries which employ biological scientists and technicians on research work and production.

Other openings, at home and overseas, occur from time to time in museums, technical libraries, agriculture and education.

Qualifications and Training

For research posts a good honours or preferably a higher degree is required.

Degree entry requirements are two or three A level passes in biology, chemistry and another science or maths. (Usually GCSE or equivalent standard in maths and physics is required.)

Technicians may enter at a variety of levels and there is a wide range of courses available depending on the qualifications already obtained. The usual course entry requirements are three or four GCSEs or equivalent. Subjects preferred are chemistry, biology, maths and a subject showing the use of English.

Personal Qualities

Biological scientists and technicians need to be patient, methodical and accurate. Details must be checked and experiments repeated to ensure absolute accuracy; the results must then be expressed clearly and concisely, verbally and in writing.

Starting Salary
Salaries vary according to the nature of employment and the level of responsibility. Graduates earn from £11,500–£15,000; technicians start at £5000+ at 16.

Further Information
Local Careers Offices

Baker

The baking trainee can learn the skills involved in the production of a wide variety of bread and confectionery goods. Master bakers have traditionally provided, and still continue to provide, an ideal environment in which to acquire craft skills, perhaps with a view to eventually setting up one's own business. Although hours of work can be unsocial (shifts or early starts), the rewards can include tremendous job satisfaction.

Baking trainees can also enter the industry by working for a supermarket in an in-store bakery or at a large manufacturing plant bakery.

In-store bakeries have seen a prolific growth over recent years. Plant bakeries can teach mass-production techniques and knowledge of operating highly sophisticated, though usually automated, equipment.

Many organisations employ research and quality control staff; normally specific qualifications will be required. Local bakery colleges will be able to give more information about exact requirements.

Both large and small firms often operate schemes by which trainees can attend their local bakery college and/or train in the workplace for National Vocational Qualifications. Modern apprenticeships are available in craft baking and bakery service.

Qualifications and Training
No formal educational qualifications are required to enter the trade and entrants may train in preparation for NVQs in craft baking at levels 2 and 3 awarded by City and Guilds or HAB.

Bakery colleges provide a wide variety of other courses, which can be studied on a full- or part-time basis. They include, for example, advanced confectionery and decorating skills. Plant bakers would normally use the NVQs in food and drink (manufacturing operations), awarded by C&G/FDQC.

Advanced bakery management and science-based courses are available from BTEC.

Candidates wishing to pursue a BTEC or degree course should enquire from their local college about the entrance requirements; these are often quite flexible. Details of both modern apprenticeships and colleges that provide bakery courses can be obtained by writing to the National Association of Master Bakers.

Personal Qualities
Willingness to learn the craft and the ability to work in a team, with an above-average concern for cleanliness and hygiene, are required.

Starting Salary
Low at 16, when qualified £150 per week, or higher depending on experience, responsibility, region and overtime.

Further Information
National Association of Master Bakers, 21 Baldock Street, Ware, Hertfordshire SG12 9DH; 01920 468061

Ballet*, see *Dancing

Banking

Banks provide a delivery point for financial services. The most obvious side of banking is the high street branches but other work areas in banking include: international, the financing of foreign trade and the provision of a complete overseas banking service for UK customers; corporate finance, the area of banking that deals with the requirements of large companies; human resources, recruitment, training and staff development; insurance; computer services; selling and marketing, promoting banking services; training; and working in the trust division, when the bank has been appointed as executor or joint executor of a will.

The High Street or Clearing Banks
These banks provide a complete financial service for their customers. This includes maintaining customers' accounts, making payments, arranging personal loans and mortgages. They also undertake the safe custody of valuables and act as executors and trustees of wills. Many of the careers in banking are in the high street, or clearing banks. The work involves: general office work, such as dealing with telephone enquiries, learning to use the mechanised accounting systems and computer terminals, and dealing with standing orders; cashier work

at the counter, and foreign and securities work. The latter includes the buying and selling of currency, import–export documentation and handling travellers' cheques. Marketing and selling skills are also required. Specialisation may take place in areas such as investment, a computer centre, an international division, personnel and marketing. To work in a British bank abroad, or for an overseas bank in London, requires specialisation in international business, finance, and development projects. The ability to speak one or more other languages is very useful.

The Bank of England

The banker to the government in this country is the Bank of England. It is also concerned with the financial structure of Great Britain and with other banks in the country as well as operating accounts for overseas central banks. The Bank of England is responsible for the printing, issue and withdrawal of British banknotes and it also controls interest rates and raises short-term government finance. The monitoring of economic developments at home and abroad provides information for the Bank, the Treasury and other government departments. It does not offer banking facilities to the general public. Specialists such as economists, statisticians and librarians are recruited in addition to other banking staff.

Investment Banks

These establishments do some general banking but specialise in financing international tradc, raising capital, takeovers and mergers. The work in merchant banks includes export credit, leasing and special credits, and in addition, their expertise is in corporate finance and investment which includes the management of pension funds and unit trusts.

Qualifications and Training

Each bank has different entry points but there are four main categories: standard, accelerated, graduate and secretarial. For standard entry banks ask for a range of GCSE grades A–C and sometimes for A levels; for accelerated entry candidates must have a minimum of two A levels or a BTEC national diploma in business and finance or GNVQ advanced. Those who join as accelerated entry candidates follow a structured training programme leading to senior clerk status. Graduate training schemes are designed for those with the potential to reach management. There are fewer vacancies for secretaries now but for those vacancies that are available, candidates need a range of GCSEs grades A–C, a typing speed of 40wpm and good English grammar and punctuation.

In Scotland the Chartered Institute of Bankers in Scotland is a separate body whose first level qualification is the certificate in financial services which requires no previous qualifications for entry. Students completing the certificate can then progress to the associateship and membership examinations.

Entry to investment banks has traditionally been by personal introduction and it is only comparatively recently that they have recruited more widely. The number of openings is small and entrants are usually graduates in accountancy, law or business studies, or people with previous experience.

Personal Qualities

Accuracy, integrity, good powers of concentration and a clear mind are essential for success in a banking career. It is important to be able to get on with people and to work as a member of a team.

Starting Salary

New entrants are paid from £5675–£6500 at age 16, to over £14,000 for someone at the top of the clerical scale. An assistant manager earns £14,500–£21,500 a year. Thereafter salaries are dependent on the job and performance of the individual. Banks operate a job evaluation salary structure and promotion is on a merit basis. Extra allowances are paid to staff serving in London and some other towns and cities.

Further Information

London Investment Banking Association (LIBA), 6 Frederick's Place, London EC2R 8BT; 0171 796 3606

The Chartered Institute of Bankers, 90 Bishopsgate, London EC2N 4AS; 0171 444 7115
(*Information about membership of the Institute, qualifications, college courses*)

The Chartered Institute of Bankers in Scotland, 19 Rutland Square, Edinburgh EH1 2DE; 0131 229 9869

Careers in Banking and Finance, Kogan Page

Barrister

The services of a barrister are required by solicitors who deal with the clients and then 'brief' the barrister. Barristers plead counsel in the higher courts and may also appear in the lower courts where they usually begin their careers. They give specialised advice on the law and may advertise their services to the public. Some barristers are employed in the Army Legal Services giving advice on all aspects of service and civil law which may affect the Army.

In Scotland, advocates are the equivalent of barristers.

Qualifications and Training

Full details of qualifications required for admission are available from the General Council of the Bar, but generally students are expected to hold a UK law degree with second class honours or better, or a non-law degree at the same standard plus a pass in a special one-year course known as the Common Professional Examination.

Every intending barrister must join one of the four Inns of Court and complete the necessary dining terms before Call.

Students intending to practise must also attend the one-year full-time vocational course. From 1997 a number of institutions will offer this course (list available from the Bar Council). Students' successful completion of the course will be assessed in the practical work, and in tests and examinations carried out during the year. Success in this is followed by Call and one-year pupillage under the personal instruction and guidance of a barrister. Pupillage may involve researching relevant details of a case, setting them out in detail and drafting documents. During the first six months' pupillage pupils may attend court but may not accept briefs.

After completing pupillage a barrister has to find a 'seat' in an existing set of barristers' chambers. Some may choose to work as employed barristers and enter the Civil Service, local government or commerce and industry. About 15 years after being established at the Bar a barrister may apply for a 'patent' as a Queen's Counsel. Although 'taking silk' (as it is known) is usual (but not obligatory) if a barrister wishes to become a high court judge, it can have financial penalties and some barristers stay 'juniors' throughout their careers at the Bar.

In Scotland, advocates must be admitted to the Faculty of Advocates usually by holding a degree in law. They must also take a course leading to the diploma in legal practice from a Scottish university. If intending to practise in court, it is necessary to serve 21 months' apprenticeship in a solicitor's office followed by nine months in unpaid pupillage to a practising member of the Faculty and pass the Faculty examination in evidence, pleading and practice.

All advocates practise from the Advocates Library in Edinburgh. Each advocate is assigned to one of ten clerks.

Personal Qualities

Since the work is confidential, an intending barrister needs to be trustworthy and discreet. An excellent command of the English language which ensures the meticulous understanding and use of words is essential. It will be necessary to understand and interpret complex legal wording in clear basic English. Barristers must understand and talk knowledgeably about technical matters in order to be able to cross-examine the most expert witness, for example, on complex aspects of technology. It is also useful if barristers can put on a 'good performance' in court and possess certain theatrical qualities.

Starting Salary
Barristers' earnings relate to the amount and type of their work, their reputation, and, if they share chambers, the apportionment and value of briefs. Barristers may find it a struggle to make a living at the beginning of their profession, but the rewards for those who succeed can be high. In 1997 there is a surplus of barristers.

Further Information
Directorate of Army Legal Services (ALSI), Ministry of Defence, AGC Centre, Worthy Down, Winchester SO21 2RG
Faculty of Advocates; The Clerk of Faculty, Advocates Library, Parliament House, 11 Parliament Square, Edinburgh EH1 1RF; 0131 226 5071
General Council of the Bar, 2/3 Cursitor Street, London EC4A 1NE; 0171 440 4000
Careers in the Law, Kogan Page

Barrister's Clerk

The barrister's clerk is the administrator or, more appropriately nowadays, manager of the business chambers. He decides which briefs to accept, which of the barristers in the chamber to give them to, and he then negotiates the fees with the solicitor. Junior clerks run errands and make tea. The accounts, barristers' appointment books, as well as the efficient day-to-day running of the office are all part of the job of an experienced clerk.

Qualifications and Training
The necessary qualifications are four GCSEs, grades A to C, to include maths and English. Training is on the job and juniors can apply through the Institute to attend a two-year part-time BTEC national certificate course studying: organisation, finance, management, law, marketing and chambers administration. On obtaining the certificate juniors may apply after five years' service for qualified membership of the Institute of Barristers' Clerks.

The Bar in Scotland is divided into ten 'stables', each of which is served by an Advocates' Clerk and a deputy clerk employed by Faculty Services Ltd. Training is provided in service. The job of advocates' clerk is very similar to that of barrister's clerk in England and Wales. Their rates of pay are linked to the Civil Service scale on a level which roughly relates to a comparable post within the courts' administration. The ten clerks have clerical and secretarial staff back-up.

Personal Qualities

In order to organise efficient chambers and the barristers who work from them, a barrister's clerk requires an orderly mind, the ability to work in a team, and to get on with the general public. A good command of written and spoken English, and an appreciation of the necessity for absolute confidentiality at all times are vital to success in this career.

Starting Salary

£7000–£8000. Juniors with two or three years' experience receive £10,000–£15,000, going up to £25,000 for very experienced juniors. Senior clerks may earn £60,000–£75,000 plus a performance-related bonus. Senior clerks were traditionally paid a fee which was a percentage of the barrister's own earnings. Some are still paid in this way and the fee is usually around 5 per cent.

Further Information

Institute of Barristers' Clerks, 4a Essex Court, Temple, London EC4Y 9AJ; 0171 353 2699

Faculty Services Ltd, Advocates Library, Parliament House, 11 Parliament Square, Edinburgh EH1 1RF; 0131 226 5071

Careers in the Law, Kogan Page

Beautician

The beautician is usually either a beauty therapist (who may also be a manicurist) or a sales consultant.

Beauty Therapist

They give treatments ranging from facials, make-up, manicuring and body treatments to electric depilation and waxing (removal of superfluous hair), and the treatment of some skin conditions such as open pores. A fully qualified therapist is capable of using various types of electrical apparatus. Therapists must know when to deal personally with skin complaints and when to refer a client to a doctor. It is usual to treat about eight clients a day in a treatment salon which may be run by a cosmetic firm, an owner-manageress, or occasionally as part of a hairdressing establishment.

Sales Consultant Beautician

They work in the perfumery departments of some large stores, in luxury hotels at home and overseas, on the big liners and at airports. They sell and promote their firm's products, answer questions from potential buyers on skin care and make-up, and may occasionally give talks at schools and colleges or to women's organisations. Some sales consultants travel for their companies at home and abroad.

Hairdresser/Beautician
The double qualification gives greater scope for employment, and some may work as make-up artists in radio or television. Some progressive psychiatric hospitals employ hairdressers/beauticians in rehabilitation centres and work of this nature plays an important part in treatment and recovery programmes. See *Hairdresser*.

Qualifications and Training

Educational qualifications vary and formal academic qualifications are not always required. However, three GCSEs are needed to take a number of courses. City and Guilds and BTEC offer awards. NVQs are available in beauty therapy, levels 1, 2 and 3. Private schools run courses leading to the award of their own diplomas to candidates who are usually over 18 years old. Most good courses last from five to six months although some are longer. Courses (lasting a few weeks) for sales consultants are usually at schools attached to cosmetic houses, some of which demand a premium which may be repayable after a period of working for the firm. The minimum age is usually 21 and experience in selling is required.

Personal Qualities

A friendly but confident manner combined with a liking for women of all ages, tact and courtesy, good health and a good skin, a smart and well-groomed appearance and stamina for a job which involves much standing are all important.

Starting Salary

Trainee beauty therapists' earnings are low and later dependent upon the number of clients; consultants from £7500 upwards plus commission on sales.

Further Information

Local Job Centres and Careers Offices
Careers in Hairdressing and Beauty Therapy, Kogan Page

Biochemist

Biochemistry is the study of chemical substances and processes which occur in living cells and tissues. Because they practise a practical science most biochemists work in laboratories. However, some make their careers in education, or industry where there are opportunities in brewing, food technology, forestry, agriculture, dietetics, pharmaceuticals management and planning.

Many biochemists are employed in hospitals where they manage and develop the service and carry out research into disease. Pharmaceutical firms also employ biochemists who are concerned with the development of new drugs and their effects on diseases and patients.

Qualified biochemists are employed too in research institutions such as the Medical Research Council, the National Institute for Medical Research and the Agricultural and Food Research Council, as well as some funded by charities such as the Imperial Cancer Research Fund (ICRF).

Laboratory Technician

Universities, institutes of higher education, hospitals and industry employ technicians to support the work of biochemists in teaching and research. Technicians are either employed straight from school, in which case they are encouraged to continue their specialist education part time, or they may be recruited at graduate level.

Qualifications and Training

Most professional biochemists are graduates, usually with an honours degree. Those working in research often have a higher degree. In addition to a degree, entrance qualifications include A level/H grade passes in chemistry and one or two others in biology, maths or physics.

Laboratory technicians and assistants work part-time for BTEC higher certificates or HNCs in appropriate subjects. Employers prefer to engage people with GCSE grade A to C or A level passes in maths and science subjects because these qualifications usually gain exemptions from parts of BTEC courses. Because the routine laboratory work is highly automated, a knowledge of the latest computer and automated systems is most useful.

Personal Qualities

The ability to work in a small or large team, patience, accuracy and powers of concentration are the prerequisites of the successful biochemist. Meticulous care of plants and other organisms, and sometimes the sympathetic and careful handling of laboratory animals, are required.

Starting Salary

Salaries vary with the type of employment and responsibility involved. Graduates start at £12,500–£15,000 and technicians at age 16 from £5500+. Additional graduate qualifications usually lead to positions of greater responsibility with commensurately higher salaries.

Further Information

Association of Clinical Biochemists, 2 Carlton House Terrace, London SW1Y 5AF; 0171 930 3333

The Education Officer, The Biochemical Society, 59 Portland Place, London W1N 3AJ; 0171 580 5530

The BioIndustry Association, 14–15 Belgrave Square, London SW1X 8PS; 0171 245 9911

'A Career for Scientists in Clinical Biochemistry' (Association of Clinical Biochemists)

'Careers Wallcharts' (The Biochemical Society)

Biologist*, see *Biochemist, Biomedical Scientist, Biotechnologist

Biomedical Scientist

Biomedical scientists (including medical laboratory scientific officers in the NHS) investigate specimens of body fluids and tissues, and play an important role in the diagnosis and treatment of diseases. Most are employed in the laboratories of hospitals, in the pathology department, but many also work for the blood transfusion service, in public health laboratories, for veterinary establishments, universities, and pharmaceutical and other manufacturing companies. There are opportunities to assist in research and to teach. There is strong competition among graduates wanting to enter this profession as trainees.

Qualifications and Training

The profession has all graduate entry. A guide to courses can be obtained from the Institute of Biomedical Science. Trainees in the National Health Service and related bodies have to proceed to state registration and need a degree to do so.

Personal Qualities

Biomedical scientists must be able to work quickly, accurately and methodically. Complicated and new equipment must be used, so technical as well as scientific ability is needed.

Starting Salary

£6918–£9064 depending on age and qualifications.

Further Information

Institute of Biomedical Science, 12 Coldbath Square, London EC1R 5HL; 0171 636 8192

Biotechnologist

Biotechnology is the application of living organisms and biological systems to industrial processes. Various aspects of biological science are involved – biochemistry, microbiology and genetics. At present the main industrial areas in which biotechnologists are employed are fermentation, waste systems, antibiotic production and animal foodstuffs.

Qualifications and Training

Degree entry requirements are a minimum of five GCSEs including maths, plus three A levels to include chemistry and two other sciences. (In Scotland four SCE H grades are needed to include chemistry, and Standard grade maths.)

Personal Qualities

Those employed in biotechnology need a high degree of accuracy, thoroughness and the ability to check and recheck details.

Starting Salary

£11,500–£15,000 for graduates.

Further Information

The Education Officer, The Biochemical Society, 59 Portland Place, London W1N 3AJ; 0171 580 5530

The BioIndustry Association, 14–15 Belgrave Square, London SW1X 8PS; 0171 245 9911

Institute of Biology, 20–22 Queensberry Place, London SW7 2DZ; 0171 581 8333 (*Please enclose an sae.*)

Blacksmith

Traditionally, the blacksmith had his forge in a village, shod horses and produced iron work and agricultural machinery. As well as using the traditional hand methods, nowadays many blacksmiths make use of modern equipment – power presses and hammers, oxy-acetylene and electric arc lamps. Blacksmiths not only work in forges, some are also employed in industry making articles that still must be produced by hand.

Qualifications and Training

Formal qualifications are not necessary. Herefordshire College of Technology runs full- and part-time courses. These must be paid for privately or by the local authority.

Farrier

Farriers practise the age-old craft of shoeing horses and ponies. They examine the hooves and diagnose the requirements of the animal based upon the conditions in which it will have to work, or any physical defects it may have that need correction.

As well as making shoes and nails by hand, farriers very often make their own tools and may also carry out blacksmithing work such as agricultural repairs, welding or specialist wrought iron work in a forge. Farriers may also travel to their customers, taking their equipment with them.

Qualifications and Training

To practise as a farrier it is necessary to be registered with the Farriers Registration Council. Registration is possible after completion of a four-year apprenticeship with an approved training farrier and after passing the diploma examination of the Worshipful Company of Farriers (DWCF).

To enter an apprenticeship applicants must have a minimum of four GCSE passes at grade D which must include English language.

Personal Qualities

Blacksmiths should have stamina, an eye for design and some knowledge of structural engineering. Farriers must be physically strong and practical and have a true interest in horses.

Starting Salary

Apprentices' wages are variable depending upon the conditions of the apprenticeship. Many qualified blacksmiths are self-employed and their salary depends upon skill and the amount of work undertaken.

Further Information

The Farriers Registration Council, Sefton House, Adam Court, Newark Road, Peterborough PE1 5PP; 01733 319911 ('Guide to Apprenticeships in Farriery' and current list of approved training farriers)

Herefordshire College of Technology, Folly Lane, Hereford HR1 1LS; 01432 352235

National Association of Farriers, Blacksmiths and Agricultural Engineers, Avenue R, Seventh Street, NAC, Stoneleigh, Kenilworth CV8 2LG; 01203 696595

The Worshipful Company of Blacksmiths, The Clerk, 27 Cheyne Walk, Grange Park, London N21 1DB; 0181 364 1522

Boat Builder

Boat building and boat repairing are an important part of the marine industry in the UK, which also covers such activities as marine engineering, electronics, equipment manufacture, chandlery, sail making etc. Boat building, as distinct from ship building, involves work on leisure and pleasure craft such as yachts, dinghies, powerboats, inflatables, and some fishing craft, and some companies also build to MoD specifications. The materials used in boat building are largely FRP (fibre reinforced plastic) and wood, with other materials such as steel and ferro-cement used by specialist companies.

Depending on the size and type of company, the boat builder/ repairer can be involved in the design and outfitting specifications with the customer.

Qualifications and Training

The British Marine Industries Federation (BMIF) have a modern apprenticeship scheme. Many companies offer on-the-job training or take on people who have trained on one of the available courses.

BMIF is the trade federation for the industry and has five N/SVQ qualifications in boat building, repair, outfitting and lamination available. An up-to-date list is available from the BMIF. There are still some BTEC and City and Guilds courses relevant to the industry which can be followed at various colleges. Other courses cover yacht and boatyard management, and leisure studies (water-based), and design diplomas and degrees are also available. Entry qualifications differ and applicants should check with the relevant college. A list of colleges and their courses is available from the BMIF. Also a list of members and their details is available for £15.

Personal Qualities

Boat builders/repairers should have an interest in boats and the water, and practical craft abilities.

Starting Salary

Depends on training to date and geographical location, and is open to negotiation. No national rates.

Further Information

British Marine Industries Federation, Meadlake Place, Thorpe Lea Road, Egham, Surrey TW20 8HE; 01784 473377

Bookmaker

Bookmaking and betting shops can be small independent units or part of a large, often international, group of companies operating in the leisure industry. The work is varied and involves counter work and general administration.

Qualifications and Training

Trainee managers need GCSE passes in maths and English and, in addition, they sit an aptitude test for employment in most of the well-known companies as part of the selection procedure. Trainee managers usually start behind the counter at age 21. Promotion follows basic on-the-job training and counter work.

Personal Qualities

Competence in dealing with cash and with the general public are necessary.

Starting Salary

Salaries are negotiable in independent shops with part-time work available.

Further Information

National Association of Bookmakers, 298 Ewell Road, Surbiton, Surrey KT6 7AQ; 0181 390 8222

Bookseller

In a bookselling career the accent is on knowing your product and on selling it. It is important to keep up to date by reading new books and reviews in order to assist customers and display the books to advantage. The ability to find information in catalogues and directories, and particularly on computer, is essential. Bookselling managers order new stock and endeavour to give their shops an image that will attract regular customers. They may build up mail order and institutional supply connections and participate in author promotions – some larger bookshops have their own marketing departments.

Qualifications and Training

A good general education is essential. Some bookshops require education to degree level. The industry recognised qualification, the Diploma in Professional Bookselling, is available through The Booksellers Association of Great Britain and Ireland together with a number of comprehensive training resources.

Personal Qualities

A liking for books and people, good general knowledge and an interest in reading and handling books are necessary, as too are good health and stamina for a job which involves much standing. Customer care is essential to create a friendly and reassuring atmosphere where book-buyers know that they are being looked after by professional, knowledgeable staff, in an efficient manner.

Starting Salary

Salaries are usually negotiable in small shops and many booksellers work part time. Salary ranges are (with London being at the top end of each range): sales assistants £7500–£9000, senior assistants £8000–£10,500, managers £10,000–£18,000. Managers of larger chains can earn up to £35,000.

Further Information

Booksellers Association of Great Britain and Ireland, Minster House, 272 Vauxhall Bridge Road, London SW1V 1BA; 0171 834 5477

Box Office*, see *Theatre

Brewing

Brewing is the complex process of making and packaging beer. Specialist technicians are responsible for the choice of all raw materials, malt, hops etc, and plant equipment. Brewing technicians and brewing scientists are required to maintain consistently high-quality products. There are opportunities for non-qualified people to work as plant operators.

Qualifications and Training

No formal qualifications are necessary for non-technical jobs in the brewing industry. For technical jobs, the main demand is for honours graduates in science and engineering, particularly if they have specialised in brewing, biochemistry or chemical engineering. Requirements to enter a degree course are GCSE or equivalent passes in English language, maths and another science and two A levels/three H grades to include chemistry. Specialist degree courses are offered at Heriot-Watt University in brewing. This degree provides exemption from the associate membership examination of the Institute of Brewing.

School-leavers with five GCSE/SCE passes including English language, maths, and two approved science A levels, or approved BTEC certificates, may study in-service to sit the associate membership examination of the Institute of Brewing.

Personal Qualities

Good health is required for a job which will inevitably involve some night- and shift-work. The ability to organise and communicate effectively at all levels and a keen interest in science and engineering are the hallmarks of successful brewers and brewing scientists.

Starting Salary

Non-technical staff earn from £8500 to £9500; technical trainees £12,000+.

Further Information

The Institute of Brewing, 33 Clarges Street, London W1Y 8EE; 0171 499 8144

Broadcasting

The aim of radio and television is communication. The range of programmes offered is enormous: news, entertainment, sport, music, documentaries, drama and education, to name some. There is also a great variety of different jobs under the general heading of 'broadcasting'. Any of the jobs in radio and television require special knowledge, training and experience. Newcomers must know what skills and qualities they have and match them to the job areas within the industry. Jobs in the BBC open to new entrants are advertised in the national press and a summary appears on CEEFAX page 696.

It is important to be able to demonstrate your enthusiasm through practical involvement in relevant activities – hospital/community radio, writing for a school/college newspaper, photography or working behind the scenes in amateur theatre, for example.

Journalist/Reporter

Journalists work in radio and television collecting information and reporting on news and general interest items. They interview people, attend public events, compile reports and may carry out background research for programmes. Keyboard skills are essential as information is put directly on to computer.

Programme Assistant
They work in radio and are responsible for the technical and artistic presentation of programmes. They need to be able to operate the equipment and to be good at dealing with other people in the team and with the people who are interviewed or who work on the programmes.

Producer's Assistant (or Secretary)
They work for the producer organising all the administrative work. They retype scripts to incorporate any changes which have been made ready for the next rehearsal or performance.

Floor Manager
Floor managers work in television doing a similar job to that of a theatrical stage manager. However, the broadcasting floor manager's job may be more strenuous since actors working on different sets cannot see each other and the floor manager's function is to cue and coordinate the cast in a drama production. The floor manager is also responsible for health and safety in the studio.

Studio Manager
Studio managers work in radio and are responsible for all studio programmes as regards the artistic and technical operation. They must know how to interpret the producer's ideas correctly and how to achieve the best sound effects.

Assistant Floor Manager and Floor Assistant
They carry out a variety of tasks according to each production. They are often in charge of the prompt book.

Production Assistant
Production assistants work as part of the production team. They must have good keyboard and organisational skills, be able to deal with a wide range of contacts and work to deadlines. Part of the job involves sitting in the control gallery timing the programme. In addition they may do research for programmes.

Director/Producer
They are often specialists in a specific area such as documentaries, children's programmes, drama etc. Both jobs require a good technical knowledge of the media with financial management and budgeting skills as well as the necessary creative ability.

Broadcast Engineer

Engineers are involved in maintaining and testing the equipment used in studios and in outside broadcasts in radio and television, together with operation and maintenance of the transmission chain. They may also be involved in project development and research work.

Vision-Mixer

They must have excellent powers of concentration and manual dexterity in order to carry out instructions from the producer, who may be using up to six cameras during a production.

Film Editor/Video Editor

Film and video editors increasingly work with both formats. The editor must be able to visualise the director/producer's ideas and make the required creative decisions. Film and video editors have usually had experience in a technical/creative capacity before moving to an editor's position.

Television Make-Up and Hairdressing

This is a highly skilled area of work. In consequence competition is keen for any vacancies. It requires a thorough knowledge of period hairstyles and the ability to understand how to combat the effects of lighting and camera on people's faces. The major difference between film and television is that the make-up designer/assistant is responsible for both make-up and hair in television; in film it is two jobs.

Costume Designer

After gaining the relevant diplomas, they should have theatrical experience. The work involves liaison with producers and make-up staff and being responsible, where necessary, for hiring and adapting costumes. They must have had basic training in pattern making, cutting and dressmaking with practical experience in a fashion house or theatrical costumier.

Costume Dressmaker

They carry out the alterations and adaptations necessary on hired or existing costumes as well as making up new designs.

Dresser

Duties involve the maintenance of costumes and the dressing of artists for performances. They must be able to sew and have had relevant experience in the theatre, the film industry or as a theatrical costumier.

Camera Operator
Camera operators work both in studios and on outside broadcasts. They have deep interest in subjects such as photography and lighting. The ability to establish good working relationships with other crew members and the director is necessary.

Audio Assistant
Audio assistants work on radio and television programme origination throughout the UK doing similar jobs to sound operators and studio managers. There is a tendency now in BBC regions for the job to split into these two categories.

Sound Operator
They help to set up and operate sound equipment in studios and on outside broadcasts. They have a deep practical interest in subjects such as hi-fi and sound. The ability to establish good working relationships is necessary.

Secretaries and Clerks
There are a large number of jobs available in broadcasting with the possibility of promotion from clerk-typist to secretary, and from secretary to producer's assistant.

Qualifications and Training
Both the BBC and some ITC companies offer in-service staff training schemes which are advertised as they occur. At a time of falling numbers in broadcasting, competition for a place on these schemes is fierce. The selection boards are impressed by good all-rounders as well as candidates with specialist knowledge.

In technical areas, engineers require, at trainee level, at least English GCSE plus A level maths and physics or a BTEC/SCOTVEC national diploma in electronics. Qualified engineers need to have a degree or HND in electronic engineering. The BBC also recruits non-electronics graduates and converts them to engineers via an in-house training scheme.

Technical operators require a good standard of education; at least GCSE grades A–C in English, maths and combined science (preferably physics). To improve their chances candidates often progress their education further. Evidence of in-depth relevant practical involvement, often through amateur interests, is always looked for.

Many training courses, as well as those to a BTEC standard, now have an equivalent in National Vocational Qualification (NVQ).

Trainee studio managers need to have knowledge of sound equipment together with practical involvement in radio. GCSEs in maths and physics are generally required.

Production trainees must have practical experience of work directly related to production either professionally or via amateur involvement. No specific qualifications are asked for but applicants must have a wide range of interests.

Journalism training opportunities require applicants to have a demonstrable interest in news and current affairs, with practical evidence of involvement. Training schemes attract a large response and the standard is high.

Secretarial and clerical staff must have a good standard of education. Qualifications for clerical posts vary, depending on the department, eg in finance an aptitude for figures is essential. Accurate keyboard skills are required for clerk-typist posts. Secretaries must have accurate typing; shorthand is an advantage.

Make-up trainees need to be involved in the professional or amateur theatre, and must have had formal training in make-up and hairdressing. Applicants should have A levels including art.

Personal Qualities

Qualities vary from job to job but all broadcasting staff must show commitment, enthusiasm, the ability to work as part of a team, and enormous stamina.

Starting Salary

There is such a wide range of salaries payable in broadcasting that it is only possible to give a few examples. BBC technical operations trainees start at £10,000 upwards; direct entry engineers £12,000 upwards; production trainees £13,500; news trainees £12,500; local radio trainee reporters £13,123. These are basic salaries, and allowances are often paid in addition.

Further Information

BBC Corporate Recruitment Services, PO Box 7000, London W5 2PA

Personnel Department, ITV Network Centre, 200 Gray's Inn Road, London WC1 8XZ; 0171 843 8000

Skillset, 124 Horseferry Road, London SW1P 2TX (the industry's lead training body)

Careers in Television and Radio, Kogan Page

Building

Building is the maintenance and construction of any structure in the UK or abroad. It is allied to civil and structural engineering, building and environmental engineering, municipal engineering, highway and transportation engineering. There are many crafts in the building industry. These include: carpenters, joiners and formwork erectors, wood machinists, mastic asphalters, bricklayers, painters and decorators, crane drivers and mechanical equipment operators, electricians, refrigeration fitters, thermal insulators, plumbers and gas fitters, plasterers, glaziers, scaffolders, paviours, steel erectors, stone-masons, roofing and wall tilers, floor and ceiling tilers, coiling fixers, heating and ventilation specialists. Each craftsman is responsible for his part of the job but works as part of a team whose collective responsibility is to produce high quality work.

Contract Manager

Contract manager is the title given in the building and construction trades to the person responsible for the overall control of a building project. He has to coordinate the subcontractors and specialist firms, the technical staff and the machine operatives and make sure that the whole project is completed within the specified time limit and to the specified budget.

Clerk of Works

A clerk of works' role on a construction project is to undertake independent inspection of the works in progress to ensure that they conform to the specification so that the client obtains value for money.

Site Manager

The site manager is the person responsible for all operations on a construction site. He recruits the necessary skilled and semi-skilled workers; in a large construction company he works in conjunction with the personnel department.

Qualifications and Training

Formal educational requirements are not required. Training is by apprenticeship – usually of three to four years' duration – but may be shortened to 12 months for entrants who have studied building subjects at school or college. Apprentices work towards NVQs awarded jointly by the City and Guilds and the Construction Industry Training Board. Technician entrants to the building industry must have a minimum of four GCSEs grades A to C or three standard grades 1 to 3 to include a science, maths and a subject showing the use of English. Anyone wanting to become a clerk of works should have a sound technical education, ideally with a construction trade background. Students can progress through the Institute of Clerks of Works examinations (intermediate and final parts 1 and 2) or alternatively gain partial exemption through the HNC/HTC/ SCOTVEC equivalent routes. Site managers will have had several years' experience of working on a building site and will probably hold a building technician qualification. The Construction Industry Training Board offers an advanced block release course in scaffolding, attendance at employer's discretion. NVQs, levels 2 and 3, are available, awarded jointly by City and Guilds and the Construction Industry Training Board.

Personal Qualities

The building worker needs the ability and desire to work accurately to technical drawings or notes, to measure very accurately, and to have an eye for straight lines. Commitment and a desire to produce good work are necessary, as too are physical fitness and a liking for outdoor work. A contract manager needs to be able to handle large amounts of paperwork and liaise with all kinds of different people from the architect to the building workers.

Starting Salary

Recommended weekly rates are: £73.90 at 16; £103.46 at 17; £147.81 at 18; and, when qualified, the craftsman rate is £178.62. Starting salary for a contract manager is about £17,500 upwards and for a site manager, £15,000 upwards.

Further Information

Construction Industry Training Board, Bircham Newton, King's Lynn, Norfolk PE31 6RH; 01553 776677 (ext 2466)

Institute of Clerks of Works of Great Britain Incorporated, 41 The Mall, Ealing, London W5 3TJ; 0181 579 2917

Scottish Regional Careers Organiser, CITB, 2 Edison Street, Hillington, Glasgow G52 4XN; 0141 882 6455

Building Control Surveyor

Building control is undertaken by local authorities and the National House Builders Council. The work is interesting and varied. The main activities involve the examination and assessment of plans, making site visits to inspect work, and liaison with designers, builders, other professionals within the construction team and the fire authorities.

A broad knowledge of the many areas of building work and skill in dealing with people need to be developed.

Qualifications and Training

The Institute has three levels of qualification. Associate level is attained through an appropriate BTEC higher certificate in building studies. Incorporated members are at first-degree level or equivalent and corporate membership is obtained by satisfying the requirements of the Institute's incorporated examinations and its Assessment of Professional Competence.

Personal Qualities
A knowledge of construction technology and legislation is necessary, plus the ability to state one's requirements firmly and to see that they are carried out.

Starting Salary
This depends on qualifications and experience and varies according to the employer.

Further Information
Institute of Building Control, 21 High Street, Ewell, Epsom, Surrey KT17 1SB; 0181 393 6860

Building Services Engineering,* see *Engineering

Building Societies

Building societies function by attracting savings and investments from the public; they then use these funds to make loans for home ownership. The Building Societies Act 1986 has allowed societies to enter many new areas, such as insurance, investment, estate agency and unsecured lending. The traditional savings and loan activities remain, however, the most important. Building societies are among the most highly automated and computerised offices in the UK and are in the forefront of those who offer in-service staff training in the latest office technology. Management and marketing methods in the building societies are aggressive and offer good career prospects.

Qualifications and Training
Four GCSE passes including English and maths, and two A levels (necessary for entry to professional career training) are the basic requirements. Time off may be allowed to study for BTEC/SCOTVEC national and higher awards in business studies, and the examinations of the Chartered Institute of Bankers. BTEC/SCOTVEC higher awards gain exemption to some parts of the Institute examinations. In-service training tends to be spread over two to five years. To gain admission to a course leading to the Associateship

Examinations of the Chartered Institute of Bankers, a recognised UK degree or a professional qualification is required. One pass at A level or two A/S levels plus GCSE English language, A–C, is sufficient to gain admission to the foundation course (known as the Pre-Associateship Route). The Institute also offers a vocational level qualification, the Certificate in Financial Services Practice. No academic qualifications are necessary for entry to this, which is aimed at clerical staff who want to learn more about how building societies work. The certificate is a recognised qualification in its own right.

National Vocational Qualifications (NVQs) or Scottish Vocational Qualifications (SVQs) levels 2 to 4 are available in some building societies. NVQs at level 2 are predominantly aimed at branch staff. Levels 3 and 4 are aimed at supervisory and managerial staff.

Personal Qualities

Since the funds come from the general public, personal honesty and discretion as well as verbal and mathematical skills need to be combined with the ability to make decisions and work methodically. A sympathetic and understanding manner with people is a definite asset for building society staff.

Starting Salary

Salaries vary from society to society, but a new entrant could expect £6500+ and a graduate £12,500.

Further Information

The Building Societies Association, 3 Savile Row, London W1X 1AF; 0171 437 0655

The Chartered Institute of Bankers, 90 Bishopsgate, London EC2N 4AS; 0171 444 7115

Careers in Banking and Finance, Kogan Page

Building Surveying,* see *Surveyor, Surveying Technician

Bus Companies

About 60 per cent or more of personnel working in passenger transport on the roads are drivers and conductors. Many work on routes within one town or city, but some are employed by coach companies taking passengers from one town to another, or right across the country. The remaining staff are divided between management, administration and engineering (which includes mechanics). Administration covers route planning, traffic surveys, publicity, fare scales, computer operation, legal work and financial management. Engineering work includes vehicle maintenance and repair as well as technical research and design.

Qualifications and Training

The traineeship schemes offered by companies to those with suitable educational backgrounds cover the requirements of bus operating staff and bus mechanics. A driving licence, sound mechanical ability and aptitude are preferred qualifications for this practical and craft-based work; formal educational qualifications are not required. NVQs are available at levels 1, 2 and 3. In-service training is an integral part of all careers with bus companies.

School-leavers and graduates are eligible for training in administration and management.

Personal Qualities

The work of bus drivers and conductors is strenuous and requires stamina and a willingness to operate early and late shift rotas. Tact and good humour are essential when dealing with the general public, as well as a liking for the old and young people who form the majority of the bus-travelling public.

Starting Salary

Salaries vary and applicants should enquire of the individual companies. London salaries are higher than those in the regions.

Further Information

Local bus and coach companies

Bus and Coach Training Ltd, Regency House, 43 High Street, Rickmansworth WD3 1ET; 01923 896607

Butcher *see Meat Industry*

Career prospects are varied in the meat industry, extending from work in a small retail shop through to supermarkets, and meat buying for large organisations such as hotels and caterers, to the manufacturing of meat and poultry products.

Qualifications and Training

A good general education is necessary but not formal educational requirements. Training is on the job and courses are available at further education establishments and technical colleges, leading to examinations of the Meat Training Council. NVQs are available at levels 1, 2, 3 and 4, and higher national diploma/certificate qualifications. Modern apprenticeships are also available. Further training, appropriate to the relevant sector of the industry, in management, meat technology, or small business ownership, may follow an apprenticeship.

Personal Qualities

An above-average attitude to hygiene is vital, as it is in all the food industries, plus a real interest in people and their eating habits in order that the meat products may be geared to the customers' needs.

Starting Salary

Around £60 per week at 16, £250 when trained.

Further Information

Meat Training Council, PO Box 141, Winterhill House, Snowdon Drive, Milton Keynes MK6 1YY; 01908 231062

National Federation of Meat and Feed Traders, 1 Belgrove, Tunbridge Wells, Kent TN1 1YW; 01892 541412

Scottish Federation of Meat Traders Association, 8 Needless Road, Perth PH2 0JW; 01738 37472

Buyer *see Purchasing Officer*

The retail price of any product or service depends to a great extent on the cost of raw materials and of labour. Buying departments in manufacturing industries are consequently engaged in the discussion and planning of all projects so that they may buy wisely the raw materials and, in some cases, the services required to supply the manufacturing process.

Buyers in the retail trade, for example, may work in the fashion department of a large multiple store. Their work requires that they keep their knowledge of the latest trends ahead of the seasons and may involve them in travel at home and abroad. They will also be involved in transactions with manufacturers and will place orders and chase deliveries.

Buying careers exist in all large organisations – whether profit making or not. Hospitals in the National Health Service, local authorities and government departments are all concerned to keep the prices of supplies at a reasonable level and ensure continuity of supplies, particularly when installing new technology and equipment. The function of the buying department is to shop around for the best value for money.

Qualifications and Training

Although some companies do not ask for GCSEs, the majority do prefer applicants with four or five GCSEs. Graduates, and those with GCE A level passes, usually enter as trainee buyers working with experienced personnel and continuing their training in-service. To take the examinations of the Chartered Institute of Purchasing and Supply five GCSE passes are necessary, to include English and a quantitative subject, and two A levels or three H levels. BTEC/SCOTVEC qualifications are acceptable. All-round experience in organisations of all types is a sound base upon which to build a career in buying – or purchasing as it is sometimes called.

Personal Qualities

The ability to think clearly, accept responsibility, and to express oneself concisely and pleasantly, plus a measure of determination when negotiating prices, and patience when dealing with one's colleagues in other departments, are necessary. A willingness to travel and to devote some of one's own time to the job are also required.

Starting Salary

Starting salaries for trainee buyers are £10,000–£11,000+ for graduates but may be much less, in the region of £8000–£9000+ for less qualified applicants.

Further Information

The Chartered Institute of Purchasing and Supply, Easton House, Easton-on-the-Hill, Stamford, Lincolnshire PE9 3NZ; 01780 56777

Careers in Retailing, Kogan Page

C

Care Assistant

They are employed in residential centres to work with children, old people, the chronically ill, the handicapped and other groups such as single parents or ex-prisoners, who need special day-to-day care unavailable at home. Such assistants do not always live-in full time themselves. They work under the supervision of a more highly qualified officer-in-charge (normally a trained social worker). Assistants are concerned not only with the physical requirements of their patients, but also with their mental well-being and happiness.

Qualifications and Training

The main professional qualification is the diploma in social work (DipSW) which can be studied for part-time while working or via a full-time college course. Entry requirements are five GCSEs plus two A levels, or five SCEs including three at H level. Mature entrants may be accepted without these qualifications.

It is also possible to work towards NVQs levels 2 and 3 in social care.

Personal Qualities

Assistants in residential homes or hostels need patience and a warm, sympathetic personality to enable them to communicate with those in their care and to inspire their confidence. Practical skills are also necessary in the day-to-day running of such establishments.

Starting Salary

About £9000, more in London.

Further Information

England: CCETSW Information Service, Derbyshire House, St Chad's Street, London WC1H 8AD; 0171 278 2455

Northern Ireland: CCETSW Information Service, 6 Malone Road, Belfast BT9 5BN; 01232 665390

Scotland: CCETSW Information Service, 78–80 George Street, Edinburgh EH2 3BU; 0131 220 0093
Wales: CCETSW Information Service, South Gate House, Wood Street, Cardiff CF1 1EW; 01222 226257

Careers Adviser

Careers advisers work in local careers centres situated in most towns. They give guidance, careers information and advice about job opportunities, both local and national, and about further education, by means of talks, discussion groups, displays and individual interviews. They also work closely with careers teachers in schools and colleges and with local employers and training organisations. Visits are made to many different workplaces and educational establishments to gain first-hand knowledge of what is involved.

Many careers advisers specialise, eg working with people who have learning difficulties, with sixth-form and college students, or with the unemployed. Careers service companies are increasingly assisting adult clients.

Qualifications and Training

A degree or equivalent is generally required, although some mature entrants may be accepted on the basis of suitable experience rather than formal qualifications. A background in teaching, in industry or personnel work can be an advantage. Candidates follow a one-year full-time course leading, after a year's supervised experience, to the diploma in careers guidance. Some careers service companies employ trainees who follow a diploma course on a full- or part-time basis over a two-year period. Flexible arrangements for training and qualifying are being steadily extended and S/NVQs up to level 4 are now available.

Personal Qualities

An ability to communicate sympathetically with people of all ages and from varied backgrounds is required, as well as the capacity to assimilate and organise a large amount of constantly changing information.

Starting Salary

From £12,000.

Further Information

The Institute of Careers Guidance, 27a Lower High Street, Stourbridge, West Midlands DY8 1TA; 01384 376464; Fax: 01384 440830

Local Government Opportunities, Local Government Management Board, Layden House, 76–86 Turnmill Street, London EC1M 5QU; 0171 296 6600
'A Career in Careers Guidance' (The Institute of Careers Guidance)
'Training for the Careers Service' (The Local Government Management Board)

Carpenter and Bench Joiner

Traditionally, joiners were responsible for smaller, more intricate jobs, and carpenters for larger jobs such as laying floor boards. Nowadays the terms are synonymous. The work involves making and fitting doors, windows, staircases, cupboards, shuttering; fitting structural joists, roof timbers, door frames, skirting boards, doors, handrails, wardrobes etc.

Carpenters may also be called upon to wall up excavations and erect shoring during demolition. Opportunities exist with a wide range of employers of all sizes such as building and civil engineering contractors, specialist carpentry and joinery firms, local authorities, in industrial and commercial maintenance, shipbuilding, shopfitting and vehicle manufacture, or as a self-employed craftsman.

Cabinet Maker

Cabinet makers use traditional hand skills to make, finish or restore high-quality items of wooden furniture. They may work in factories for furniture manufacturers or be self-employed in small workshops.

Qualifications and Training

A general education to secondary level is the only academic requirement, although some arithmetical ability is useful. Training is by a two- to three-year period with courses leading to NVQs awarded jointly by City and Guilds and the Construction Industry Training Board.

Personal Qualities

As qualified craftspeople, carpenters and joiners must be able to work from technical drawings or notes without close supervision and produce neat accurate work. They must be manually skilled, possessing a steady hand and a head for heights. A good eye for form is necessary, plus a willingness to work outside in all weathers.

Starting Salary

When qualified the craftsman rate is about £175.

Further Information

Construction Industry Training Board, Bircham Newton, King's Lynn, Norfolk PE31 6RH; 01553 776677 (ext 2466)
Institute of Carpenters, Central Office, 35 Hayworth Road, Sandiacre, Nottingham NG10 5LL; 0115 9490641
Practical Guide to Woodworking Careers and Educational Facilities, Guild of Master Craftsmen

Carpet Fitter

Carpet retailers, furniture stores and department stores all employ their own trained personnel who deliver and fit carpets and other floor coverings to customers' homes, shops, offices or hotels. Many fitters are also self-employed.

Qualifications and Training

GCSE English and maths or equivalents are usually required. Training is mainly given on the job working with an experienced fitter, although in some firms there are possible opportunities for day release courses leading to the examinations of the National Institute of Carpet Fitters.

Personal Qualities

Strength and fitness are important in order to handle heavy rolls of carpet. A good head for calculations and an eye for detail (such as matching patterns) are also essential. Generally, too, it is necessary to be able to drive.

Starting Salary

About £180 a week, more in London.

Further Information

Local Jobcentres and Careers Offices
National Institute of Carpet Fitters, 4D St Mary's Place, The Lace Market, Nottingham NG1 1PH; 0115 958 3077

Cartography *see Ordnance Survey Work*

Cartography embraces not only all aspects of map-making from the initial collection and editing of material (by cartographers) to the actual drawing and production of the finished product (by cartographic draughtsmen and assistants), but also the making of charts, globes and models of the earth. Most cartographic work is undertaken in government departments such as the Ordnance Survey, the Ministry of Defence, the Meteorological Office and the Department of the Environment; other vacancies sometimes occur in local authority planning departments, specialist publishing houses or with survey companies. Computers are reducing the need for manual draughtsmen, especially in repetitive work, and the increasing application of Geographical Information Systems (GIS) via a graphics workstation is significantly modifying the work of a professional cartographer. (Cartographers working for the Ordnance Survey are known as mapping and charting officers.)

Qualifications and Training

Cartographers are increasingly being recruited from among graduates who have relevant undergraduate or postgraduate training (and usually include geography in their A levels). There are few actual degree courses in cartography, GIS, topographic science or surveying and mapping science. Cartographic assistants need a minimum two GCSEs and draughtsmen three. One of the following must be included: English language, maths, geography, art or technical drawing. If they have at least four GCSEs at A, B or C level, they may attend a BTEC National Certificate course (NVQ level 3) on a day release basis. GCSEs must include maths and a subject demonstrating fluency in the use of English.

Personal Qualities

Neatness, precision, aesthetic appreciation and a fine attention to detail are important, as is also mathematical awareness.

Starting Salary

For a graduate, from £13,000; mapping and charting technicians from £11,000, and assistants £8500+.

Further Information

British Cartographic Society, R W Anson, School of Construction and Earth Sciences, Division of Geology and Cartography, Oxford Brookes University, Headington, Oxford OX3 0BP; 01865 483346

Personnel Division, Ordnance Survey, Romsey Road, Maybush, Southampton SO9 4DH; 01703 792639/40 (*enquiries only from those who hold the minimum entry qualifications*)

Catering and Accommodation Management *see Chef/Cook, Health Service, Hotel Work*

There is a wide variety of job opportunities in this category at all levels: managers, supervisors and craft workers, although sometimes these dividing lines are not clear-cut and it is quite usual for individuals to move up from one to another.

Management

Catering management can cover work in a roadside or motorway restaurant, a luxury restaurant, a hospital meals service, a snack bar, a take-away service, university and college restaurants, the armed forces, outdoor events or contract catering (providing meals and snacks to the management and staff of the contractor, eg a bank or insurance company). The manager in charge is normally responsible for budgeting, menu planning, stock monitoring and seeing that good food is served as and when it is required (often round the clock). He or she has to keep customers satisfied and supervise staff.

Accommodation management is concerned with the domestic side of colleges and universities (where managers are sometimes known as bursars), hospitals, local authority day centres and residential homes (for the aged or handicapped, for instance). A manager's duties are just as demanding as those in hotel management, with responsibilities for accommodation and catering (particularly in halls of residence which may be used as conference centres during the vacation). The work can involve personal contact with the residents (in homes, for instance, where the population is fairly permanent) or be more in the nature of housekeeping (as in hospitals where the patients are constantly changing and are not the direct concern of the domestic staff).

Kitchen

In the kitchen there are opportunities at all levels, from the chef in charge of a select restaurant to the dish-washer in a snack bar. There are also opportunities for freelance work – catering for directors' dining rooms, private parties and business lunches, for instance. It is demanding work, often in 'unsocial hours' when most people are out enjoying themselves. Some cooking can be repetitious (such as take-away menus), some creatively satisfying.

Food Service Assistants

Waiters and waitresses, as well as serving, may cook special dishes at table or specialise in particular skills such as wine-waiting. As well as serving food and drink they have to maintain contact with their customers; unfriendly servers may ruin the reputation of a whole restaurant; promotion is to head waiter/waitress.

Qualifications and Training

There are two main routes to qualification: attending a college or university as a full-time student, or joining a training programme operated by an employer or an organisation that works with employers to provide training, such as the Hotel and Catering Training Company (HCTC). In the latter case entrants learn on the job and by attending college or a training centre on a short course or day-release basis. Recruits on the work-based training programme will generally acquire NVQ/SVQ awards.

An increasing number of employers are offering modern apprenticeships. These provide a route to higher level technical or supervisory skills, NVQ/SVQ level 3, for 16 and 17 year olds. They take two and a half to three years. There are four routes: accommodation services, chef, fast food, restaurant and pub.

The standard entry requirements for a college-based course are as follows:

NVQs, SVQs, GNVQs, GSVQs, SCOTVEC national certificate: motivation and potential to succeed.

GNVQ levels 2 and 3, HCIMA professional certificate: four GCSEs.

Some two-year SCOTVEC national certificate programmes, HCIMA professional certificate: four Standard grades.

BTEC higher national: one A level and four or five GCSEs.

SCOTVEC higher national: two SCE Highers and three Standards.

Degree: two or three A levels or a combination of A and AS levels or four to five SCE Highers.

Personal Qualities

Managers need to be confident and independent with a smart appearance and good speech. They have to command respect and trust as well as understand the various aspects of modern management techniques such as budgeting, profit making and so on. Craft workers usually need physical fitness and stamina as well as high standards of personal hygiene. Skin complaints may disqualify entrants.

Starting Salary

The following are average salaries: hotel and restaurant staff earn about £160 a week and contract catering staff £150+, hotel managers about £16,000, restaurant managers slightly less at £15,000+ and contract catering managers also £15,000+.

Further Information

Careers Information Service, Hotel and Catering Training Company, International House, High Street, London W5 5DB; 0181 579 2400

Hotel and Catering International Management Association, 191 Trinity Road, London SW17 7HN; 0181 672 4251

Springboard Careers Advice Centre, 1 Denmark Street, London WC2H 8LP; 0171 497 8654

Careers in Catering and Hotel Management, Kogan Page

Kogan Page Guide to Careers in the Catering, Travel and Leisure Industries, Kogan Page

Chartered Clinical Psychologist,* see *Clinical Psychologist

Chauffeur

Chauffeurs are skilled car drivers who are employed either by one person or by companies or organisations where senior personnel (such as chairmen, managing directors and so on) need their own reliable transport on hand at all times. Private chauffeurs may often live in accommodation provided and have various other duties. Apart from the actual driving, the job will also involve making sure the car (or cars) is well maintained and clean.

Qualifications and Training

Obviously the first requirement is to have a 'clean' driving licence with no endorsements, and proven experience. Mechanical and/or geographical knowledge may be required depending on the individual demands of the job. Some of the better-known car manufacturers run their own training schemes – Rolls-Royce, for instance, have their own driving school (enquiries to the head office at Crewe in Cheshire; 01270 255155).

Personal Qualities

Essential attributes are a calm, unflappable nature when under pressure (in heavy traffic and late for an appointment, for instance), patience (as much time will be spent waiting for passengers), politeness and the discretion not to repeat confidential conversations which may well be overheard.

Starting Salary

Salaries vary from £180 a week to £285. Accommodation may be provided.

Further Information

Local Jobcentres and Careers Offices

The Lady, 39–40 Bedford Street, London WC2E 9ER; 0171 379 4717 (*job advertisements*)

Chef/Cook

In addition to creating and supervising the preparation of all kinds of different dishes, a head chef/cook has to be trained in the management of a kitchen, being responsible for the staff and the organisation of their work load, planning the menus, budgeting, ordering and approving the necessary ingredients and maintaining high standards of efficiency and hygiene. Chefs are employed in hotels, restaurants, industrial organisations (such as offices or factories), institutions (such as hospitals, schools and universities or colleges) and in the armed forces. In large establishments the *chef de cuisine* is in overall charge while there may be a number of *chefs de partie* (in charge of their part of the kitchen) and a number of *commis chefs* (still learning the trade).

Qualifications and Training

Qualifications are the same as for Catering and Accommodation Management, see page 61.

Personal Qualities

Requirements include the ability to work under pressure in frequently hot and noisy conditions, and to enjoy practical as well as creative work. The higher chefs rise in their profession, the more they need to be able to take responsibility and the more management skills they require.

Starting Salary

Salaries are similar to those on page 61 for Catering and Accommodation Management. Experienced chefs may command very high salaries.

Further Information

Careers Information Service, Hotel and Catering Training Company, International House, High Street, London W5 5DB; 0181 579 2400

Springboard Careers Advice Centre, 1 Denmark Street, London WC2H 8LP; 0171 497 8654

Chemical Engineering, see *Engineering*

Chemist

Chemistry is the basis of a wide range of careers. The majority of trained chemists work in the manufacturing industries within organisations producing such materials as foodstuffs, plastics, pharmaceuticals, cosmetics, petroleum, detergents, fertilisers and so on; large numbers teach in schools, colleges and universities, generally combining teaching with research work; there are also openings with local authorities, the Health Service, the Civil Service and the nationalised industries, as well as in marketing and sales, information and patents and specialised publishing. Professional chemists are often assisted by laboratory technicians and assistants. Chemistry is essential in many other careers as a basic qualification – in medicine, for instance, or veterinary science.

Qualifications and Training

Most professional chemists belong to the Royal Society of Chemistry. A degree or equivalent qualification is necessary to become a Society member. Entry requirements for degree courses generally include at least two A level or three H grade passes in science subjects, including chemistry and another distinct scientific or mathematical subject. A good BTEC/SCOTVEC award or a GNVQ (advanced) can provide an alternative method of entry. Royal Society of Chemistry courses are offered, one year part time, at five institutions. This combined with HNC/HND is equivalent to a pass degree. A BTEC higher national diploma in chemistry may also be appropriate as it is approximately equivalent to a pass degree. Entry to such courses (which are either two-year full-time, three-year part-time or sandwich courses) normally requires one A level or two H grade passes, including chemistry, a GNVQ (advanced) or a BTEC/ SCOTVEC award. Further study is necessary after gaining the higher diploma to reach full professional status, generally through part-time study leading to a degree.

Chemistry technicians usually need three GCSE or SCE Standard grade passes to gain entry to a BTEC certificate in science course or SCOTVEC certificate in chemistry – these are generally part-time courses with day release. This can be followed by a BTEC/SCOTVEC higher certificate in chemistry course which may then lead to acceptance on a degree course. After gaining a degree further study is generally required and individual employers normally run their own training schemes.

Personal Qualities
Chemists usually form part of a team, so an ability to work alongside others is helpful. The actual work varies enormously but generally they also need enquiring minds and practical experimental ability and experience.

Starting Salary
Varies according to type of employment. Newly qualified graduates can generally expect salaries of £13,000–£15,000+.

Further Information
The Royal Society of Chemistry, Burlington House, Piccadilly, London W1V 0BN; 0171 437 8656

Child Care*, see *Nanny, Nursery Nurse

Child Guidance*, see *Educational Psychologist, Psychologist, Psychotherapist

Chiropodist

Chiropodists (also known as podiatrists) are concerned with the health of feet; they diagnose and treat ailments such as corns, bunions, malformed nails and sports injuries and also give foot health advice. They perform minor operations under local anaesthetic. They may work in the NHS in hospitals, clinics or health centres; in private practice or large organisations.

Qualifications and Training
A recognised BSc degree in chiropody/podiatry or podiatric medicine is required for state registration, which is a compulsory requirement for employment in the health service. There are fifteen recognised chiropody/podiatry schools attached to universities and institutions throughout the country (contact the Society of Chiropodists and Podiatrists for details). Normally five GCSE passes are required, together with two A levels, but individual institutions may have their own requirements.

In private practice it is essential to belong to a reputable chiropodial association which operates a strict ethical code and professional liability insurance.

Personal Qualities
Chiropodists need good eyesight (with or without spectacles) and nimble hands as well as an ability to inspire confidence in the people they are treating. Organising ability is essential in private practice.

Starting Salary
£13,900 when qualified. For those working in the National Health Service, London weighting is payable.

Further Information
Institute of Chiropodists, 27 Wright Street, Southport PR9 0TL; 01704 546141

Society of Chiropodists and Podiatrists, 53 Welbeck Street, London W1M 7HE; 0171 486 3381

Chiropractor

Chiropractic is a health care profession concerned with, but not limited to, the diagnosis, treatment and prevention of structural and functional disorders affecting the musculo-skeletal system. Common complaints which patients may present to chiropractors include: low back and leg pain, headaches, neck and arm pain as well as sports injuries. As a primary contact profession, patients may directly seek help from a qualified chiropractor without a medical referral.

Chiropractors are trained to utilise a wide variety of diagnostic techniques including x-ray. Manual manipulation (adjustment) of spinal and extremity joints as well as soft tissue structures is the most common treatment method employed. However, chiropractors are also trained to utilise a range of complementary treatment techniques such as physical therapy modalities, braces and supports as well as offer advice on nutrition, rehabilitative exercises and modifications to activities of daily living.

With ever increasing demand for chiropractic services, the prospects for graduates are bright both in the United Kingdom and Europe for the foreseeable future.

Qualifications and Training
Training is at the Anglo-European College of Chiropractic and leads to a BSc (Chiropractic) degree. Entry qualifications are five GCSEs to include English and physics and two A levels to include biology or zoology and chemistry. After successfully completing the course, applicants may apply to become members of the British Chiropractic Association.

Personal Qualities
Manual dexterity and practical skills as well as a sound theoretical knowledge of the body are necessary. An ability to communicate with patients and inspire confidence is important.

Starting Salary
Salaries vary according to number of patients and how well established the practice is. Patients are usually charged per session.

Further Information
Anglo-European College of Chiropractic, Parkwood Road, Bournemouth, Dorset BH5 2DF; 01202 436200

British Chiropractic Association, 29 Whitley Street, Reading, Berkshire RG2 0EG; 01734 757557

Choreography*, see *Dancing

The Church

Work within the church, in all denominations, is done by ordained ministers and priests and also by lay men and women. Some denominations allow the ordination of women but not the Roman Catholic church; the Church of England ordains women as deacons and, following the vote of General Synod in November 1992, now ordains women priests. Most clergy work in their own parishes or individual churches, preaching, conducting baptisms, weddings and funerals, teaching the faith and generally caring for the spiritual welfare of their own community. Nowadays, with the upsurge of ecumenical projects and changing social trends, a minister's horizons are much wider than they were in the past and a good deal of his time may be spent outside the traditional confines of parish work. Since going to church is no longer an accepted part of life for many people, the clergyman of today has to go out and meet them on their own ground in all kinds of social contexts. Other ordained ministers and priests work as full-time chaplains – in schools, universities and colleges, hospitals, prisons and in the armed forces. A number are also concerned with church administration or public relations (such as religious advisers to the media).

Religious Orders

Within the Anglican and Roman Catholic churches there are also opportunities – for both men and women – to work within a religious order. Such a community may either be a contemplative 'closed' order, where the emphasis is on prayer, or an 'active' order working as teachers or nurses, running homes for orphans, the chronically sick, the aged, unmarried mothers or delinquents.

Lay Work

Full-time (and part-time) work is also done by the laity (men and women who are not ordained but who are confirmed followers of their particular faith and trained by the various denominations). They may work as preachers, parish workers, teachers or social workers. Laity are also needed for administrative work in central church offices, for running the various welfare agencies, dealing with finances and so on. Church work can also offer opportunities abroad for the ordained and the laity in the missionary field. For laity, their witness is usually through their work in education, health or technical projects.

Qualifications and Training

Prospective ministers normally require at least two A level or three H grade passes, and a degree is desirable. These requirements are by no means vital in every case or in every denomination and may well be varied according to an individual's other attributes and suitability. Training does not normally begin before candidates have reached the age of 18. Length of courses varies between two and six years, again depending on the denomination involved. Entry to religious orders frequently demands qualifications similar to those of a prospective ordinand, although here too an individual's overall suitability is taken into account. Training for such orders is often longer than for the ministry or priesthood and it can take up to nine years or more to reach the stage of final vows. Full-time (and part-time) lay workers are recruited from a wide variety of backgrounds, with and without professional qualifications.

Personal Qualities

Working for the church is not a job; it is a way of life and entering such work requires a deep and strong commitment to one's chosen faith. It also requires sufficient maturity to cope with the intellectual, physical and emotional demands involved. A minister, particularly, needs a strong personality to inspire and lead his congregation and high moral values and integrity. There is little room for a materialist as the rewards of such work are virtually all spiritual and self-sacrifice is often required. Spouses of married clergy will need to share their partners' commitment.

Starting Salary

Varies according to denomination. Some ministers receive a basic stipend together with free accommodation. In some cases 'office' expenses such as postal and telephone charges or running expenses for a car are provided. In the Church of England, curates' salaries begin at £11,940 (the same salary is payable to licensed lay workers) and vicars in charge of a parish at £13,760.

Further Information

Those who feel drawn towards church work should, of course, consult their own minister or priest as a first step. Further information can also be obtained from the following:

The Vocations Officer, Advisory Board of Ministry, Church House, Great Smith Street, London SW1P 3NZ; 0171 222 9011 (*Anglican Church*)

Christians Abroad, 1 Stockwell Green, London SW9 9HP; 0171 737 7811 (*work overseas with development agencies and mission organisations, offer free information, career counselling and publish Opportunities Abroad – job list*)

Agency for Jewish Education, Woburn House, Tavistock Square, London WC1H 0EZ; 0171 387 4300 (*Jewish religion*)

Cinema Management

A cinema manager is responsible for the smooth running of the cinema, the box-office takings and the staff. Most cinemas are now controlled by the major distribution companies and so the manager has little say about what films are shown, but there are also some independents. There may be special functions to organise such as live performances, late night shows and so on.

Cinema Projectionist

A projectionist is responsible for showing the correct films, in the correct sequence and for maintaining the necessary equipment. The work may often be repetitious and the hours 'unsocial' (since it is mainly afternoons and evenings).

Cinema Attendant

Staff are also needed to assist the public to their places, check and sell tickets, distribute refreshments and keep public rooms clean and tidy. This kind of work can be full or part time.

Qualifications and Training

Formal qualifications are not always specified but candidates for managerial positions need to show intelligence and aptitude (often working their way up from more junior positions). The main distributing companies have their own training programmes for cinema managers and projectionists and most of the training is done on the job.

Personal Qualities

A manager needs to enjoy responsibility and be able to handle a variety of demands and/or complaints with courtesy and forbearance. He must be a good leader to get the best teamwork from his staff. A projectionist needs technical ability, organisation, and should not be bored by repetitious work. Attendants need pleasant personalities as they will be dealing with the general public.

Starting Salary

Salaries vary according to organisation and there is often a considerable supplement for Sunday working. The basic weekly salaries are in the region of £180 for a manager, £160 for a projectionist and £130 for other staff.

Further Information

Local Jobcentres and Careers Offices

Civil Aviation

Pilot

Commercial pilots in the UK fly fixed wing aircraft and helicopters. Before take-off the pilot must prepare a flight plan, study the weather, make sure that the craft is airworthy, that the cargo and fuel are safely loaded, and work out estimated times of arrival. Little time is spent actually flying the aeroplane manually. The pilot spends most of his time carefully monitoring sophisticated computer-controlled automatic flying, navigational and communications systems. He must keep in touch with air traffic control and be prepared to deal with sudden changes in weather and other conditions. Pilots work very irregular hours but their actual flying time is strictly controlled.

Most UK pilots are employed by one of the major carriers of passengers and goods, and when flying large aircraft they are part of a team of two or three pilots and possibly a flight engineer. Opportunities for pilots of small aircraft and helicopters are to be found in flying executive jets, or in the field of air taxiing (especially in the North Sea), spraying crops, conducting aerial surveys and also as test pilots or flying instructors.

Flight Engineer
Flight engineers may be employed on long-haul, international flights as a link between maintenance engineers on the ground and the flying crew. They are rarely needed on modern aircraft. They make pre-flight inspections and are responsible for the efficient performance of the aircraft during the flight; they must be able to diagnose and deal with any systems failures, making possible repairs, reporting any defects to maintenance and later checking that they have been dealt with; they may also be responsible for refuelling.

Air Cabin Crew
Stewards and stewardesses look after the safety, comfort and welfare of passengers; before a flight they check stocks of equipment, welcome passengers on board and go through safety routines. During the flight they will serve ready-cooked meals and drinks, sell duty-free goods and on short haul, domestic routes they may also issue tickets. Flight reports are prepared by senior stewards or the cabin staff officer who also attends to first-class passengers and supervises junior staff.

Aircraft Maintenance Engineer
Aircraft maintenance engineers make sure that aircraft are airworthy; they maintain, service and overhaul the craft, their engines and equipment, working to very high standards set by the National Air Traffic Services (NATS), and every part of every job is checked and certified. Engineers usually specialise in either mechanics or avionics and work on major overhaul or in 'turn arounds', ie the work carried out after each flight. Apart from working with the airlines, other opportunities are found with firms that specialise in aircraft maintenance. There are also a few openings for professional engineers in works management, production, planning, and research and development.

Air Traffic Control
The safe and efficient movement of all aircraft through British air space and airports is the responsibility of the NATS air traffic control officers and assistants. With the aid of sophisticated radio, radar and computer systems and with visual checks on visibility and weather conditions, made from the control tower, they ensure that aircraft are kept a safe distance apart, that pilots are well advised as to their position and prevailing conditions, give clearance to land, directions to loading bays etc.

Air traffic controllers working for employers other than the NATS, such as local authorities or an aircraft manufacturer, must hold a NATS licence stipulating the service they are qualified to give, and where they can operate. Some of the more routine tasks such as checking flight plans, updating weather information, logging aircraft movements and keeping runways clear are carried out by the air traffic control assistants. Prospects for promotion to officer level are good but air traffic control staff are employed to work at any location within the country.

Air Traffic Engineer
Air traffic engineers are responsible for the efficient operation of the wide range of sophisticated telecommunications, electronic systems and specialist equipment needed in air traffic control centres, airports and other specialist centres. This involves the installation, calibration and maintenance of radar, air to ground communication systems, navigational and landing aids, computer data and processing equipment, visual display units etc. Opportunities may exist for engineers, to look after day-to-day maintenance, and, at graduate level, for field management, installation and development work.

Qualifications and Training

Pilot
UK pilots are required to hold a professional pilot's licence issued by the NATS indicating, by a series of ratings, exactly what type of aircraft, and under what conditions, the pilot is qualified to fly. Applications for a professional pilot's licence and instrument rating can only be made by candidates who have successfully completed a college of air training course and have 200 hours of flying experience. Residential air training courses lasting approximately one year are available for aeroplanes at Air Services Training, Perth, the Oxford Air Training School, Cabair, Cranfield, and Prestwick and, for helicopter pilots, at Bristow Helicopters Ltd, Redhill and at the Oxford Air Training School. For full-time approved courses the student must have obtained at least five GCSEs including English language, maths and a science subject or the equivalent. Those who do not meet this minimum educational standard should seek advice on their acceptability from the flying training organisation at which the course is to be conducted. A good entry route is via a short service flying commission with either the RAF or RN as this is where many airlines recruit. Further training is completed by the airlines themselves with a combination of ground training and job experience, and throughout a pilot's career he will be expected to attend retraining and refresher courses.

Flight Engineer
Flight engineers usually begin their careers as maintenance engineering apprentices. Applications for a flight engineer's licence can only

be made by candidates aged at least 21. Before being permitted to fly as a flight engineer under training in fulfilment of the requirements, or being permitted to enter for the technical examinations or flight tests, a prospective candidate for the licence must satisfy the NATS that he has acceptable experience as an aircraft engineer, or as a professional pilot, or as an RAF air engineer. Forms for obtaining an assessment of acceptability of experience may be obtained from the Directorate of Flight Crew Licensing, Civil Aviation Authority, Safety Regulation Group, Aviation House, South Area, Gatwick Airport, Gatwick, West Sussex RH6 0YR; 01293 573563.

Air Cabin Crew

Airlines usually train their own air cabin crews at special centres where courses are provided lasting four to six weeks.

Applicants should be over 18 and have a good level of general education to GCSE standard, preferably including English, maths and conversational fluency in at least one European language. Some experience of catering or nursing is also helpful.

Aircraft Maintenance Engineer

Entry to aircraft maintenance engineering is via craft, technician or student apprenticeships; entry qualifications depend upon the type of apprenticeship. The apprenticeships take the form of on-the-job training and part-time study at local colleges to prepare for aeronautical engineering qualifications offered by City and Guilds and BTEC/SCOTVEC or the NATS. Qualified aircraft engineers (including those from the armed forces) have to meet certain practical experience requirements before they can take NATS examinations to become licensed aircraft maintenance engineers. There are some full-time courses in aeronautical engineering available, usually lasting two and a half years.

Air Traffic Control

Entrants for the NATS scheme must be eligible for work within the UK, have security clearance, be aged between 18 and 27 and pass a medical. The training lasts just under 18 months and includes practice at Bournemouth Airport. This is followed by an extensive period of practical training at a designated site.

Air Traffic Engineer

NATS runs a training scheme for graduate electrical/electronic engineers lasting a minimum of 15 months. The training is approved by the Institute of Electrical and Electronic Engineering and will lead after approximately three years to chartered engineering status.

Personal Qualities

Pilot

Pilots must be very well balanced, physically fit, have stamina, good eyesight and colour vision; they must be mentally and physically alert and ready to respond quickly to changing conditions. They must be unflappable, confident, self-assured leaders with considerable technical skill.

Flight Engineer

Flight engineers must be physically fit and have a sound technical understanding of aircraft maintenance, flying techniques and operations. The ability to work in a small team and get on well with people in a confined space is necessary.

Air Cabin Crew

Air cabin crew must be reassuring and approachable, smart, have lots of energy and stamina, confidence and the ability to act quickly, decisively and in a firm but polite and tactful manner.

Maintenance Engineer

Maintenance engineering requires a combination of practical interest, mechanical aptitude, accuracy and manual dexterity. Engineers must be willing to adapt and to retrain. Very high standards and a responsible attitude are also most important.

Air Traffic Control

Air traffic control officers must be able to read and interpret a great deal of different information instantly and act upon it. They must be able to act quickly if conditions suddenly change, be healthy, reliable and well balanced emotionally; good eyesight and colour vision are important.

Air Traffic Engineer

Colour vision, great care, accuracy and a basic understanding of electricity and magnetism and their practical applications are required of the air traffic engineer, who must work to very high standards and be reliable.

Starting Salary

Salaries vary but the following is a guide: pilots £17,000–£26,000; cabin crew £7000+; student air traffic controller £14,699, air traffic control officer £25,247.

Further Information

National Air Traffic Services, 45–59 Kingsway, London WC2B 6TE; 0171 379 7311

Recruitment Services, T1213, CAA House, 45–59 Kingsway, London WC2B 6TE; 0171 832 6696

The Royal Aeronautical Society, 4 Hamilton Place, London W1V 0BQ; 0171 499 3515

Individual airlines

Civil Engineer*, see *Engineering

Civil Service

Civil servants work for the government in a variety of departments and agencies that recruit individually. These include the Ministry of Defence, the Foreign and Commonwealth Office, the Departments of Health and Social Security, the Department of the Environment, the Inland Revenue, the Home Office (including the Prison Service), the Department of Trade and Industry, and the Ministry of Agriculture, Fisheries and Food. They also work in the new Executive Agencies set up to provide a more efficient and cost-effective service to the public and to other departments, for example, the Stationery Office, Companies House and the Driver and Vehicle Licensing Agency. Consequently job opportunities are many and varied, but generally they fall into the following categories.

Administrative Staff

This is the largest group and members work in all departments, carrying out the work of government. At the top level it is responsible for policy and management. At a lower level are executive officers who are responsible for carrying out the daily work. They are the junior management – often in charge of a section or acting as the personal assistant to a more senior civil servant. Graduates may enter the diplomatic service or as executive officers or administration trainees. The administrative assistant (clerical) level is responsible for routine office work, such as answering straightforward enquiries, sending out forms and filing, as well as for providing secretaries/typists; administrative officers have wider responsibilities such as keeping records and figures and assisting the public.

Scientific Staff

They are employed in government laboratories and research establishments, working in research, design and development. Most opportunities here are in physics and engineering although there are also opportunities in maths and computing, chemical and life sciences. The majority of candidates are recruited at scientific officer grade (working on routine testing and analysis). Those with fewer qualifications can join as assistant scientific officers.

Professionally Qualified Staff

Professionally qualified staff (particularly in the field of technology) are employed in great numbers since the government needs its own architects, accountants, computer personnel, lawyers, librarians, statisticians, photographers, surveyors, draughtsmen, valuers and even veterinary surgeons and so on in the various departments.

Location

Eighty per cent of civil servants work outside London. Employees of the government must be prepared to work anywhere in the UK and (sometimes) abroad.

Qualifications and Training

Requirements vary from GCSE/GCE O level passes for junior posts to an honours degree for professional and higher administrative posts. Some typical examples are: a good honours degree (or equivalent) is essential for fast-stream administration trainees, scientific officers and other professional posts. Candidates with BTEC/SCOTVEC higher awards may be considered for some scientific jobs.

A level and H grade passes (or equivalent) are required for executive officers, engineering apprentices and grade 9 officers in the diplomatic service.

Specified passes at GCSE/GCE O level or SCE Standard grade (or technical qualifications) are normally required for administrative officers, assistant scientific officers and technician apprentices. NVQs at the appropriate level in a relevant subject may be acceptable for many posts. Much of the training is given on the job and is supplemented with attendance at formal courses (such as those in managerial or tax skills) when necessary. A large number of in-service training courses are also available (part time, full time and sandwich to assist in gaining appropriate qualifications).

Personal Qualities

Qualities required vary considerably from department to department. Much of the government's work is confidential, however, so loyalty and discretion are needed whatever the work.

Starting Salary

Salary compares favourably to those of outside staff. Some departments may pay a retention and recruitment allowance.

It is possible to gain promotion, and therefore higher salaries, from all grades.

Further Information

Recruitment & Assessment Services Ltd, Alençon Link, Basingstoke RG21 7JB; 01256 29222

Clerk

Clerks are employed in most offices and their duties vary enormously from firm to firm. They generally begin as office juniors and handle such routine tasks as dealing with the post, filing or photocopying. Most of their traditional work has been concerned with filling in forms and looking after paperwork – making out invoices/receipts, keeping customers' records, production sheets, answering postal (and telephone) enquiries, mailing catalogues, advertising materials and so on. Clerking jobs of this kind are much less numerous these days, however, since computer-based systems have taken over, particularly in record keeping where the VDU is replacing traditional filing. Practically all clerical jobs now require word-processing skills or a willingness to learn on the job.

Qualifications and Training

Most employers prefer some GCSEs (particularly English and maths) for even the most junior positions. Basic clerical skills can be learnt on the job but knowledge of office practice, word processing skills and/or secretarial training are necessary depending on the demands of individual employers.

Personal Qualities

Clerks should be methodical and organised. They have to be able to take orders and also be discreet about the information they may deal with.

Starting Salary

Varies depending upon duties and skills but for a junior generally about £5500+, considerably more in London. With experience, clerks earn on average £13,000–£14,000.

Further Information
Local Jobcentres and Careers Offices

Clockmaker,* see *Jewellery Trade, Watch and Clock Maker/Repairer

Clothing Industry *see Fashion*

The clothing industry is diverse and complex, with products ranging from off-the-peg garments which are turned out in hundreds and thousands, to exclusive *haute couture* designs from top fashion houses. There are job opportunities in large factories and in small workrooms, with large wholesaling firms and in small family businesses, and production lines may turn out high-fashion clothes where designs change radically and frequently, or more conservative lines such as underwear where the demand is fairly steady. The most important sections of the industry are men's and boys' outerwear, women's and girls' outerwear, children's clothing, bespoke tailoring (made to measure) and dressmaking. More specialised areas like millinery and glove making are relatively small.

Skilled workers are generally in great demand in most areas; main craft jobs are pattern cutting and grading, lay-making (how to position the pattern so as to make the best and most economical use of the cloth), cutting, marking or fixing (putting the different pieces of an individual garment together and marking the stitch lines), hand-sewing and pressing. There are also plenty of opportunities for semi-skilled workers and operators, particularly machinists. Much of this work is repetitive – frequently production lines are arranged so that each machinist sews only one part of a garment – but there may be opportunities to move up to more skilled work later (such as sample machining).

Technology is making itself felt in the clothing industry and more advanced sewing machines, computer-controlled pattern laying and die cutting of bulk quantities are only a few of the more recent developments. The industry in the future will need more skilled mechanics to maintain and care for the increasingly sophisticated machines. More and higher-skilled operatives will also be required. The clothing industry also employs people in its commercial sections – marketing and sales, for instance, or purchasing and supply – where there are often very close links with the major textile and fibre companies.

Qualifications and Training

Formal educational qualifications are not always needed to train for the craft skills. These are traditionally learnt by courses leading to City and Guilds examinations. Trainee tailors and cutters normally serve a four and a half year apprenticeship. Machinists are trained on the job by the employing company.

For more senior or technical jobs GCSEs are needed. The London College of Fashion and Clothing Technology runs a four-year full-time course for would-be managers (entry requires candidates to be over 18 with a minimum of five GCSEs and two A levels). There is a three-year full-time course (requiring five GCSEs to include maths and English) in tailoring as well as two-year courses in clothing and tailoring and one-year courses in clothing production and garment making. No formal academic qualifications are needed for the garment making course. The Mabel Fletcher Technical College, Liverpool, offers a three-year full-time diploma course in tailoring.

Personal Qualities

These vary according to the particular sector of the industry concerned. It is generally advantageous to be deft with one's hands and have high standards of neatness and precision. In factories a willingness to be part of a team is needed, while in bespoke tailoring a candidate should have a pleasant manner and be able to put potential customers at their ease.

Starting Salary

Depends upon individual employer, but generally low.

Further Information

CAPITB Trust, 80 Richardshaw Lane, Pudsey, Leeds LS28 6BN; 0113 239 3355

The Clothing and Footwear Institute, 105 Butlers Wharf Business Centre, Curlew Street, London SE1 2ND; 0171 403 9926

Coach

Football and cricket are the main sports where there are opportunities for coaches and these are for ex-professionals only. Sports centres, clubs, schools and swimming baths also provide opportunities for coaches on a part-time basis.

Some local authorities employ coaches to offer facilities for local schools at one or more centres in the authority. The sports offered are likely to be: badminton, basketball, climbing (indoor walls), ice skating, swimming, squash, tennis, trampolining and weight training. A coach employed in these circumstances must be able to coach in all or nearly all of the above.

Increasingly there is a need for coaches in the summer months to work in outdoor pursuits centres.

Qualifications and Training
Coaches must gain recognised coaching qualifications which are awarded by the governing bodies of the various sports and acquired either at evening class or weekend school. Swimming coaches must also hold a national lifeguard award.

Personal Qualities
Coaches need the ability to communicate as well as perseverance, patience and tact. The ability to inspire children or adults of very different abilities, often in less than ideal situations, is also needed.

Starting Salary
Salaries vary greatly. Coaches paid by the hour by local authorities receive £10.15–£11.30 an hour.

Further Information
The Sports Council, 16 Upper Woburn Place, London WC1H 0QP; 0171 388 1277

The Scottish Sports Council, Caledonia House, South Gyle, Edinburgh EH12 9DQ; 0131 317 7200

The Sports Council for Wales, Sophia Gardens, Cardiff CF1 9SW; 01222 397571

Coach Driver*, see *Bus Companies*, *Road Transport

Coastguard

When vessels and small craft are in trouble or missing off the coast it is the coastguard who is called in to organise and coordinate the necessary search and rescue measures. The UK area of responsibility is divided into six regions, each headed by a regional controller who is based at a Maritime Rescue Coordination Centre. These centres have officers who keep a constant watch on international distress frequencies and are trained to handle radio, telephone and telex messages which are received automatically. At other stations, regular officers are helped by auxiliaries. New technology is making it possible for the coastguard to provide a greatly enhanced service.

Qualifications and Training

Most coastguard officers are ex-seamen who have done previous marine work in services such as the Royal Navy or the Merchant Navy. They must have a strong maritime background, with at least six years' sea-going experience, a knowledge of communications or navigation and three GCSEs to include maths and English. There is an eight-week training course at the Coastguard Training School in Highcliffe (Dorset) for new entrants, who subsequently train on the job, complete a task book then attend a further short course and take a proficiency test.

Personal Qualities

Good eyesight and hearing are essential and candidates are expected to pass a strict medical. Candidates must be prepared to adapt to shift work and to serve anywhere in the UK.

Starting Salary

£12,000 for a probationer, which rises to £13,000 once qualified.

Further Information

The Coastguard Agency, Personnel Section, Spring Place, 105 Commercial Road, Southampton SO15 1EG; 01703 329461

Colour Science and Technology

Colour technologists are concerned with producing dyes and pigments that have a wide range of applications, including those in the textile, paint, rubber, plastics, paper, leather and foodstuffs industries. They must ensure that exact colours can be produced at an economic price and in the right quantities whenever they are needed. They are often involved in research and development projects. Technologists are also employed in sales, management, buying, development and research, quality control, customer liaison and technical services departments (depending on the industry involved and the expertise needed).

Textile Technologist

Technologists may work in the design, manufacture and operation of textile machinery; the design, production, coloration, finishing and manufacture of fibres, yarns and fabrics of all types.

Qualifications and Training

Two, preferably three, A levels or three H grades, one of which must be chemistry or a subject including chemistry, or a relevant BTEC/SCOTVEC award or an ND or NC in sciences are required for entry to a degree course in colour chemistry or textile chemistry. Minimum entry requirements for part-time technician courses leading to the BTEC/SCOTVEC certificate and higher certificate in textile coloration (textile dyeing) are GCSE or SCE Standard grade passes in mathematics, an appropriate science and English.

For textile technologists, the basic professional qualification is the Associateship and Chartered Textile Technologist (CText ATI) of The Textile Institute, awarded on the fulfilment of the academic and industrial/professional experience requirements. The professional qualification for a specialist in colour technology is the Associateship of the Society of Dyers and Colourists.

Personal Qualities

Good colour vision is essential, as is scientific or technical ability and the ability to work as one of a team.

Starting Salary

£11,500–£12,000+ with a degree; £8000+ for a textile technologist.

Further Information

The Society of Dyers and Colourists, PO Box 244, 82 Grattan Road, Bradford, West Yorkshire BD1 2JB; 01274 725138

Community Work

Community workers are concerned with areas where deprivation such as bad housing, unemployment or lack of community facilities is adding to the problems faced by the local community. The role of the community worker is to encourage residents to work together to improve the community's situation. The type of help given will depend on the needs of the neighbourhood but may include liaising with government and voluntary bodies, establishing social clubs and welfare services for the old and/or handicapped and developing play facilities for children.

Community workers are usually employed by local authorities or voluntary organisations. The work overlaps to some extent with that of youth and community workers and social workers.

Qualifications and Training

The main professional qualification is the diploma in social work (DipSW) which can be studied part time while working or via a full-time college course. Entry requirements are five GCSEs plus two A levels or five SCEs including three at H level. Mature entrants may be accepted without these qualifications. NVQs are also available.

Personal Qualities

Community workers must be able to get on with people from all backgrounds, listen to people, weigh up any conflicting interests and come to a fair decision, as well as having the necessary organisational and administrative skills to get things done.

Starting Salary

£13,581–£19,818 for qualified workers.

Further Information

England: CCETSW Information Service, Derbyshire House, St Chad's Street, London WC1H 8AD; 0171 278 2455

Northern Ireland: CCETSW Information Service, 6 Malone Road, Belfast BT9 5BN; 01232 665390

Scotland: CCETSW Information Service, 78–80 George Street, Edinburgh EH2 3BU; 0131 220 0093

Wales: CCETSW Information Service, South Gate House, Wood Street, Cardiff CF1 1EW; 01222 226257

Company Secretary

The company secretary provides the formal link between a company registered under the Companies Acts and its shareholders. They are responsible for all the legal requirements under the Acts, and duties include organising board meetings, shareholders' meetings, registration of shareholders and issue of shares, paying dividends, preparing agendas and minutes, advising on law, taxation and financial matters.

Qualifications and Training

Most company secretaries are chartered secretaries, holding the professional qualifications awarded by the Institute of Chartered Secretaries and Administrators. To become an associate or a fellow, success in Institute examinations must be allied with practical experience, although students can start to study without the relevant experience and gain this over the years.

Applicants must be 17 years of age or over. The Institute has an open access policy for entry to its foundation programme and a range of access points for holders of particular qualifications. The full ICSA qualification is recognised by the Department of Education and Science as equivalent to a university degree.

Holders of BTEC HNC/HNDs gain credit from the foundation programme, while holders of UK degrees gain credit from the foundation and pre-professional programmes. In both cases additional credits are available for courses which have been developed in collaboration with the Institute. Additional exemptions are also available for a variety of professional qualifications.

Personal Qualities

Company secretaries need good judgement and common sense, together with a flair for administration and organisation. Communication skills – both written and oral – are essential, as well as a clear understanding of figures and an interest in current affairs.

Starting Salary

Those with little previous experience can expect a starting salary of at least £16,000. Fully qualified company secretaries can expect to earn up to six-figure salaries.

Further Information

The Education Help Desk, The Institute of Chartered Secretaries and Administrators (ICSA), 16 Park Crescent, London W1N 4AH; 0171 580 4741

Computing

Computers have now taken their place in virtually every aspect of modern life and the demand for trained personnel is likely to be high for some time to come. The uses of computers are almost limitless; there are applications in industry (on production lines), in commerce (for preparing salaries, invoices and all kinds of routine paperwork), in retailing (for stock control), in scientific research (for analysing and comparing results), in travel (for making and confirming bookings and flight reservations) and in banking (for storing information about accounts). These are but a fraction of the tasks a computer may be asked to perform. Computer personnel may be divided into several specialised categories.

Systems Analyst

This work involves analysing the problem and designing a system which the computer can use to solve it. They have to work out what type of computer is necessary, how the information available should be fed into it and how the results should be presented, bearing in mind the amount and type of data the computer will be given, what the customer proposes to do with the results and the likely direction of expansion and future development.

Computer Operator

Networked PCs are more common these days and they are operated by their users, eg market analysts, accounts clerks, nurses, archivists or toolsetters. The computer operator is responsible for the actual running of the computer and is important in mainframe systems; he/she loads the magnetic disks or tapes which carry the program and the data, monitors the running of a program and is responsible for record keeping and storage. It is, however, a decreasing trade, now being replaced by systems support. Support staff install, maintain and update networked systems of PCs and workstations, and stand-alone PCs; they are responsible for both the hardware and the software.

Computer Programmer

A computer programmer composes the instructions and puts them into the special computer language so that the computer is able to carry out the tasks in the way the systems analyst has designed.

Software Engineer

He/she designs, tests and maintains large-scale software, frequently utilising 'library routines', written by programmers. He/she will work in teams, which include systems analysts, programmers and systems engineers. Much of the work is with people, and team skills are developed.

Data Processing

Data preparation operators organise the routine input of data into the programs, often via keyboards and screens (VDUs). Much of the work is now done by users, especially in commercial installations.

Training

Modern sophisticated packages run more efficiently if used by trained personnel. Trainers are employed by software vendors, by training companies and by user companies for their own staff. They need to be familiar with the packages at all levels, and have people and teaching skills, and may have to develop training materials.

In addition to these categories there are also openings in sales and marketing and in the service engineering side of computing. Computer (maintenance) engineers/service engineers install, maintain and annually clean computers.

Qualifications and Training

There are no rigid academic qualifications demanded as employers tend to set their own entry requirements. There are, however, a large number of relevant courses and these do have set requirements. Potential systems analysts are generally expected to hold degrees and/or programming and/or business qualifications (entry for such courses requires A levels, often in mathematical subjects). Programmers are usually expected to have A levels/H grade or HNC/HND passes as well as GCSEs or equivalent in English and maths. Some firms recruit graduates as trainee programmers.

Computer operators need at least three GCSE/SCE Standard grades including maths and English and one of these in computer studies can be an added asset. Data processors do not always require formal qualifications although experience in typing is advisable. Secretarial word processing courses may require GCSEs. Trainee service engineers need maths and physics qualifications (usually at least GCSE level/Standard grade passes).

Training opportunities are wide and varied. Many companies run their own training programmes as well as sending their trainees on relevant outside courses. Most candidates are asked to take an aptitude test before embarking on their training, to assess their numeracy, logic, accuracy and thinking speed. There are various courses available full and part time leading to BTEC and City and Guilds qualifications. Twenty-six NVQs are available at levels 1 to 4, in systems development and service provision areas. Awarding bodies include the BCS, BTEC, City and Guilds and in Scotland SCOTVEC.

Personal Qualities

Clear communications abilities and team working should come high on the list, together with the ability to both give out and receive information.

Starting Salary

Typical minimum salaries are: data preparation VDU operator £9000+; data preparation supervisor £12,000+; computer operator £11,000; senior operator £14,500+; junior programmer/graduate trainee £12,000+; programmer £14,500+; senior programmer £18,500+; systems analyst £18,500+; senior systems analyst £21,000+.

Further Information

Association of Computer Professionals, 204 Barnett Wood Lane, Ashtead, Surrey KT21 2DB; 01372 273442

British Computer Society, 1 Sanford Street, Swindon, Wiltshire SN1 1HJ; 01793 417417

Institution of Analysts and Programmers, Charles House, 36 Culmington Road, London W13 9NH; 0181 567 2118

Conference Organiser

A number of large companies and industrial concerns have their own department with staff responsible for making and coordinating the necessary arrangements for regular sales conferences, staff conferences, product launches and special events. Some institutions, associations and charities also employ staff specialising in the organisation of meetings and events. In several firms, the organising work is combined with other promotional or administrative duties. Other firms employ professional conference organisers.

Conference organisers must select and book the most suitable venue, organise the invitations and accommodation (if necessary) of the various participants, the relevant paperwork, the catering and reception facilities, any specialist equipment necessary (such as video, microphones, projectors, closed-circuit television and so on), media coverage (if applicable), and a host of minor details. Some firms of professional organisers have a small staff and also employ temporary freelances as and when necessary.

Conference centres and hotels specialising in conference facilities have their own conference staff who are responsible for arrangements for conferences already booked and for advertising and encouraging further bookings.

Qualifications and Training

There are currently no formal educational requirements, but occupational standards and NVQs are being established. Useful experience could include sales and marketing, knowledge of hotel and venue operations, and language skills, as well as secretarial duties. Computer literacy is important. Scottish Vocational Qualifications should be available in 1997.

Personal Qualities

A flair for organisation and forward planning is needed, as are tact, discretion and the ability to talk to all kinds of people and anticipate their various demands. In addition, conference organisers should be prepared to organise events abroad.

Starting Salary

£14,000–£16,000 is the salary a large firm might offer. Salaries for freelances vary as to the type and amount of work undertaken.

Further Information

Association for Conferences and Events, ACE International, Riverside House, High Street, Huntingdon, Cambridgeshire PE18 6SG; 01480 457595

How to Organise Effective Conferences and Meetings, Kogan Page

Conservation (Environmental)

Conservation is the term used for the careful preservation and protection of a natural resource: the land itself, plants or animals. Government departments are actively and extensively involved in conservation.

Countryside Commission is uniquely responsible for conserving and enhancing the beauty of the countryside, making it accessible for people to enjoy, and also sustaining its value to the local and national economy. The work of the Commission includes protecting National Parks and other valued landscapes, helping land managers to improve the environmental and recreational potential of farmland, conserving hedgerows, ancient orchards and other much loved features of the countryside, planting woodlands on the edges of great cities, or improving the thousands of kilometres of rights of way.

English Nature is the statutory adviser to government on nature conservation in England and promotes the conservation of England's wildlife and natural features. Its work includes the selection, establishment and management of national nature reserves and marine nature reserves, the identification and provision of advice and information about nature conservation, and the support and conduct of research relevant to these functions.

Countryside Council for Wales is the Government's statutory adviser on wildlife, countryside and maritime conservation matters in Wales. It is the executive authority for the conservation of habitats and wildlife. Through partners it promotes the protection of landscape, opportunities for enjoyment and the support of those who live and work in and manage the countryside.

Department of the Environment supervises and advises upon land reclamation and coastline protection schemes carried out by local authorities. It is also involved with national parks projects and the restoration of derelict country sites.

National Environment Research Council involves itself in a broad range of activities concerned with conservation (mainly involving scientists), including geological surveys, studies of the ocean, terrestrial ecology and the British Antarctic Survey which studies atmospheric, earth and life sciences.

Scottish Natural Heritage fulfils a similar role for Scotland as the Countryside Council does for Wales.

In addition there are non-government bodies.

National Trust owns vast amounts of land and is the largest single private landowner in the country. It is concerned with the conservation of places of natural beauty and historic buildings. It employs land agents and various specialist staff to care for such sites and supervise the visiting public.

Royal Society for the Protection of Birds has its own protected reserves and employs nature wardens, researchers and surveyors in reserve management, although such posts are relatively few.

In addition conservation includes a large number of voluntary societies such as the Councils for Protection of Rural England, Wales and Scotland, the Commons Open Spaces and Footpaths Preservation Society and Wildlife Trusts. Such organisations have few full-time posts and these are mainly confined to administrative staff.

Qualifications and Training

Qualifications vary as there are many different jobs: conservation officers and science specialists need relevant degrees or equivalent; much of the training is done on the job but the advent of National Vocational Qualifications in landscapes and ecosystems provides an important set of standards and defines levels of competence for most people working in the environmental conservation field. Administrative officers need at least five GCSEs or equivalent, one of which must be English language; reserve wardens do not always need formal qualifications although A level biology is an advantage. Much of the training is done on the job. Competition for posts in conservation is strong.

Personal Qualities

Conservationists must show dedication in their chosen field and be prepared to work as one of a team.

Starting Salary

Salaries vary but are in the region of: scientific officer £11,500–£19,000, administrative assistant £5000–£10,000, administrative officer £5500–£11,500, estate worker £150 a week.

Further Information

Countryside Commission, John Dower House, Crescent Place, Cheltenham GL50 3RA; 01242 531381

Countryside Council for Wales, Plas Penrhos, Ffordd Penrhos, Bangor, Gwynedd LL57 2LQ; 01248 370444

English Nature, Northminster House, Peterborough PE1 1UA; 01733 455000

National Trust, 36 Queen Anne's Gate, London SW1H 9AS; 0171 222 9251

Natural Environment Research Council, Polaris House, North Star Avenue, Swindon SN2 1EU; 01793 411500

The Royal Society for the Protection of Birds, The Lodge, Sandy, Bedfordshire SG19 2DL; 01767 680551

Scottish Natural Heritage, 12 Hope Terrace, Edinburgh EH9 2AS; 0131 447 4784

Careers in Environmental Conservation, Kogan Page

Brochures and leaflets, English Nature

Conservation (Historical) *see Museum and Art Gallery Work*

Conservation is the preservation and restoration of works of art such as paintings and sculptures; historic buildings; furniture; fabrics, such as tapestries; manuscripts; clocks; and china. Some museums and art galleries employ specialist conservation officers who are responsible for restoring, repairing and protecting the exhibits in their charge, using the latest scientific techniques. Such work generally calls for scientific training and artistic knowledge. There are a number of conservators working in the private sector, many working alone or with one partner. Museums and art galleries are sending out more of their objects to private conservators rather than increasing the in-house staff.

Qualifications and Training

Requirements vary a good deal according to the organisation involved. The training courses for museum conservation officers are mainly at degree or postgraduate level with the exception of the more craft-based subjects such as clocks or ceramics restoration which are available as college diplomas.

Personal Qualities

Those working in conservation need imagination, scientific ability, a flair for improvisation, meticulous attention to detail and great patience.

Starting salary
Public sector: £13,000–£15,000+. Many one-person businesses have a turnover of less than £10,000.

Further Information
Association of British Picture Restorers, Station Avenue, Kew, Richmond TW9 3QA; 0181 948 5644
The Conservation Unit, Museum and Galleries Commission, 16 Queen Anne's Gate, London SW1H 9AA; 0171 233 4200
Institute of Paper Conservation, Leigh Lodge, Leigh, Worcester WR6 5LB; 01886 832323
Museums Association, 42 Clerkenwell Close, London EC1R 0PA; 0171 608 2933
Historic Scotland, Longmore House, Salisbury Place, Edinburgh EH9 1SH; 0131 668 8600
Scottish Society for Conservation and Restoration, The Glasite Meeting House, 33 Barony Street, Edinburgh EH3 6NX
Society of Archivists, Information House, 20–24 Old Street, London EC1V 9AP; 0171 253 5087
United Kingdom Institute for Conservation of Historic and Artistic Works, 6 Whitehorse Mews, Westminster Bridge Road, London SE1 7QD; 0171 620 3371

Constituency Agent*, see *Politics

Courier (Messenger)

Couriers deliver and collect parcels. The work is generally done in the larger towns and cities. Mostly the delivery or collection is in the same town, sometimes a different one and, occasionally, another country. Most couriers travel by motorcycle which they may be required to buy. Couriers carrying packages abroad travel by air.

Qualifications and Training
No formal educational qualifications are necessary. Motorcycle couriers must be 17 and hold a clean motorcycle licence.

Personal Qualities
Couriers are generally required when speed is important or when the package cannot be entrusted to the post. Therefore reliability is most important as too is the ability to arrive without undue delays. Common sense and initiative are also useful.

Starting Salary

Some couriers are self-employed, the firm paying a certain amount per mile, and the messenger being responsible for petrol, insurance and other overheads. Others are employees and receive vouchers for petrol which they cash at a nominated garage. Starting salaries vary, but an employed courier can earn £180+ a week and a self-employed person much more.

Some air couriers are employed on a one-off basis and receive a free or reduced-cost flight in lieu of salary and baggage allowance.

Further Information

Local Jobcentres and Careers Offices

Courier (Travel)

Couriers are employed by the major tour companies as official guides for parties of tourists travelling with them from country to country and town to town. The courier is responsible for the welfare of the tourists and must attend to any worries or complaints. In addition, they are responsible for all the paperwork necessary when the party stays overnight in a hotel or crosses a frontier post. Much of their work is seasonal and generally only senior staff are kept on a permanent basis.

Qualifications and Training

A good general education including GCSE passes in English, geography and maths is usually required by the travel trade. Qualifications in relevant languages and experience of living and working abroad are an obvious advantage, and couriers must be conversant with local customs and fluent in the various languages needed on a particular tour. Most training takes place on the job and there are NVQs available. The Institute of Travel and Tourism has professional examinations (three to four GCSEs required) but these are not intended for trainees, rather experienced staff wishing to gain more senior positions in the travel industry.

Personal Qualities

A courier must have infinite patience, tact and a pleasant personality. They need to be able to get on with a wide variety of people of all nationalities and from all walks of life, without becoming flustered or panic-stricken when a crisis arises.

Starting Salary

Couriers may expect to earn £130+ a week with full accommodation. There are also opportunities to earn more money by organising extra trips.

Further Information

Institute of Travel and Tourism, 113 Victoria Street, St Albans, Hertfordshire AL1 3TJ; 01727 854395

Major tour operators

Careers Using Languages, Kogan Page

Careers in the Travel Industry, Kogan Page

Court Staff

Court Reporter

Court reporters attend court sittings and take down a complete report of all the evidence, the summing-up or judgment and, on occasions, the speeches of counsel in the various cases. Formerly the proceedings were taken down in shorthand; now a stenograph, a typewriter-like machine, is used which enables reporters to achieve 200 words per minute. In addition, computers may be used to prepare transcripts with all the advantages of on-screen editing and speed of preparation. The work sometimes involves travelling to a number of different courts.

Justices' Clerk

They are either solicitors or barristers. Their job is to advise and assist lay magistrates by providing them with guidance on the law and the procedure relevant in any particular case. The clerk will often sit in court while cases are being heard and remind the bench of their powers and give general advice.

Justices' Clerks' Assistant

Administrative assistants and administrative officers assist justices' clerks in the administration of the magistrates' courts. Their work involves the preparing of summonses and warrants, the issuing of licences and fine notices and seeing that correct court procedures are followed.

In Scotland, the administration of the court comes under the province of the Scottish Court Administration – part of the Civil Service. This includes staff who do a similar job to justices' clerks' assistants.

Qualifications and Training

No specific academic qualifications are demanded for court reporters although GCSE and A level passes can be an advantage. Applicants do need to have proven ability in shorthand or steno-typing (usually over 150 words per minute), good typing speeds, and a thorough knowledge of grammar and punctuation. Legal experience can also be an asset. Training is undertaken by a number of specialist firms who supply shorthand writers to the courts. On successful completion of the training, trainees are awarded a certificate issued by the Institute of Shorthand Writers or the Association of Professional Shorthand Writers.

Justices' clerks must be solicitors or barristers with five years' experience. Administrative assistants need two GCSE passes (grade C or above), one of which must be English. Administrative officers need five GCSE passes (grade C or above), one of which must be English.

Scottish Court Service applicants need several Standard grades and preferably H grades. Training lasts for two to three years during which time trainees both work and undertake courses run by the Court Service.

Personal Qualities

Anyone concerned with the courts must be discreet, honest and trustworthy, as most of the work is confidential. Reporters must show a high degree of accuracy.

Starting Salary

A newly qualified court reporter earns over £11,000, trainees about £8000; justices' clerks £20,000; administrative assistants from £5000 and administrative officers from £8000. Additional payments are made to those working in London.

Further Information

British Institute of Verbatim Reporters, 61 Carey Street, London WC2A 2JG; (*please enclose sae*) (*court reporters*)

Individual Courts of Law

Northern Ireland Court Service, Windsor House, Bedford Street, Belfast BT2 7LT; 01232 328594

The Law Society of Scotland, 26 Drumsheugh Gardens, Edinburgh EH3 7YR; 0131 226 7411

Careers in the Law, Kogan Page

Crane Driver*, see *Building

Croupier

Croupiers work at the gaming tables of gaming clubs and casinos. They are in charge of accepting the bets, allocating chips, spinning the roulette wheel or dealing the cards and giving out the winnings (or raking in what customers have lost).

Qualifications and Training

No formal educational qualifications are demanded but a good head for figures is vital, and GCSE level maths is an advantage. A good appearance and pleasant personality are assets; a clean record is essential – no one with a criminal record can be granted a gaming licence by the Government Gaming Board; without such a licence it is not possible to be legally employed as a croupier in Britain. Most of the major gaming clubs have their own training schools where candidates are taught how to dress, how to behave and how to treat the customers as well as the rules of the various games, the special skills for counting chips, memorising and calculating the bets and so on.

Personal Qualities

Nimble fingers and an agile brain are essential, as are a pride in one's appearance and an unflappable nature. The job involves working with people so good communication skills and an ability to defuse potentially awkward situations are also needed (though these are, to a certain extent, taught). A croupier must also be scrupulously honest, and willing to work shifts and anti-social hours.

Starting Salary

Salaries vary but a trained croupier in London or abroad could expect to earn £400+ a week. A starting salary in Britain would be over £10,000, depending on area.

Further Information

British Casino Association, 29 Castle Street, Reading, Berkshire RG1 7SL; 01734 589 191 (*for list of members and training notes*); Fax: 01734 590 592

Local Jobcentres and Careers Offices

Major gambling groups

Curator*, see *Museum and Art Gallery Work

Customs and Excise

HM Customs and Excise is responsible for collecting about 40 per cent of central government taxation and protects society against illegal importations of drugs and other prohibited goods.

Most new entrants to the Department begin their careers in a local VAT office. There they give advice to local businesses and are responsible for ensuring that the correct amount of tax is paid. Executive officers are likely to spend four days out of five visiting companies to find out what they do and to audit their records.

The Department is also responsible for collecting excise duties; for example, on petrol, spirits, cigarettes, and betting and gaming. Again, the Department's role is to ensure that businesses understand their responsibilities.

Probably the most familiar role is the control of imported and exported goods at ports and airports throughout the UK. As well as checking passengers' baggage, commercial importations of cargo are examined.

The work is interesting and varied, with opportunities to get out of the office. With offices all over the country, there are opportunities to work near home.

Qualifications and Training

There are three main entry levels into Customs and Excise. The bottom rung of the ladder is administrative assistant. To join at this level you require two GCSEs at C grade or above including English language. Administrative officers require five GCSEs at C grade or above including English language. Alternatively, if you have two A levels and three GCSEs including English language, it is possible to join at junior management level as an executive officer.

Full training is given as necessary. This may involve a combination of classroom training, self-learning packages and on-the-job training.

Personal Qualities

To do this job well you need to be able to get on with people. Tact, sensitivity and firmness are all useful qualities. You also need to be able to use your initiative and common sense.

Starting Salary

Varies depending on age and location but is in the region of; administrative assistants £7300 to £7900, administrative officers £10,755–£11,250 and executive officers £12,675–£14,000. Rates are higher in London.

Further Information
HM Customs and Excise, New King's Beam House, 22 Upper Ground, London SE1 9PJ; 0171 620 1313

Dancing

Most people regard dancing as recreation or as a form of exercise; exceptionally few make performance their career.

Ballet

To achieve brilliance, and the necessary levels of physical fitness, total dedication is essential, and hours every day must be spent in practice. Competition is fierce for the 300 or so places in the UK ballet companies. Training must start at a very early age, no later than 13, and it is improbable that a dancer's career will extend beyond the mid-thirties.

Contemporary Dance

This is a much freer form of dance than ballet, the movements are less formal and the whole floor space is more widely used. As regards work opportunities, the number of positions is strictly limited by the fact that few professional companies exist and these tend not to change their personnel very often.

Modern Dance

This includes jazz and tap dancing, disco and acrobatics, and in fact anything that is currently popular. Rather more opportunities exist here than in ballet. Dancers may find themselves working in musical stage shows, television, films or cabaret, but these are all too often seasonal, short-term contracts which do not lend themselves to security of employment. Modern dance is not so demanding a discipline as ballet; nevertheless rehearsals and practice will take up a great deal of the dancer's time. Many modern dancers begin by studying ballet but the age at which they begin training is not so crucial.

Choreography

The ability to create and arrange dance requires an imaginative understanding, usually gained from years of experience of music and dance. A few performers will graduate into choreography while others arrive via specialist courses, or other related areas such as teaching. By definition, places will be fewer than those for performers and opportunities for secure employment even less.

Dance Animateur

Dance animateurs are employed by regional arts authorities or local authorities to initiate dance projects in schools, colleges and the local community. As well as relevant dance qualifications they must have administrative and organisational abilities plus the ability to drive, as they must visit a number of venues in their regional arts authority.

Qualifications and Training

Ideally ballet students should attend a recognised, residential establishment such as the Royal Ballet School from the age of 11. Financial assistance may be available for those showing great promise. Full-time courses for the 11–16 age group and school-leavers are available which offer a wide range of training in the performing arts generally and part-time instruction, allowing students to prepare for the recognised examinations of their chosen specialisation.

GCSE, A level, A/S level and BTEC courses in dance exist, but are not widely available.

The London School of Contemporary Dance offers specialist courses, some leading to a degree and many universities and colleges offer dance as part of their curriculum but these courses are not usually intended for performers. Dancers who wish to become teachers must obtain the relevant qualifications for which full- or part-time courses will be available; these may have academic qualifications such as GCSEs as an entry requirement. The Royal Academy of Dancing offers a three-year teaching certificate programme and a BA in the art and teaching of ballet. Northern Ballet School offers a three-year dance teacher's diploma. While entry to most dancing courses and schools is based upon audition, students should attain some academic qualifications as an insurance against unemployment in such a short-lived profession.

Personal Qualities

To succeed, dancers must be hard-working, self-disciplined both physically and mentally, dedicated, determined and healthy. They must also be the right height, shape and size, graceful, well poised and attractive. They must be imaginative, able to express themselves artistically and possess a good sense of timing and an ear for music.

Starting Salary

Salaries vary according to company, but should be about £200 a week. Dance animateurs earn £12,000+.

Further Information

The Benesh Institute, 12 Lisson Grove, London NW1 6TS; 0171 258 3041

Central School of Ballet, 10 Herbal Hill, Clerkenwell Road, London EC1R 5EJ; 0171 837 6332

The Council for Dance Education and Training (UK), Riverside Studios, Crisp Road, London W6 9RL; 0181 741 5084

London Contemporary Dance School, The Place, 17 Dukes Road, London WC1H 9AB; 0171 387 0152

Northern Ballet School, The Dancehouse, 10 Oxford Road, Manchester M1 5QA; 0161 237 1406

Royal Academy of Dancing, 36 Battersea Square, London SW11; 0171 223 0091

Royal Ballet School (upper), 155 Talgarth Road, London W14 9DE; 0181 748 6335

Royal Ballet School (lower), White Lodge, Richmond Park, Surrey TW10 5HR; 0181 876 5547

Regional Arts Authorities (dance animateurs)

Data Processing*, see *Computing

Dentistry

Dentist

Dentists aim to prevent gum disease and tooth decay and to identify and treat such diseases. This involves filling, crowning and extracting first teeth, scaling and cleaning teeth and gums. They design and fit dentures and plates and take corrective measures for teeth growing abnormally. They are also involved with the rectification of fractured jaws etc, and with surgery of the mouth. Opportunities exist both in this country and abroad. In general dental practice, dentists work on contract to the National Health Service, and some may treat patients privately. Many work in hospitals or in community or school services. Vacancies are also to be found in armed forces, research and industry.

Dental Hygienist

Dental hygienists clean, polish and scale teeth and in some cases they prepare patients for oral operations. Through lectures and practical experience they also endeavour to educate children and adults as to the importance of proper dental care.

Dental Nurse

Dental nurses, formerly known as surgery assistants, look after all aspects of the surgery from clerical tasks such as updating patients' records, looking after reception and keeping the books, to care of the dentist's instruments, the preparation of fillings and processing x-rays.

Dental Technician

Dental technicians are crafts people employing a wide variety of different materials and equipment to make crowns, dentures, metal plates, bridges and other appliances as instructed by dental surgeons.

Dental Therapist

Dental therapists work in local authority clinics and hospitals assisting dentists by carrying out simpler forms of treatment such as fillings and the extraction of first teeth, under the dentist's direction, of course. They also give guidance on general dental care.

Qualifications and Training

Dentist

To qualify, a dentist must have a degree in dental surgery. All dentists must be registered to the Dentists' Register, which is maintained by the General Dental Council. From the age of 17, students may enter one of the 14 UK dental schools. Competition for places is stiff and the A level grades required in physics, chemistry and biology will be high; these will vary, however, and some schools have pre-dental courses for students who have not attained the appropriate A levels. Courses usually last five years. In the armed forces dental cadetships leading to a commission are open to candidates who have completed part of their training at a dental school.

Dental Hygienist

At least five GCSE passes are required for entry to the course which leads to the diploma in dental hygiene; preferred subjects are biology and English language. Students must be over 18, although the average age is 21, and a grant is available for the duration of the one-year course (may extend to two years) which may be taken at most dental hospitals. Previous dental surgery experience is required, and some hospitals insist on candidates already having a dental surgery assistant qualification.

Dental Nurse

No set qualifications are needed to become a dental nurse. Many dentists like to train their own assistants but they will probably expect applicants to be educated to GCSE standard. Students may enter for the national certificate of the examining board for dental nurses. Preparation for this exam can be obtained either at evening or day-release classes or by full-time attendance on a course lasting between one and two years. A certificate is awarded on passing the exam and completing 24 months' practical experience. Courses are offered by colleges of further education and dental hospitals.

Dental Technician

The usual entry requirements for courses are five GCSEs or equivalents (English, maths, physics and chemistry). Prospective dental technicians may train by working with a dental surgeon or in a commercial laboratory as apprentices for five years, with a part-time study at a technical college leading to the BTEC diploma in dental technology, or they may take a full time course lasting three to four years leading to the dental technicians diploma.

Dental Therapist

To become a dental therapist it is necessary to take a two-year, full-time course at the Dental Auxiliary School, London Hospital Medical College. The minimum course entry requirement is five GCSE passes or equivalents; these should include English and biology. Applicants should also hold the national certificate for dental nurses, which requires at least two years' practical experience. As competition for places is fierce, actual requirements are likely to be higher than this.

Personal Qualities

Manual and visual dexterity combined with medical knowledge and clinical skills are essential. Candidates should be equable, sympathetic and have an agreeable nature and an ability to communicate.

Starting Salary

Typical minimum salaries are: dental hygienist £11,334+; dental nurses £4940 rising to £8606 after eight years' experience; dental technicians £4681–£7801 rising to £10,401+ when qualified; dental therapists £11,718+ on qualification; dental surgeons in practice work under the National Health Service regulations and the recommended target net income is £36,350. In the Community Dental Service, the salaries for clinical dental officers range from £19,320–£28,390. In the hospital service the salaries are the same as for medical grades.

Further Information

British Association of Dental Nurses, 110 London Street, Fleetwood, Lancashire FY7 6EU; 01253 778631 (*Please enclose a sae*)

British Association of Dental Therapists, Dental Auxiliary School, London Hospital Medical College, 6–8 Walden Street, London E1 2AN

The British Dental Association, 64 Wimpole Street, London W1M 8AL; 0171 935 0875

British Dental Hygienists' Association, 64 Wimpole Street, London W1M 8AL; 0171 935 0875

The Dental Technicians' Education and Training Advisory Board (DTETAB), 5 Oxford Court, St James Road, Brackley, Northamptonshire NN13 7XY; 01280 702600

General Dental Council, 37 Wimpole Street, London W1M 8DQ; 0171 486 2171

Designer*, see *Artist, Fashion, Industrial Designer, Interior Designer, Jewellery Trade, Publishing, Theatre

Detective/Private Investigator

A private detective can either work alone, ie self-employed, or as part of an agency. The investigation profession has a diverse workload and is therefore difficult to categorise. A small cross-section of the subjects that an investigator may be instructed to assist with are as follows: tracing missing persons, debtors, witnesses and taking statements; video and photographic surveillance for matrimonial or insurance company fraud; process serving (the correct delivery of legal documents); pre sue and means enquiries; verifying credit worthiness; road traffic and industrial accident investigations involving sketch plans and photographs; land registry searches; land and property repossession; test purchases.

Qualifications and Training

No formal qualifications are necessary but a good standard of education will be an advantage for the preparation of reports and the taking of statements. Training seminars are run by the Association of British Investigators. A sound knowledge of computers, experience in credit control, or a service industry with direct contact dealing with public are useful. NVQs level 3 and 4 are available in investigation techniques.

Personal Qualities

Honesty, integrity, and discretion are vital. Patience, perseverance, self motivation, ability to work on own initiative, adaptability and a good outgoing personality are all useful qualities.

Starting Salary

This is regional and depends upon experience. An agency can charge approximately £20 per hour but will pay lower rates to staff. The self-employed may be able to charge similar rates. (Check with local legal aid board for acceptable hourly rate.)

Further Information

Association of British Investigators, ABI House, 10 Bonner Hill Road, Kingston-upon-Thames, Surrey KT1 3EP (The general secretary can assist with finding a local agency that may offer further information.)

Local Jobcentres and Careers Offices

Libraries also hold directories of investigators

You will need personal indemnity and public liability insurance, also to register with the Office of Fair Trading and the Data Protection Registrar. It is also advisable to obtain membership of a recognised association.

Dietitian

A dietitian is an authority on diet and on the application of the principles of nutrition. There are a great many opportunities and interesting posts for dietitians, particularly in the National Health Service. Hospital dietitians, for example, collaborate with doctors and catering staff in planning the correct balance of foods for all the patients, depending on their general state of health and medical requirements. Their work involves instructing patients and their relatives, the medical, nursing and catering staff. Dietitians are also employed by local health authorities to work with general practitioners, in health centres and clinics dealing with infant welfare and ante-natal treatment. Some dietitians may now be employed directly by fund-holding GPs. They are also called upon to educate other healthcare professionals in nutrition. Other opportunities for dietitians exist in education, industrial research, the food industry and the media. Increasingly, dietitians work as freelances.

Qualifications and Training

GCSEs in maths and English are required, and two or three A levels, preferably chemistry and another science subject, are required for entry to a dietetics degree course. BTEC qualifications may be acceptable and mature students may also apply. Dietitians are all university graduates.

It is possible to take a degree in dietetics or nutrition and dietetics. Graduates with a degree with an acceptable level of human physiology and biochemistry may take a postgraduate diploma course in dietetics. Leeds Metropolitan University, University of Ulster, Coleraine, University of Wales Institute, Cardiff, and Glasgow Caledonian University offer two-year full-time courses.

Personal Qualities

Dietitians' special skill is to translate scientific and medical decisions relating to food and health into terms which everyone can understand. An interest in food, coupled with an understanding of how different cultural, social and economic factors can determine a person's dietary requirements, are needed by the dietitian. Dietitians must therefore be interested in people and not just the scientific aspects of their problems.

Starting Salary

£13,120. Senior Dietitians earn £15,500–£19,000 and managers up to £29,000.

Further Information

British Dietetic Association, Seventh Floor, Elizabeth House, 22 Suffolk Street, Queensway, Birmingham B1 1LS; 0121 643 5483; Fax: 0121 633 4399 (*Please send an sae*)

Diplomat*, see *Civil Service

Disc Jockey

Disc jockeys present records (compact discs) in a variety of situations: hospital radio, where many djs start out; local and national radio and in clubs. Radio 1 prides itself on not only playing the music available but on going out and finding new bands.

Disc jockeys talk to their audience and must be able to hold their interest, think of something different and keep the balance right between music and chat.

Qualifications and Training

A strong interest in and a wide knowledge of different bands is necessary. Some djs have had experience at school or in hospital radio. Some have previously worked for radio in another capacity and moved from that to being a disc jockey.

Personal Qualities

Disc jockeys need to have lively enquiring minds and be good communicators.

Starting Salary

This varies tremendously depending on hours worked and where. Big name djs command high salaries.

Further Information

Local and national radio (*those applying to radio stations should generally enclose a tape showing what they can do*).

District Nurse *see Nurse*

District nurses are employed by NHS Community Trusts. They work closely with general practitioners, health visitors, practice nurses and other community nurses, providing skilled nursing care for patients and their families in their own homes, in surgeries and in other health and community centres. The district nurse is the leader of the district nursing team, which includes staff nurses, district enrolled nurses and care assistants.

Qualifications and Training

Applicants must be registered general/adult nurses, usually with post-registration experience. Programmes are offered at institutions of higher education.

From 1995 new courses lead to the award of Specialist Practitioner (district nursing) and are at degree level. By October 1998 all courses will be replaced by this new Specialist Practitioner qualification.

Personal Qualities

The district nurse must have good leadership skills, the ability to understand the needs of individuals and families in the community. She or he will have the confidence to work independently and also to relate well to other members of the primary health care team. As well as the ability to work efficiently and manage his or her own work, good communication skills, and often a sense of humour, are important qualities.

Starting Salary

Dependent upon previous experience but from £18,156–£21,007; district nurses employed in the London zone or outer London zone receive London weighting.

Further Information

ENB Careers, PO Box 2EN, London, W1A 2EN; 0171 391 6200/6205
Careers in Nursing and Related Professions, Kogan Page

Diver

Until the mid-1970s professional divers were mainly employed in ports, harbours, docks, by water authorities and in support of 'wet' civil engineering work. The growth in offshore oil and gas exploration greatly increased the opportunities open to qualified divers, but there has recently been a decline in demand. The growth of diving as a popular sport has created a limited number of positions for full-time instructors. Fairly large numbers of divers are employed by the police force and the Royal Navy, while a few find employment in salvage work.

Qualifications and Training

Diving is potentially hazardous and efficient training is absolutely essential to ensure maximum safety. HSE-approved diving schools provide full-time courses of instruction; these courses are expensive: in the region of £5000 for the HSE I course for air divers offshore; HSE parts III and IV courses for inshore work are shorter and less expensive. Applicants must be at least 18 years of age. Clubs and diving schools offer amateur qualifications which should be recognised by the World Underwater Federation (Confédération Mondiale d'Activités Subaquatiques or CMAS). Training is given for their own personnel by the Royal Navy and the police force. In the case of the latter, pupils must have a minimum of two years' experience as a constable. All divers who are paid for the work which they do must attend and pass a course which has been approved by the Health and Safety Executive (HSE).

Personal Qualities

Divers must be sound swimmers and physically fit; all professional divers have to pass a full commercial diving medical which complies with Health and Safety Executive Diving Operations at Work Regulations. They must be able to tolerate hard exercise, extreme conditions and recognise and work within their own personal limits. They must be very responsible and willing and able to work as part of a team.

Starting Salary

An occupation for the few with some openings in water authorities at around £15,000. The potential rewards for deep sea and oil rig divers are much greater but as there are at present (1997) more divers than work available for them it is difficult for the newly trained to obtain work.

Further Information

The International Marine Contractors' Association, 177A High Street, Beckenham, Kent BR3 1AH; 0181 663 3859
Health and Safety Executive, Rose Court, 2 Southwark Bridge, London SE1 9HS; 0171 717 6000
Fort Bovisand Underwater Centre, Plymouth, Devon PL9 0AB
Society for Underwater Technology, 76 Mark Lane, London EC3R 7JN; 0171 481 0750
The Underwater Centre, Fort William, Highland PH33 6LZ
Local police forces
Local Royal Navy Careers Information Offices

Doctor of Medicine,* see *Medicine

Dog Groomer

Dog grooming is a growing industry, with more and more dog owners taking advantage of the services provided by grooming salons. There are over 2000 grooming salons, the majority of which are individual premises, and increasing numbers are part of other pet-related establishments such as pet shops, garden centres, boarding and breeding kennels. There are also mobile groomers who visit the animals in their own homes. Each breed has different requirements and there are many types of coat which all require specialist skills and techniques in their preparation. The work involves bathing, shampooing, drying, clipping, trimming and brushing a variety of long- and short-coated dogs.

Qualifications and Training

There are three main routes into training: a fee paying course at a private grooming training centre, learning on the job or, for 16 and 17 year olds, a training place as part of a youth training programme. Those with one year's practical experience should enrol for the City and Guilds Dog Grooming Certificate 775. A further qualification is the Advanced Grooming Diploma.

Personal Qualities

A love of animals is essential for this type of work, and a good deal of patience is required with a firm but gentle way of handling. Good customer care plays a large part of the job, and a pleasant courteous manner combined with a neat and tidy appearance is essential.

Starting Salary

This varies from area to area and hours and rates of pay are negotiable.

Further Information

British Dog Groomers Association, Bedford Business Centre, 170 Mile Road, Bedford MK42 9TW; 01234 273933; Fax: 01234 273550

Our Dogs, 5 Oxford Road, Station Approach, Manchester M60 1SX; 0161 236 2660 (job advertisements)

Local Jobcentres and Careers Offices

Domestic Service

Although far fewer people are engaged in domestic service than in the past, there are still some job openings. Posts include: butler, cook, housekeeper, maid and, occasionally, footman and valet.

Butlers' duties involve announcing guests, serving drinks and supervising other staff; cooks are responsible for preparing food; housekeepers for the general running of a household, often in the absence of the owner; and maids for waiting at table, cleaning and/or looking after the lady of the house's clothes.

It is possible to do some of these jobs such as buttling on a temporary basis, and agencies exist to provide domestic staff for special occasions.

Qualifications and Training

Formal educational qualifications are not necessary, although a City and Guilds or other catering qualification may be a bonus. Experience and good recommendations are important.

Personal Qualities
Discretion, tact, and the ability to put someone else first are important.

Starting Salary
Salaries vary depending on whether full board and lodging are provided, hours worked and individual employers.

Further Information
Local Jobcentres and Careers Offices

The Lady, 39–40 Bedford Street, Strand, London WC2E 9EN; 0171 379 4717 (*job advertisements*)

Drama Therapist

Dramatherapy's main focus is the intentional use of drama and theatre as a therapeutic process. It is a method of working and playing that uses action methods to facilitate creativity, imagination, learning, insight and growth.

Qualifications and Training
In order to train as a dramatherapist a person usually needs to have a relevant first degree, either in drama, theatre or performing arts or a nursing qualification. There are currently six postgraduate training courses in dramatherapy in Britain. These are at University of Hertfordshire, College of Art and Design, St Albans; University College of Ripon and York St John, York; South Devon College of Arts and Technology, Torquay; Sesame/Central School of Speech and Drama, London; the Institute of Dramatherapy at Roehampton, London; and City College Manchester.

Personal Qualities
This is demanding work which requires awareness, insight, integrity and compassion.

Starting Salary
Salaries vary according to whether the work is full- or part-time and the type of setting eg mental health, training centres, education, prison and probation, child care and private practice. Many dramatherapists work on a freelance basis or they practise dramatherapy whilst being employed in some other capacity: eg teacher, social worker, nurse, occupational therapist, psychiatrist or manager.

Further Information

British Association for Dramatherapists, 41 Broomhouse Lane, London SW6 3DP

Draughtsman *see Architectural Technician, Technical Illustrator*

The job is to produce clear, detailed scale drawings of a design concept with the object of showing a craftsman exactly what he has to do. Draughtsmen or technicians, as they are often called, are employed in a variety of industries: architecture, building services, cartography, construction engineering, electrical and electronic engineering and surveying.

Qualifications and Training

It is possible to train as a craft apprentice in any field except architecture. GCSEs are not required, but candidates should be able to show mathematical, artistic and mechanical aptitudes. These should include maths, a mathematical science and a subject showing the use of English. For entry to areas of work other than as a craft apprentice, requirements vary from firm to firm. Some will ask for GCSEs and some require two A levels. Training is on the job and by day and block release and leads to a City and Guilds qualification or a BTEC certificate or diploma.

Personal Qualities

Draughtsmen must be accurate and neat in their work and have the capacity to pay great attention to detail.

Starting Salary

Trainee £8000–£9000, fully qualified £15,000+.

Further Information

Local Jobcentres and Careers Offices

Dresser

Dressers may find employment in theatre, television, films and fashion houses. They prepare and maintain costumes and help the performers and models to dress, especially where quick changes are needed.

Qualifications and Training
No formal qualifications are necessary; experience, especially in the theatre, is helpful as too is an ability to sew.

Personal Qualities
Calmness and speed, a soothing and sympathetic nature, discretion and tact are all helpful.

Starting Salary
Dependent on age, experience and employer, but generally low.

Further Information
The Stage and Television Today, 47 Bermondsey Street, London SE1 3XT; 0171 403 1818 (*job advertisements*)

Dressmaker

Opportunities for dressmakers occur in fashion couture houses where they make specially designed costumes for a particular collection or customer, in wholesale fashion houses making mass-produced garments, in theatres both making and adapting costumes. Dressmakers may also be employed by large stores to do alterations, or they may be self-employed making clothes etc for people either from home or from a workshop. Teachers of dressmaking are employed in schools, colleges and by evening centres.

Qualifications and Training
No formal qualifications are necessary; however, a City and Guilds qualification may be obtained by full-time study at a technical college or by entering a workroom on leaving school and studying on a day-release basis.

Personal Qualities
Dressmakers need to combine artistic and practical skills with an ability to follow instructions and to recognise problems as they arise and make the necessary adaptations. They must be able to deal with both temperamental designers and their customers.

Starting Salary
Dependent on experience and practical ability and specialisations, about £105–£155 a week when qualified.

Further Information
Local Jobcentres and Careers Offices

Driving Examiner

Driving examiners must ensure that candidates are competent to drive without endangering other road users and that they drive with due consideration for other drivers and pedestrians. To ascertain this, the examiner directs learner drivers over an approved route and asks them to carry out various exercises. While doing this the examiner must take notes without distracting candidates' concentration and must make a fair assessment.

Qualifications and Training
Driving examiners are required to complete a strict selection process, followed by four weeks' training. They must have detailed knowledge of the Highway Code, of road and traffic safety problems, some mechanical understanding, have held positions of responsibility and dealt with the public. Driving examiners must be over 25 years of age and have had extensive experience of a variety of different vehicle types. Vacancies are advertised both locally and nationally by the Driving Standards Agency. Selection is dependent upon passing a special driving test and interview, and for those who are successful there are continuous checks by a supervising examiner to ensure the maintenance of a high standard.

Personal Qualities
Examiners should be fair, sympathetic, friendly, clear spoken and have a calm, unflappable nature. The ability to work to a strict timetable is important.

Starting Salary
£11,433; London £11,907.

Further Information
Driving Standards Agency, Stanley House, Talbot Street, Nottingham NG1 5GU; 0115 901 2805
Local Jobcentres and Careers Offices

Driving Instructor

Driving instructors teach their pupils how to drive as a 'life skill' in preparation for all categories of the Driving Standards Agency's theory and practical driving tests. Instructors can also provide post-test training for the Pass Plus scheme as well as prepare clients for advanced driving tests, such as the DIAmond Advanced Motorists test.

Qualifications and Training

In order to provide tuition for money, car driving instructors must either be registered or licensed by the Registrar of Approved Driving Instructors. This requires them to have passed a stringent three-part qualifying test within the space of two years. The test consists of: a written test, a practical driving test and a practical test of the ability to instruct. Training is available from any of the Approved Training Establishments inspected and listed by the Driving Instructors' Association and Driving Standards Agency in the starter packs listed below. Approved Training Establishments are those which regularly satisfy the inspection criteria under the voluntary scheme of minimum required standards set up and agreed by the Driver Training Industry and the Driving Standards Agency.

Personal Qualities

Driving instructors must have a calm and friendly nature, be very alert and quick to react and should be clear spoken and able to express themselves well. Patience, confidence and tact are also important characteristics, as is the willingness to abide by a professional code of practice.

Starting Salary

The driving instruction industry is now very much structured to self-employment as an own business or independent operation within a franchise agreement. Typical earnings, after business or franchise fees, will vary widely, depending on tuition hours worked and operating costs. Annual gross income can vary between £10,000 and £20,000.

Further Information

Driving Instructors' Association, Safety House, Beddington Farm Road, Croydon CR0 4XZ; 0181 665 5151; Fax: 0181 665 5565 (*So You Want To Be A Driving Instructor?* starter pack, including information on DIA-RTE Approved Training Establishments, £3.99, payable to DIA)

Registrar of Approved Driving Instructors, Driving Standards Agency, Stanley House, 56 Talbot Street, Nottingham NG1 5GU; 0115 955 7600

(*Your Road To Becoming an Approved Driving Instructor*, starter pack, including application forms, £2.50, payable to Driving Standards Agency)

Local driving schools, Jobcentres and Careers offices

The Driving Instructor's Handbook, Kogan Page

The Driving Instructor's Manual, DIA Publishing

Dry Cleaning Work,* see *Laundry and Dry Cleaning Work

Ecologist, see *Conservation (Environmental)*

Economist

Economists study the use and organisation of the world's resources, and the way in which they are distributed. The field of investigation is very wide, but may include the study of such topics as the reasons for balance of payments crises, the effects of different forms of taxation, international trade or business economics. Economics is not a precise science; it is only possible to forecast degrees of probability of a particular economic model having certain results. Economists are employed in government, nationalised industries, large industrial and commercial companies, teaching and research, banking and stock-broking, journalism, international organisations and independent consultancies. Their primary task is to give advice on the probable consequences of a course of action; for example, they might advise a company on the effects of a rise in the price of its products. Economists are concerned too with collecting data, preparing reports, and, to an increasing extent, with building complex mathematical models.

Qualifications and Training

A good honours degree in economics, or in one of the specialised branches of the subject, is needed. In addition, many economists take a postgraduate qualification.

Some degree courses are mathematically biased, and for these an A level pass in maths is essential. For most other courses, GCSEs in maths or English are required. A levels in arts subjects, such as history and modern languages, are useful.

Personal Qualities

An analytical mind, numeracy and the ability to express oneself clearly, verbally and in writing, are required.

Starting Salary
£13,000–£21,000.

Further Information
Institute of Economic Affairs, 2 Lord North Street, London SW1P 3LA; 0171 799 3745

Education Welfare Officer *see Social Work*

Education welfare officers are social workers, employed by local authorities to liaise between schools and families. They help with problems affecting children's behaviour at school. One of their main roles is to ensure regular school attendance, and to deal with persistent cases of truancy. They also work in child guidance clinics.

In Scotland, there are relatively few posts for education welfare officers as such, the responsibility for school welfare being shared between social work and education departments.

Qualifications and Training
The main professional qualification is the diploma in social work (DipSW) which can be studied part time while working or via a full-time college course. Entry requirements are five GCSEs including two at A level or five SCEs including three at H level. Mature entrants may be accepted without these qualifications.

Personal Qualities
Maturity, emotional stability, tact and patience are necessary.

Starting Salary
£13,581–£19,818

Further Information
Institute of Welfare Officers, 3rd Floor, Newlands House, 137–139 Hagley Road, Edgbaston, Birmingham B16 8UA; 0121 454 8883

Electrician

There are a number of different jobs which come under the title of 'electrician'.

Installation Industry
This has the biggest electrical training scheme in the country. The industry in the main comprises thousands of private firms of electrical contractors; some installation apprenticeships are also offered by electricity boards and local councils. The electrical installation industry works on new construction and refurbishment sites and also, on contract, on repair and maintenance work.

Factory Maintenance
Most factories employ maintenance electricians.

Servicing
Service engineers usually concentrate on a particular range of equipment and travel from house to house or firm to firm. They repair domestic equipment such as televisions, office equipment or electrical equipment in factories.

Manufacturing
Electricians are involved in inspection and testing.

Auto Industry
Auto electricians check, repair and replace the electrical/electronic circuiting and components in all types of motor vehicle.

Theatre Industry
Theatre electricians are responsible for the lighting of theatres: rigging and lights, operating them during performances and dealing with any problems.

Qualifications and Training

At craft level GCSEs in maths, science and English are helpful. Training is by apprenticeship and lasts three to four years. NVQs are available in electrical installation engineering and electricity generation, supply and distribution. Technician engineers need four GCSEs or equivalents including maths, a science subject and English. Training takes four years and usually leads to a BTEC or SCOTVEC certificate.

Installation apprenticeships include City and Guilds qualifications and a comprehensive practical Achievement Measurement Test is also taken, irrespective of the time needed to do so or the age of the apprentice. Success in all elements leads to NVQ level 3.

Personal Qualities

Technical aptitude is essential, and service electricians must have the ability to deal with the public. The work can be strenuous and it may be necessary to work from heights. Poor vision and colour-blindness will also cause problems.

Starting Salary
Low to start with but upwards of £200 a week when qualified.

Further Information
JTL, South Block, Central Court, Knoll Rise, Orpington, Kent BR6 0JA; 01689 891676

Engineering

The British engineering industry is a major wealth producer, and almost every other industry depends upon engineering in some way. A simple definition of engineering is that it 'is to do with the application of science and mathematics to the solving of practical problems and the making of useful things' (Engineering Council). The variety of specialisms is described below.

Aeronautical Engineering
A relatively small branch of the engineering industry, aeronautical engineering involves design, construction, operation and testing of aircraft. Employment is mostly with the armed services, the Civil Service, aircraft and aircraft engine manufacturers or with airlines.

Agricultural Engineering
The main fields in which agricultural engineers are involved are: design and production of agricultural machinery – planning, design and construction of farm buildings and associated equipment; field engineering – irrigation, drainage and land resource planning; and service engineering, involving sale, servicing, repairing and installation of farm machinery. They are also involved in forestry engineering, amenity and ecological engineering, and precision farming using satellite positioning systems.

Air Conditioning, see *Building Services Engineering*

Automobile Engineering
When engaged in vehicle manufacture, engineers tend to be qualified at higher technician graduate levels. In motor vehicle servicing, the work involved spans the craft, engineering technician and higher technician grades, with some engineers using their technical base to

develop into motor vehicle engineering management. Currently the relevant N/SVQs on offer are at levels 2 and 3, entitled 'Vehicle Mechanical and Electronic Systems Maintenance and Repair'. Engineering registration through a professional body rests exclusively with the Institute of Road Transport Engineers.

Biochemical Engineering

Involves the application of engineering principles to industrial processing. Biochemical engineers are involved in the research, design, construction and operation of plant used for the processing of biochemicals such as those used in effluent treatment, fermentation and the production of drugs.

Biomedical Engineering

Involves the application of engineering techniques and principles to medicine and biology. Most biomedical engineers are employed in hospitals or by companies manufacturing medical equipment.

Building Services Engineering

The term 'building services engineering' covers the work of engineers concerned with heating and ventilation, refrigeration, lighting, air conditioning, electrical services, internal water supply, waste disposal, fire protection, lifts, and acoustic and communication systems. The work involves planning and design of engineering systems, and supervision of contracts, working in collaboration with architects, surveyors, structural engineers and builders.

Chemical Engineering

Chemical engineers are concerned with large-scale processes – not always in the chemical industry. The term 'process engineering' is often used to describe their work, as they are more interested in the physical factors involved in a process than in the chemical reaction itself. Chemical engineers are employed in the oil, chemical, pharmaceutical, food, brewing and process industries.

Civil Engineering

Civil engineering involves design and construction of roads, dams, harbours, railroad systems, airports and similar projects. Civil engineers also play an important part in the provision of electricity and water supplies, and in managing traffic and transport. They are employed by local authorities, government departments, private contractors, engineering consultancies and nationalised industries.

Control Engineering
A multi-disciplinary field involving electrical and electronic engineering, mathematics, computer science, instrument and mechanical engineering. Specialisation in control engineering often follows the study of another branch of engineering.

Drainage Engineering, see *Building Services Engineering, Civil Engineering, Water Engineering*

Electrical and Electronic Engineering
The technology of electrical engineering is quite different from that of electronic engineering, electrical dealing with heavy current, electronic with light current. Applications of heavy current include electrical machinery of all kinds, generating stations and distribution systems. Light current is used for such products as transistors, microprocessors and telecommunications equipment. The two fields are often interdependent and training is closely related. Electronics is a rapidly developing field, and offers excellent opportunities, as do the allied disciplines of computer and software engineering.

NVQ/SVQs will be available, levels 1 to 5, in the future. The Institution of Electrical Engineers (IEE) is involved with the development of level 5 (equivalent to chartered engineer) and The Institution of Electronics and Electrical Incorporated Engineers with levels 4 and 3.

Energy Engineering
This branch of engineering is concerned with the use, production, distribution, conversion and conservation of energy, with due regard to the environment. Energy engineers are employed across the whole spectrum of industry as energy management and control are essential elements in containing costs, reducing pollution and addressing environmental concerns. The majority of openings are in major fuel industries (including renewables), consultancy and research.

Environmental Engineering, see *Building Services Engineering*

Flight Engineer, see *Civil Aviation*

Fire Engineering
This involves the application of engineering principles to the assessment, prevention and inhibition of fire risk within buildings, manufacturing plant and industrial processes. The various stages include the use of mathematical principles in the assessment of fire risk, the application of scientific principles to fire safety practices and the use

of management techniques to the inhibition and prevention of the onset and spread of fire.

As such, fire engineers are employed in the fire services, architectural and building design, project management, insurance assessment, industrial processing, the aircraft industry, environmental health and any area of safety where the possibility of fire or combustion represents a hazard.

Gas Engineering

Gas engineering involves specialisation in the use, transmission and distribution of gas (natural or manufactured), or in the production of gas, or in related fields such as exploration.

Heating and Ventilation Engineering, see *Building Services Engineering*

Highway Engineering, see *Transport Engineering*

Instrument Engineering

Instrument engineers are concerned with the measurement of pressure, temperature etc. They design, install and maintain instrument systems. See also *Control Engineering*.

Manufacturing Systems Engineering

This new branch of engineering deals with the skills required to operate new manufacturing systems: computerised production, computer-controlled assembly, robotic systems and flexible manufacturing systems.

Marine Engineering

This discipline is inter-related with offshore-engineering under a general title 'maritime engineering' which involves engineering systems and equipment in a maritime environment. Both marine and offshore engineers are involved in design, research, consultancy, survey, manufacture, installation and maintenance activities, the former with vessels of all sizes and types, the latter with offshore platforms, subsea installations and undersea vehicles. Employment opportunities exist with firms offering design and research activities, engine and ship building firms, classification societies, government bodies, the Merchant Navy and the Royal Navy.

Mechanical Engineering

Mechanical engineering is the biggest branch of the engineering industry. It involves the skills of designing, developing, producing, installing and operating machinery and mechanical products of many types. The field is enormous in scope, and most engineers specialise in a particular area. Other branches of engineering, such as electrical and civil engineering, overlap with mechanical engineering to a certain extent. Mechanical engineers are employed in almost every sector of industry. Some of the largest areas of employment are machine tools, railway engineering, aerospace and the automobile industry. NVQ/SVQs will be available, levels 1 to 5, in the future. The Institution of Mechanical Engineers (IMechE) is involved with the development of level 4 (equivalent to incorporated engineer) and level 5 (chartered engineer).

Mining Engineering

In Britain, most mining engineers are employed by companies in mining areas, working for consultants who monitor mining activity and subsidence. They need some knowledge of related disciplines such as mechanical, electrical and civil engineering, and to understand geology and surveying in relation to mining.

The majority of openings in metal mining are overseas.

Municipal Engineering

Municipal engineering is the application of civil engineering to the public service; municipal engineers are employed by local authorities or other public bodies. They work on a wide range of projects concerned with public works, and in such fields as traffic engineering, lighting and refuse collection.

Naval Architecture

Naval architects are engineers who play a key role as project leaders and specialists in the design, building and marketing of all systems which have to move just above, on or under the sea. They include: merchant ships, warships, drilling platforms and semi-submersibles, submarines and underwater vehicles, hovercraft, SWATH ships and hydrofoil craft and yachts and other small craft.

Naval architects work for: ship and repair yards, offshore rig fabricators and operators, government departments, classification societies, consultants, equipment manufacturers, small craft and yacht builders, research organisations, universities and colleges and shipping companies.

Nuclear Engineering

Nuclear engineering involves the applications of nuclear energy and associated research and development. The work of designing and constructing nuclear reactors, and the management of nuclear power stations, are carried out by nuclear engineers.

Offshore Engineering
Offshore engineers are concerned with the construction and operation of drilling platforms and wellheads, and other engineering problems related to the exploitation of offshore oil and gas.

Petroleum Engineering
Petroleum engineers are concerned with exploration and drilling for oil. They obtain and interpret information – for example, the quantities and quality of oil discovered.

Production Engineering
Production engineers develop and improve manufacturing techniques. They are responsible for designing production systems to ensure that products can be manufactured to the specified design, in the right quantities, at the right price and by the required date. Their work overlaps with production management.

Recording Engineering
Recording engineering is a specialised branch of electronic/radio engineering. Recording engineers are mainly employed by broadcasting authorities and recording studios, and vacancies are limited. See *Broadcasting.*

Refrigeration Engineering, see *Building Services Engineering*

Structural Engineering
Structural engineers are concerned with the design and maintenance of the framework and fabric of large structures such as bridges, motorways and office blocks.

Transport Engineering
Transport (or traffic) engineers try to plan the best use of roads and other traffic facilities, and work mainly with road traffic. Transportation planners, who are not necessarily engineers, are concerned with the provision of all types of transport.

Water Engineering
Water engineers mostly work for water boards and river authorities, ensuring the supply of fresh water, and dealing with the reclamation and disposal of water which has been used.

Qualifications and Training
There are five main grades of employment in the engineering industry.

1. Graduate and Chartered Engineers

Graduate and chartered engineers analyse and solve engineering problems. Their work is rarely routine, and they must constantly keep up with technological advances and developments. Their main activities are research, design and development, manufacture, production planning and control, commissioning equipment and technical sales. Two or three A levels, including maths and a science (generally chemistry or physics), and four GCSE/SCE passes (or equivalent) are the usual entry requirements. A BTEC or SCOTVEC certificate or diploma in appropriate subjects is also acceptable. Entry is normally by means of an accredited degree course (full time or sandwich). In addition to an accredited degree, a period of industrial training is necessary together with a period of working experience at a suitable level of responsibility, before qualification as a chartered engineer.

It is still possible to qualify as a chartered engineer without taking a degree, by taking the professional examinations of the Engineering Council.

Chartered civil engineers, however, must have an accredited degree in either civil or general engineering, and must also complete the Professional Qualification Scheme of the Institution of Civil Engineers. This involves a period of approved practical training and examinations.

2. Incorporated Engineers

The work of an incorporated engineer overlaps with that of an engineering technician (see below), but is at a more senior level; they work in the areas of design, manufacturing, commerce and quality control. An incorporated engineer might, for example, lead a team of technicians. The range of technical knowledge required is broader than that of a technician. Education is by means of a BTEC/SCOTVEC higher award course. Five years' training and experience in the industry is needed before one can register with the Engineering Council as an Incorporated Engineer. It is possible to proceed to a BTEC/SCOTVEC higher award after taking a BTEC or SCOTVEC national certificate or diploma, in which case GCSE passes may not be required.

3. Engineering Technicians

Engineering technicians usually have less responsibility than incorporated engineers, but their work is broadly similar. Many employers require four GCSE/SCE passes (or equivalent), including maths, science and English. Training is by means of an apprenticeship scheme, with release for a part-time or full-time course leading to a BTEC/SCOTVEC national certificate or diploma.

4. Craft Workers

Craft workers specialise in a particular practical skill, such as tool-making or welding. They must be able to interpret engineering drawings, and to work with a minimum of supervision. Entry is normally at 16 or 17, to an apprenticeship lasting three to four years. GCSE/SCE passes in maths, science and English are an advantage, though not absolutely essential. On-the-job training, together with day or block release, leads to NVQs awarded by the City and Guilds and the Engineering Industry Training Board. With very good exam results, transfer to technician courses is possible.

5. Operators

Operators are employed in a wide range of jobs, and make up about a third of the engineering industry's labour force. Their work is often simple and routine, but in some cases they may require some skill or skills similar to those of craft workers.

No specific academic requirements are needed, but aptitude in English and arithmetic and knowledge of metal work or technical drawing are useful. Operators may work towards NVQs at an appropriate level.

Personal Qualities

Graduate and chartered engineers need academic ability, an imaginative and problem-solving approach and social and communication skills. Incorporated engineers and engineering technicians should have reasoning ability, numeracy and the ability to communicate. Craft workers, as well as manual dexterity, need basic mathematical ability, patience and self-discipline. Operators should show reliability, patience and the ability to work with others.

Starting Salary

Newly qualified graduate engineers start at £14,000+.

Further Information

The British Computer Society, 1 Sanford Street, Swindon SN1 1HJ; 01793 417417

Civil Engineering Careers Service, 1–7 Great George Street, London SW1P 3AA; 0171 222 7722

The Chartered Institution of Building Services Engineers, Delta House, 222 Balham High Road, London SW12 9BS; 0181 675 5211

The Engineering Council, 10 Maltravers Street, London WC2R 3ER; 0171 240 7891

The Institute of Energy, 18 Devonshire Street, London W1N 2AU; 0171 580 7124

The Institute of Marine Engineers, The Memorial Building, 76 Mark Lane, London EC3R 7JN; 0171 481 8493
The Institute of Measurement and Control, 87 Gower Street, London WC1E 6AA; 0171 387 4949
The Institute of Road Transport Engineers, 22 Greencoat Place, London SW1P 1PR; 0171 630 1111
The Institution of Agricultural Engineers, West End Road, Silsoe, Bedford MK45 4DU; 01525 861096
The Institution of Chemical Engineers, 165–171 Railway Terrace, Rugby CV21 3HQ; 01788 578214
The Institution of Electrical Engineers, Savoy Place, London WC2R 0BL; 0171 240 1871
The Institution of Electronics and Electrical Incorporated Engineers, Savoy Hill House, Savoy Hill, London WC2R 0BS; 0171 836 3357
The Institution of Fire Engineers, 148 New Walk, Leicester LE1 7QB; 0116 2553654
The Institution of Gas Engineers, 21 Portland Place, London W1N 3AF; 0171 636 6603
The Institution of Highway Incorporated Engineers, 20 Queensbury Place, London SW7 2DR; 0171 823 9093
The Institution of Mechanical Engineers, 1 Birdcage Walk, London SW1H 9JJ; 0171 222 7899
The Institution of Mechanical Incorporated Engineers, 3 Birdcage Walk, London SW1H 9JH; 0171 799 1808
The Institution of Mining Engineers, Danum House, South Parade, Doncaster DN1 2DY; 01302 320486
The Institution of Nuclear Engineers, 1 Penerley Road, London SE6 2LQ; 0181 698 1500
The Institution of Structural Engineers, 11 Upper Belgrave Street, London SW1X 8BH; 0171 235 4535
The Royal Aeronautical Society, 4 Hamilton Place, London W1V 0BQ; 0171 499 3515
The Royal Institution of Naval Architects, 10 Upper Belgrave Street, London SW1X 8BQ; 0171 235 4622

The Environment Agency

The Environment Agency (formerly the National Rivers Authority) or inland waterways employees are concerned with the organisation, maintenance and running of Britain's canals, rivers, lakes and reservoirs for recreational and commercial purposes. The main employers are the Environment Agency and British Waterways, but local authorities and private companies are also concerned with waterways. The Environment Agency employs people concerned with pollution control, chemists, engineers, surveyors, fishing officers and water bailiffs, among others. British Waterways is concerned with the maintenance of inland waterways, particularly the canal system, its development and its use for leisure pursuits.

Qualifications and Training

British Waterways employs people with many different skills, from waterway operatives to engineers and professional support staff. Requirements vary from no academic qualifications to a degree and professional qualifications.

British Waterways is the industry lead body for the inland waterways and in conjunction with the Environment Agency will be setting standards and competence levels for occupations within the industry.

Personal Qualities

These vary widely depending on the nature of the job, but a technical bias, sound health and the ability to work well in a team are desirable. A liking for the outdoors is also important for many aspects of the work.

Starting Salary

Salaries vary depending on type of occupation.

Further Information

The Environment Agency, Coverdale House, Aviator Court, Clifton Moor, York YO3 4UZ; 01904 692296

British Waterways, Willow Grange, Church Road, Watford WD1 3QA; 01923 226422

Environmental Health Officer

Environmental health officers are enforcers, educators and advisers. They are employed in both the public and private sectors, and their aim is to protect the public from environmental health risks. Their responsibilities include pollution control and environmental protection, the inspection of food and food premises, health and safety in workplaces and in the leisure industry, and the control of housing standards, particularly in the private rented sector. Much of their time is spent out of the office, dealing with the public and visiting premises of all types.

Qualifications and Training

Training involves a four-year sandwich course leading to a degree in environmental health, or a two-year postgraduate sandwich course, for those with a good honours degree in a natural science. (The course must be accredited by the Institution of Environmental Health Officers.) Degree entry qualifications are a matter for the college concerned.

In Scotland candidates for the professional qualification (Diploma in Environmental Health, awarded by REHIS) must hold an honours degree in environmental health. Applicants for the four-year degree course offered by the University of Strathclyde must have four H grade passes (B level) in maths, chemistry, biology or physics and one other subject. Before being awarded the Diploma, candidates must have undergone a minimum of 48 weeks' training with a local authority.

Personal Qualities

These should include social responsibility, tact, integrity, an enquiring mind and good communication skills.

Starting Salary

Trainee grade £10,000+, qualified officers £16,000–£18,000.

Further Information

The Chartered Institution of Environmental Health Officers, 15 Hatfields, London SE1 8DJ; 0171 928 6006

The Royal Environmental Health Institute of Scotland, 3 Manor Place, Edinburgh EH3 7DH; 0131 225 6999

Estate Agent

Estate agents are responsible for the sale, letting and management of any kind of property – factories, shops, offices and farms as well as houses. They also, in many cases, deal with valuation and auctioneering, and often they are qualified surveyors. Large firms may employ specialists to deal with surveying, auctioneering and valuing, and sales staff as property negotiators. Smaller firms may consist of just one or two agents, carrying out some or all of the various functions.

Qualifications and Training

The principal professional bodies are the National Association of Estate Agents (NAEA), the Royal Institution of Chartered Surveyors (RICS) and the Incorporated Society of Valuers and Auctioneers (ISVA). Minimum entry requirements for the RICS are three GCSEs and two A levels, and for the ISVA, five GCSEs to include English and maths. Full- or part-time training courses are available, and practical experience is required before qualification. N/SVQs levels 3 and 4 in residential estate agency are available through the NAEA's national assessment centre.

Professional qualifications are an asset, but not essential: anyone can set up in business as an estate agent unless he has been forbidden to do so by the Director of Fair Trading, or is bankrupt, and established firms take on unqualified staff for property negotiation.

Personal Qualities

For most people the purchase or sale of their home is the biggest financial transaction they will ever carry out, and there are bound to be attendant worries and problems. Estate agents must be able to deal with their clients' problems sympathetically, but in a businesslike way. They should be numerate and able to express themselves well, verbally and in writing.

Starting Salary

£5000 upwards for a school-leaver with A levels, graduates £11,000+. Firms of estate agents charge a commission for selling or letting a property; the rate for a sale is usually 1½ to 2 per cent of the selling price.

Further Information

ISVA (The Incorporated Society of Valuers and Auctioneers), 3 Cadogan Gate, London SW1X 0AS; 0171 235 2282

The National Association of Estate Agents, Arbon House, 21 Jury Street, Warwick CV34 4EH; 01926 496800

The Royal Institution of Chartered Surveyors, Surveyor Court, Westwood Way, Coventry, West Midlands CV4 8JE; 0171 222 7000/01203 694757

Estate Manager*, see *Land Agent

Events Officer

Events officers generally work for a place visited by the public such as a national park or a stately home. Events officers may also be appointed on a temporary basis to cover a festival lasting one or two weeks only.

Events officers are responsible for organising long-standing events such as a series of waymarked walks, and also extra activities such as a music festival or summer holiday entertainment for children. If appropriate, the events officer will be in contact with the local education department to encourage school visits.

Events officers working for a large concern will coordinate their work with other members of staff such as the information officer and press officer.

Qualifications and Training

Events officers do not necessarily need formal qualifications but a background in marketing and experience at promoting events and campaigns is useful. A knowledge of simple financial planning is looked for and, often, experience in preparing material for print. The ability to drive is essential.

Personal Qualities

Events officers should be energetic, sociable and adaptable, able to talk to a variety of people, have the ability to think up new ideas and have organisational skills.

Starting Salary

£12,500–£13,500.

Further Information

Jobs are advertised in the Monday edition of *The Guardian*.

Exhibition Organiser

Exhibition organisers usually work for specialist companies. They plan and coordinate exhibitions, negotiating with all those concerned – managers of the exhibition, exhibitors, stand suppliers, and designers and caterers. With overseas exhibitions, government departments are often involved.

Qualifications and Training

Training is usually on the job and graduates or those with HNDs in business or marketing are preferred. CAM or Institute of Marketing qualifications are a useful asset. NVQs are to be introduced.

Personal Qualities

Applicants should be good at dealing with people and at administration with the ability to keep a large amount of information at their fingertips. Physical and mental stamina is essential.

Starting Salary
£12,000–£16,000.

Further Information
Association of Exhibition Organisers, 26 Chapter Street, London SW1P 4ND; 0171 932 0252

Factory Inspector, see *Specialist Inspector*

Factory Worker

Factories employ people in three different areas: production, research and development or administration. In production, depending on the product being made and the processes involved, varying proportions of skilled, semi-skilled and unskilled workers may be employed.

Skilled craftsmen operate sophisticated machines such as lathes and precision grinders; they may be welders, sheet metal workers, tool-makers or fitters responsible for the assembly of precision engines and machines. As tool-setters they may 'set' assembly lines ready for operation by the semi-skilled workers who feed in materials and semi-finished components and who ensure that the production process runs as smoothly as possible.

Unskilled labourers are mainly employed to fetch, carry and clean. There are many other jobs related to the production process such as store keeping, purchasing, tool-room maintenance and repair, transportation and quality control. Prospects for promotion are often good in factories and government legislation ensures that conditions of working and engagement are fair.

In research and development, opportunities exist for scientists, engineers, technicians, designers and draughtsmen, and for general office workers; financial, marketing and sales staff are employed in administration. The functions carried out in these two areas are similar to those performed in other job areas and individual entries should be referred to for further details.

Qualifications and Training

To work in a factory as an unskilled or semi-skilled worker no formal qualifications are required. Training is given on the job and may vary in length from one hour to weeks or months, depending on the type of work to be done.

Those wishing to follow a career as a skilled craftsman must follow a three- to four-year apprenticeship scheme starting at the age of 16 or 17; a minimum qualification of two or three GCSE grades D–E passes (or equivalent) in maths and science will probably be required, and other useful subjects are technical and engineering drawing, metalwork, woodwork and English. Apprenticeships, when available, take the form of training at work with day release to attend colleges and study for City and Guilds or other craft certificates.

Personal Qualities

Craftsmen must have a sound understanding of machinery, manual dexterity, a good eye for shape, sound eyesight, patience and concentration. Semi-skilled workers, especially on production lines, must be able to cope with repetitive work and be able to work quickly. All factory workers must be safety-conscious and able to tolerate dirt and noise.

Starting Salary

Dependent upon industry; however, £70+ a week at 16 rising to over £200 is average, and this may be helped by incentives, bonus schemes and shift allowances.

Further Information

Local Jobcentres and Careers Offices

Farming

In recent years economic conditions and increasing mechanisation have resulted in larger farms and a tendency towards greater specialisation. Mixed farms are now in a minority and most farmers choose to specialise in one or two areas of production. The most common of these are milk, cereals, poultry, sheep, pigs or beef. In order to make his farm profitable, the modern farmer needs a thorough working knowledge of the type of farming to be undertaken, an understanding of general agricultural science, years of practical experience and an aptitude for farming and farm management.

Opportunities are few, however, since it is now very expensive to buy land and equip even the smallest farm. While most of today's farmers start with smallholdings, land prices have now made the chances of a beginner becoming a tenant farmer almost impossible.

Farm Manager

Farm managers are responsible in the same way as farmers for all aspects of the day to day working of the farm. They must plan ahead, organise the staff and work schedules, decide which crops to plant or which animals to rear and keep a check on buildings and machinery. In addition they must deal with the office work and accounts.

Farm Worker

Specialisation and large-scale farming have led to a fall in demand for the farm worker who can turn his hand to anything. There is now a need for highly skilled personnel and new entrants should aim at becoming skilled in a special area such as animal husbandry, mechanics or food, flower or fruit production.

Qualifications and Training

There are a number of possible qualifications for a farmer/farm manager: a degree in agriculture or agricultural science or a national diploma in general agriculture. Farm workers may work towards the preliminary certificate in agriculture offered by the National Council for Vocational Qualifications. Various NVQ awards are available at different levels, eg crop and livestock production, levels 1, 2 and 3.

Starting Salary

Farm managers' salaries start at £12,000+ and with experience £16,000–£20,000 may be paid. Managers may be provided with rent-free accommodation and the use of a vehicle and may also be part of a profit-sharing scheme. Farm workers receive from about £80 at 16 to £145 at 20, with additional payments for specific skills or NVQ awards.

Further Information

Careers Education and Training Advice Centre, Warwickshire County Council, 22 Northgate Street, Warwick CV34 4SK; 01926 410410

Fashion *see Clothing Industry*

The fashion industry covers all aspects of clothing and accessories for men, women and children and falls into three main sectors: *haute couture* houses where original model garments are made for individual customers; wholesale *couture* where trends set by the *haute couture* houses are closely followed, and limited numbers of model garments in stock sizes are made for retail; and wholesale manufacture which occupies the largest sector of the fashion industry. Here the latest trends are adapted to styles attractive to the main market and mass produced at acceptable prices.

Designer

Designers do more than produce stylish sketches. Their work will, depending on the size and organisation of the particular establishment, include a wide variety of tasks. The work of the *haute couture* designer is both highly creative and intricate; unfortunately there is little scope for young designers or assistants as many houses are designer owned; they are nevertheless an excellent training ground for future designers willing to work as sketchers, stylists, fitters, hands etc. In wholesale *couture*, designers produce original garments, but they generally follow the instructions of an employer as far as style and cost are concerned.

The wholesale manufacture designer must be able to predict future trends, combine this perhaps with the firm's own 'brand image', match it to available fabrics and produce a garment which can be produced economically and will appeal to their particular section of the market. When sketches have been drawn, it is necessary to produce working drawings and translate the drawings into flat patterns, so that sample garments can be made to show to buyers and estimates can be made about the garment costs in fabric and manufacturing time.

Pattern Cutters

At this stage the drawings are passed on to the pattern cutter, who has to translate the designer's working drawings into a pattern suitable for factory production. The pattern cutter may use two main approaches to develop these patterns: modelling directly on to an industrial dress form to achieve the designer's style, or flat pattern cutting, which is using a standard block pattern shape and manipulating it to an almost unlimited range of styles. The pattern cutter also has the responsibility to cut a production pattern which is used for grading into a range of sizes by the grader.

The grader needs to be able to work carefully and accurately and be able to follow size charts. The grader must also be able to assess garment proportion and style and have an understanding of pattern cutting methods. In some companies patterns are graded on computers.

The set of graded production patterns is then passed on to the cutting room to the cutters and marker makers. Cutters and marker makers work in factories mass producing clothes.

Cutters

Each area of technical design demands a high standard of skill and experience. Cutters' work involves arranging lengths of cloth in a pile called a 'lay' so that all the pieces for a number of garments can be cut out in one operation. The pieces of the pattern are arranged on the lay in such a way that the pattern in the fabric will match up when the garment is sewn together and so that the minimum of material is wasted. The lay is then cut with the aid of either a hand-operated electric cutter called a 'knife' or with a mechanical press known as a die cutter. In addition there are fully automatic, computer controlled cutting machines. Promotion prospects in a cutting room are generally good. It is possible for cutters to become production or factory managers or to move into design and pattern cutting.

Fitter

The duties of a fitter vary considerably throughout the industry, from being in entire charge of a workroom where garments are made up, to improving original designs or altering individual garments.

Hand

In a *couture* workroom the hand would oversee the work of juniors and undertake the most important making-up herself. This position is often used as a stepping stone to designer.

Sample Machinist

This job involves working with the designer and pattern cutters in order to produce the original sample garment range.

Qualifications and Training

Clothing production workers such as cutters are required to have a general level of secondary education, although no specific qualifications are requested. Training is on the job with day release college attendance to take City and Guilds examinations. It takes four years to train as a cutter and there is a City and Guilds cutters and trimmers certificate available. It is also possible to study for craft certificates in tailoring and women's light clothing manufacture; these courses deal not only with cutting but also with make-up and design. Successful candidates may progress to advanced craft certificates and the technician's certificate in clothing manufacture. In the field of design, employers always look for entrants who have already taken a full-time course of further education study in art and design. Certain colleges and universities offer a BA (Hons) degree in textile/fashion. This is a three-year full-time or four-year sandwich course and the minimum entry requirements are five GCSE passes plus two A levels or a standard of education equivalent to that. A full-time course in art and design of at least one year and five GCSEs plus an A level, or equivalent, is also acceptable.

BTEC courses lasting for two years lead to the fashion certificate or diploma and provide a good entry route to the industry; successful students may take a further two-year course leading to the higher diploma.

Various colleges offer their own certificates and diplomas, three GCSEs usually being requested for entry. The London College of Fashion offers a four-year course for potential managers in the clothing industry; entrance requirements are five GCSEs plus two A levels. Whatever qualifications are obtained prior to employment in the fashion industry, further training on the job is essential.

S/NVQs are now available which attest to workplace competence. No formal entry requirements are necessary. NVQs currently exist for cutters and machinists at levels 1 and 2, pressers at level 1, handcraft tailors at level 3 and product development staff at level 3.

Personal Qualities

Clothing production workers should be able to work quickly and adjust to standing for long periods of time. They should be accurate, nimble, neat and have good eyesight. Designers are required to display both a high level of creative ability and a technical understanding of production methods. Fashion awareness, colour and shape sense are also important; they must be able to work to schedule, as part of a team and alone.

Starting Salary

Design assistants earn from £10,000 rising to £18,000+; for a top designer the sky's the limit.

Further Information

CAPITB Trust, 80 Richardshaw Lane, Pudsey, Leeds LS28 6BN; 0113 239 3355

Qualifications for Industry Ltd (QFI) (*address as above*)

Textile Institute, 10 Blackfriars Street, Manchester M3 5DR; 0161 834 8457

Careers in Fashion, Kogan Page

Film Production *see Broadcasting*

Opportunities to work in film production arise in television, film companies and advertising. It can be permanent work or increasingly on a freelance basis, in which case periods of unemployment between jobs are to be expected. Film production involves both studio and location work. Jobs within film production are much sought after but vacancies are few and competition is consequently fierce.

Animation

Animation involves the design, creation and operation of animated production and effects.

Announcers
Announcers work to detailed and carefully timed scripts, communicating information to the viewer from a soundproof 'behind the scenes' office. They sometimes write or adapt their own material.

Archivists/Librarians
Archivists and librarians collect, collate, preserve and make available collections of recorded visual, sound, written and other materials for use by various productions.

Art and Design
The art and design function is to create a visual effect to meet the needs of the production, creating manual or computer generated graphics.

Costume/Wardrobe
The wardrobe department interprets the production requirements in terms of costumes and accessories to ensure historical accuracy and an accurate portrayal of the style and ethos of the period.

Direction
The director is responsible for achieving the creative, visual and auditory effect of a production.

Engineering
Engineers provide a design, maintenance and installation service to the production site and equipment. Research specialists are usually employed by the equipment manufacturers or design consultancies.

Film, Video and Audio Tape Editing
Raw tape or film is shaped to interpret the requirements of the director, either by physical cutting (film) or by selecting sequences and rerecording onto a master tape using sophisticated machinery.

IT Specialists
IT specialists support many aspects of broadcasting, film and video, either within the companies or as consultants, providing and maintaining relevant systems and software.

Journalists
Generate and report on local, national or international stories, and research relevant background information. Bi-media (radio and TV) contracts are increasing. Some journalists present their own work.

Laboratory
Lab technicians develop and process film, duplicate and check video tapes, ensuring high technical quality.

Lighting
Lighting specialists ensure that the stage or set is correctly lit to meet the needs of the production.

Make-up and Hairdressing
Make-up and hairdressing professionals interpret the requirements of the production and research to ensure accurate representation of the historical or design concept. They maintain a continuity of approach throughout the production in studio or on location.

Management
Directs and coordinates the different elements of the industry to ensure their efficient function – ranging from commissioning a production to negotiating international rights.

Marketing and Sales
Marketing and sales staff work in an international marketplace to raise revenue for broadcasters or film makers. Airtime is sold, sponsorship and co-production rights negotiated and spin-off products developed, eg books, toys, videos.

Producers
Producers perform a variety of management and operational roles to bring together the many elements of a production either in studio or on location. Often responsible both for the initial concept and raising the essential finance, they are the team leaders.

Production Assistants
Production assistants provide high-quality administrative and secretarial support to the producer and director at every stage of production, coordinating all activities and preparing schedules and scripts.

Production Management
Production managers organise all essential support facilities for the team – accommodation, catering, transport etc. They will also roster crews and arrange payments.

Production Operatives
Perform the operational duties of the production such as vision mixing and autocue operations.

Researchers
Support the producer, helping to turn ideas into reality – providing and following up ideas, contacting and interviewing people, acquiring relevant factual material, and writing briefings for presenters.

Recording Still and Moving Images (Camerawork)
Workers in this area operate and assist with still, film and video cameras to record images as directed, using different techniques.

Runners/Gofers
The traditional entry-level job for the industry. Bright, highly motivated – often highly qualified – people act as general assistants, taking messages, making deliveries, being indispensable . . . and learning the basics of the commercial business.

Setcraft/Props
People working in this area construct the scenery, sets and backdrops to meet the production brief reflecting both historical accuracy and required design and style. They also maintain sets during a production, and operate any mechanical features as directed. Props (hired or made) are used to dress the set.

Sound
Sound craftspeople interpret requirements of a production in terms of sound collection. During post-production they may be involved in recording, editing and dubbing, using a range of sophisticated equipment.

Special Effects
Special effects designers create and operate effects for a production, within technical limitations and budget, and operate the necessary machines.

Support Staff
Many people working in film, video, television and radio fulfil essential support roles, including administration, catering, driving, cleaning.

Transmission
Technicians and engineers work to exhibit the production in a high quality form which can involve projecting images or operating transmission equipment linking electronic signals from the studios to a transmitter.

Writers
Writers work to produce or edit scripts for a variety of radio, TV, video or film productions.

Qualifications and Training
BECTU (Broadcasting Entertainment, Cinematograph and Theatre Union) and BKSTS (British Kinematograph, Sound and Television Society) are working with Skillset, the industry training organisation, in developing a system of accreditation of courses at film schools. The National Film and Television School runs a three-year course in film making taking about 25 students each year, but none of these is a complete beginner; most are graduates and all will have shown some previous ability in either writing, direction, production or photography. Also offering previously accredited courses are: the London International Film School, the University of Westminster, the West Surrey College of Art and Design, Bristol University's Film and Television Department, the London College of Printing and Distributive Trades, and Bournemouth and Poole College of Art and Design. New entrant training is offered by FT2 but competition for places is fierce.

Camera operators train differently in different sectors of the industry. At present, the industry's leading body, Skillset, is developing standards for NVQs. A good general level of education is required (to GCSE level standard for the BBC) and some operators start off as film loaders or clapper board operators. One way into continuity work is via shorthand typing; a general education to GCSE standard is required and a foreign language would be helpful. Film editors may be promoted from the position of assistant cutter which, although a fetch and carry job, provides valuable experience.

Personal Qualities
In film work it is important to combine artistic with technical ability, to pay attention to detail, to have patience, good powers of concentration and an interest in colour and design. An even-tempered, logical and visually imaginative approach is necessary. It is important to keep in touch with what is happening in your branch of the industry, and to be able to make friends and contacts.

Starting Salary
Employees in the film industry start usually as assistants at a salary of over £300 per week; with further experience the rewards can be very high.

Further Information
Broadcasting Entertainment, Cinematograph and Theatre Union (BECTU), 111 Wardour Street, London W1V 4AY; 0171 437 8506

British Film Institute, 21 Stephen Street, London W1P 2LN; 0171 255 1444
British Kinematograph, Sound and Television Society (BKSTS), M6–14 Victoria House, Vernon Place, London WC1B 4DF; 0171 242 8400
FT2 (Film and Television Freelance Training), Fourth Floor, Warwick House, 9 Warwick Street, London W1R 5RA; 0171 734 5141
Skillset (the industry training organisation for broadcast, film and video), 124 Horseferry Road, London SW1P 2TX; 0171 306 8585

Fire Service

Firefighters attend fires and numerous other emergencies, often requiring new techniques, to save life and property. They give a 24-hour service; typical emergencies other than fires include tanker spillages, car, train and aeroplane crashes, flooding and building collapse, and explosions where people and animals may have to be rescued. Some firefighters specialise in particular areas such as training or communications and the Fire Service also provides advice on fire protection and prevention by inspecting existing properties and studying proposals for new buildings. In addition they must enforce legal regulations to reduce risks of injury by fire such as the provision of secure escape routes.

The Fire Service is administered by local authorities in the UK; in addition, the Ministry of Defence, Army, Royal Air Force, Royal Navy and the British Airports Authority all have their own brigades.

Qualifications and Training

Firefighters should have a good general level of secondary education. Qualifications in English, maths and science are useful but not essential. The minimum age is 18 though it is possible to join the service as a junior at 16. There are strict requirements for entrants concerning physical fitness, hearing, eyesight, height and physique. Initially training takes place in a training school and is followed by regular courses of instruction for special situations and the use of specialist equipment.

Personal Qualities

Members of the Fire Service must be practical, courageous, able to use their own initiative, prepared to work shifts and work as part of a team. Some scientific understanding is helpful when dealing with dangerous chemicals.

Starting Salary

£13,644 rising to £17,073 after five years' service. Leading firefighters earn £17,286–£17,994 and sub-officers £18,747–£20,220. Various allowances increase these basic wage figures, and London firefighters are paid London weighting.

Further Information

BAA Plc, Jubilee House, Furlong Way, North Terminal, Gatwick Airport, Gatwick, West Sussex RH6 0JN; 01293 595323

Home Office (Fire Department), Horseferry House, Dean Ryle Street, London SW1P 2AW; 0171 217 8752

The Secretary, The Emergency Fire Services Lead Body, Room 662, Horseferry House, Dean Ryle Street, London SW1P 2AW

The Scottish Office Home and Health Department, Fire Service & Emergency Planning Division, St Andrew's House, Edinburgh EH1 3DG; 0131 244 2170

Local Chief Fire Officer/Firemaster, Fire Brigade Headquarters (*address in your local phone book*)

Ministry of Defence: contact your nearest Ministry of Defence establishment with a fire service.

Fisherman

Fishermen have many tasks; they cast out and haul in the nets when they are full, gut, clean and stow away the catch, mend nets, maintain the tackle and wash down the decks. Fishermen may work on deep sea trawlers in the North Sea or on 'factory' stern vessels which prepare and deep freeze the catches of cod, haddock, plaice, halibut and sole at sea; they fish as far away as Newfoundland and stay at sea for weeks at a time. While fishing is actually taking place, all hands must work for stretches of up to 18 hours. On the older ships all work is done on the decks but the more modern factory ships process the catch below decks. Catering staff, engineers and radio operators are also employed on these large vessels.

Fishermen on drifters carry out similar tasks but these boats follow fish around the coast and land a catch every day. Small seine-net boats with a crew of only four stay at sea for two weeks. Inshore fishing boats are usually family concerns using a variety of different methods to catch white fish, herring, cod, haddock, whiting, shrimps, lobster and crab.

As an industry, fishing is in decline; the opportunities still existing are to be found at the five main ports of Grimsby, Hull, Lowestoft, Fleetwood and Aberdeen.

Qualifications and Training

No formal education qualifications are necessary for a career in fishing, although an understanding of maths would be helpful and the local nautical college at Hull requires 100 days to have been spent at sea before attending its pre-seagoing course. Other courses are available at Fleetwood, Grimsby, Lowestoft and Aberdeen. Further training is gained in employment and further qualifications can be obtained leading to promotion from deck hand to third hand, second hand and then skipper.

Personal Qualities

Physical fitness, stamina and courage are essential for fishermen, who have to be able to withstand terrible Arctic conditions and long periods of very hard work. They must also be good sailors, able to turn their hand to any task, react quickly to emergencies, and be able to work in a team.

Starting Salary

Inshore fishermen all take a share of the catch and if there's no catch, there's no money. However, for someone starting, wages average out at about £100 a week or just over, more for deep sea work.

Further Information

Jobcentres and Careers Offices in towns which are ports.

Fish Farmer

In Britain there are some 500 fish farms producing quality fish for consumption and sport. This is a growing activity; although most farms are owner run, opportunities exist for farm managers and workers. Opportunities exist for scientists to test new methods for improving conditions, stocks and disease control and for bailiffs who look after the general welfare of the fish from hatchery to harvesting. In the future, as food manufacturers move into fish farming, there is likely to be a need for marketing staff.

Qualifications and Training

NVQs are offered in fish husbandry, level 2. Certificates, diploma and degree courses on fish farming and agriculture are offered by universities and specialist colleges. A diploma in fisheries management is offered by the Institute of Fisheries Management to students who have first taken their correspondence course and passed the certificate. No formal qualifications are required to become a bailiff, although correspondence courses are available from the Institute of Fisheries Management. Graduate and postgraduate biologists are employed on the scientific side and specialist courses are available, as too are courses dealing with the more sporting aspect of fish farming.

Personal Qualities

Physical fitness, a willingness to work outside, in remote areas and in all conditions, and an ability to think ahead and act independently are necessary.

Starting Salary

£10,000+ for technicians, £11,000+ for bailiffs and £14,000–£15,000+ for scientists, managers £15,000–£20,000.

Further Information

British Trout Association, 8 Lambton Place, London W11 4PH; 0171 221 6065 (*Send sae for list of courses.*)

The Secretary, The Institute of Fisheries Management, Balmaha, Coldwells Road, Holmer, Hereford & Worcester HR1 1LH

The Environment Agency, Coverdale House, Aviator Court, Clifton Moor, York YO3 4UZ; 01904 692296

Flight Engineer*, see *Civil Aviation

Florist

The florist's job involves visiting flower markets early in the morning to buy flowers, plants and other stock. As well as selling cut flowers and plants, they make up plant and flower displays such as table decorations, bouquets, sprays and wreaths. Some florists also work outside the shop, providing office displays, making arrangements for banquets, functions and receptions, and decorating hotels and public buildings.

Qualifications and Training

The industry has a well-established qualifications structure, giving recognition to those who achieve floristry skills, and professional standing to those who achieve the industry's highest accolade – the national diploma of the Society of Floristry.

National Vocational Qualifications (NVQs, SVQs in Scotland) in floristry are established at levels 2 and 3. These qualifications are offered by the National Examinations Board for Agriculture and

Horticulture and Allied Industries (NEBAHAI) which also offers a business qualification and a national certificate in floristry for more senior florists.

BTEC qualifications are also offered by some colleges, from the first certificate in floristry, through to the ND and the HND in floristry which is newly available.

The Society of Floristry offers two professional qualifications, the intermediate certificate (ICSF) and the national diploma (NDSF).

Personal Qualities

Imagination and creative flair, colour sense, organisational ability, an ability to work to deadlines, a friendly manner, patience and dexterity. Good health and stamina are essential because the work can be physically demanding.

Starting Salary

Generally a 40-hour week, including Saturdays. Rates of pay vary according to size and location of the business, and according to the individual's own skills and qualifications, experience and seniority. Rates of pay are on a similar scale to other retail work. Part-time work may be available.

Further Information

Floristry Training Council, Roebuck House, Hampstead Norreys Road, Hermitage, Thatcham, Berkshire RG18 9RZ; 01635 200465

The Secretary, The Society of Floristry, 70a Reigate Road, Epsom, Surrey; 01372 463688

Food Science and Technology

Food scientists study the properties and behaviour of foods from raw materials through processing to the final product, using a variety of scientific disciplines, notably chemistry and biology, but also physics and nutrition. Food technologists use food science and other technological know-how to turn raw materials into finished products for the consumer in an industry which is becoming increasingly sophisticated.

The majority of those qualifying in food science or technology will readily find employment in a variety of positions in the food industry which covers not only the manufacture of food but its ingredients, food packaging and the manufacture of food processing machinery. Positions exist in production, quality assurance or in product or process development. The growth of 'own label' products has led to additional opportunities in the food retailing sector where technologists are responsible for developing new products, identifying suppliers, and ensuring the quality of the product from manufacture, through distribution to the store and ultimately the consumer's table. Those keen to secure a career in research will find opportunities in government service, in research associations, as well as commercial organisations and the universities. There are additional opportunities in environmental health, education, consultancy, public health laboratories and in technical publishing and journalism.

Qualifications and Training

Food science and technology qualifications may be gained at three different levels: BTEC/SCOTVEC national certificates and diplomas, HNC and HND, and degree courses. Qualifications at all levels can be taken as full-time and sandwich courses. There are also a few part-time courses.

Minimum entry requirements for BTEC certificates are four GCSEs to include maths, a science and English, for National Certificate/Diploma, five GCSEs to include maths and English, plus one A level, preferably in chemistry for HND/HNC. For a degree level course at least two A level passes at the appropriate grade from the science subjects, of which chemistry may well be compulsory for certain courses. Many institutions of higher education will accept a good BTEC qualification as an alternative to A levels.

Membership of the Institute of Food Science and Technology depends upon satisfying both academic qualifications (minimum HND) and having several years' experience at a responsible level for higher grades.

Personal Qualities

Food scientists and technologists require a sound theoretical knowledge and scientific ability, a practical approach and an ability to communicate with people, and a willingness to work as one of a team.

Starting Salary

Technologists with A levels or equivalent would earn £10,000+; graduates or HND holders £10,500+ to £13,000+ depending on qualifications, employer and location.

Further Information

The Food and Drink Industry Training Organisation, 6 Catherine Street, London WC2B 5JJ; 0171 836 2460

Institute of Food Science and Technology, 5 Cambridge Court, 210 Shepherds Bush Road, London W6 7NJ; 0171 603 6316

Forensic Scientist

The Forensic Science Service, administered by the Home Office, employs scientists both for research and operational forensic science. Their backgrounds are mostly as chemists and biologists, and as forensic scientists they examine and try to identify, by means of analytical chemistry, molecular biology and microscopic analysis, samples of such materials as clothing, hair, blood, glass, paint and handwriting, in order to provide evidence to expose criminals, the location of a crime, the weapons used etc.

Qualifications and Training

Scientific officers must have a degree or equivalent. The progression is then to higher scientific officer (for which a degree and postgraduate laboratory experience are necessary) and to senior science officer, which requires four years' postgraduate laboratory experience. NVQs will become available in document examination, scenes of crime examination and the recovery of evidential material.

Personal Qualities

Forensic scientists should adopt a logical, practical and methodical approach, paying great attention to detail, and willing to try every possible permutation. A naturally inquisitive, unsqueamish nature and a concern for accuracy are also important.

Starting Salary

A scientific officer in the Civil Service earns from approximately £11,500.

Further Information

The Forensic Science Service, Headquarters, Priory House, Gooch Street North, Birmingham B5 6QQ; 0121 666 6606

The Forensic Science Society, Clarke House, 18a Mount Parade, Harrogate HG1 1BX; 01423 506068

Local police forces

A Career in Forensic Science (The Forensic Science Society)

Forestry

The main business of the forestry industry in Britain is to grow trees to provide timber, but this has never been its sole purpose. As well as their involvement in timber production, foresters are acutely conscious of the impact of forestry on the environment, both in visual terms and its effect on wildlife.

Forest Officer

Forest officers have a variety of roles to perform depending on the level they reach in their career. In the lower grades they are technical supervisors with responsibility for planning and controlling operations. As an individual's career progresses he or she will be asked to perform a variety of management functions and be expected to plan, control and implement policies and operations. There are opportunities to undertake more specialised work and most officers will find themselves in regular contact with the general public and professional people.

Forest Worker

The forest worker's role is mainly manual or operating machines in the forest with a wide range of work including planting, fencing, draining, weeding and timber harvesting.

Qualifications and Training

Forest officers' qualifications range from a BTEC/SCOTVEC diploma in forestry to an honours degree in forestry and membership of the professional body, the Institute of Chartered Foresters (MICFor). Forest workers are encouraged to obtain NVQs levels 1 and 2, City and Guilds certificates or equivalent; however, entry to the job is by application only.

Personal Qualities

Forestry work requires a good standard of physical fitness, a willingness to work outside, all year round, in all weathers and in remote areas. Foresters and managers should be able to organise others and be prepared to do varying amounts of office work.

Starting Salary

Trainee forest workers earn about £90 a week at 16 rising to £150 for a forest craftsman. Forest officers start at about £14,000.

Further Information

The Forestry Commission, Personnel Management Branch, 231 Corstorphine Road, Edinburgh EH12 7AT; 0131 334 0303

Institute of Chartered Foresters, 7a St Colme Street, Edinburgh EH3 6AA; 0131 225 2705

The Royal Forestry Society of England, Wales and Northern Ireland, 102 High Street, Tring, Hertfordshire HP23 4AF; 01442 822028

The Royal Scottish Forestry Society Office, 62 Queen Street, Edinburgh EH2 4NA; 0131 225 8142

Careers Working Outdoors, Kogan Page

Foundry Work *see Engineering*

Foundry work is craft based. The industry provides metal cast components for a wide range of other industries such as propellers, turbines, crank shafts, all types of machinery, and domestic items such as fireplaces.

Craftsmen are employed in foundry work as pattern, mould and model makers and to maintain the equipment. Technical engineering staff are concerned with estimating, inspection and laboratory work. There are many opportunities for operatives in foundry work as die casters, dressers, finishers, moulders, coremakers and in metal melting. There are also limited openings for foundry technologists, metallurgists, chemists and engineers and, as the industry becomes more sophisticated, the demand for specialist skills will increase in research and development. Graduate managers are also in greater demand for both production and administrative posts.

Qualifications and Training

To become a corporate member of the Institute of British Foundrymen it is necessary to have a degree in metallurgy or engineering. HND and HNC qualifications are also acceptable when backed by appropriate endorsements or a metallurgical engineering qualification.

For the craftsman there is a three-year craft apprenticeship scheme resulting in the Foundry Institute Training Committee craft certificate; training is at a special centre, at work and with day release to attend college.

Entrants to the industry with three GCSE passes (or equivalent) in maths, a science and English can take NC or ND courses which cover the basics of cast metal technology. Successful students and school-leavers who have followed A level courses can then progress to HNC and HND courses in foundry technology which combine theoretical and technological study with supervisory techniques.

City and Guilds also offer courses intended to complement industrial training, and NVQs are available in various areas of engineering.

Personal Qualities

Workers in the foundry industry must be fit and strong as the work is heavy; they should have good eyesight and be skilful in the employment of tools; they must be willing to work in noisy conditions and possibly work shifts.

Starting Salary

Production workers £80+ a week at 16, £200+ when trained.

Further Information
Local Jobcentres and Careers Offices

Freight Forwarding

Moving goods internationally can be very complicated and it is usual to employ the services of a freight forwarding firm which will arrange for the most efficient means of transport and will also ensure that all documentation, legal and insurance requirements are met and customs duties paid etc. Freight forwarders may be individuals or firms; they may specialise in a particular method of transportation, certain goods or countries. They may arrange for a number of different shipments to be grouped together for more economical transport. Some very large organisations have their own freight forwarding department or a subsidiary company. They are usually located near ports or airports and in the provincial centres. They employ people to deal with a wide range of clerical and administrative tasks such as sales, personnel, timetabling, accounting and computer work. The most likely entry route to freight forwarding is as a clerk and then to progress through supervisory to managerial positions. There are opportunities also to work abroad.

Qualifications and Training

Some large organisations recruit graduates, usually with degrees in transport subjects or business studies with a transport bias, as trainees, but generally there are opportunities for people at all levels. For freight forwarding, training is mainly through practical experience and part-time study. A minimum of one A level is recommended for enrolment to the part-time and correspondence courses of the Institute of Freight Forwarders. BTEC and SCOTVEC national certificate courses are available at colleges of further education, and there is a Network option in freight forwarding. An NVQ/SVQ at levels 2, 3 and 4 in international trade and services is in place and a modern apprenticeship framework is being developed.

For promotion prospects A levels and languages are an advantage. Five GCSEs including maths and English are required for the Chartered Institute of Transport's (CIT) qualifying examination course or the CIT certificate in transport (road freight).

Personal Qualities

People working in freight forwarding need a good working knowledge of commercial geography; they may be required to work unsocial hours and will find that scheduling requires a logical, detailed and accurate approach.

Starting Salary
Minimum clerical salaries are in the region of £6000–£7000; management trainees start at £10,000+.

Further Information
British International Freight Association, Institute of Freight Forwarders, Redfern House, Browells Lane, Feltham, Middlesex TW13 7EP; 0181 844 2266

The Chartered Institute of Transport, 80 Portland Place, London W1N 4DP; 0171 636 9952

The Freight Transport Association, Hermes House, St John's Road, Tunbridge Wells, Kent TN4 9UZ; 01892 526171

Institute of Transport Administration, 32 Palmerston Road, Southampton SO14 1LL; 01703 631380

'A Career in Freight Forwarding' (British International Freight Association)

Funeral Director

Funeral directors collect bodies from hospital or the residence of the deceased and prepare them for burial or cremation – this may include embalming. Most funeral premises include private viewing rooms for family visitations. On behalf of the family, at their request, and after ascertaining their wishes, the funeral director usually makes all the funeral arrangements such as the date, time and place of the service and interment or cremation. He/she places the relevant notice of death and acknowledgement of thanks for sympathy in newspapers, pays all the fees and arranges flowers if required. The funeral director also transports the coffin and mourners to and from church and will act as a collection point for flowers, or donations in lieu, if so desired. Funeral directors may be employed by large firms such as cooperative societies, or by small family-run concerns. In remote rural areas the local carpenter or other craftsman may also work as a funeral director.

Qualifications and Training
Those wishing to obtain their diploma in funeral directing must register with the National Association of Funeral Directors (NAFD) and will also have student membership of the British Institute of Funeral Directors (BIFD). Full details of the diploma course are forwarded to each student. Every student must follow the foundation module – there are no exceptions.

A satisfactory standard must be reached in the foundation module before proceeding to the diploma. A student will be required to have

24 months' experience and have arranged 25 funerals before the diploma is awarded.

NVQs levels 2 and 3 are available for funeral directors under the subject heading of Care.

Personal Qualities

Tact and sympathy and a reassuring, helpful nature are essential to funeral directors when they are advising the bereaved. They also need to combine administrative ability with technical expertise in the varied preparations in the funeral arrangements. On-call and out of hours work is an integral part of the job and an ability to adapt to irregular hours is essential.

Starting Salary

Salaries vary greatly depending on size of firm – many are family concerns.

Further Information

British Institute of Embalmers, Anubis House, 21c Station Road, Knowle, Solihull, West Midlands B93 0HL; 01564 778991

National Association of Funeral Directors, 618 Warwick Road, Solihull, West Midlands B91 1AA; 0121 711 1343

Furniture and Furnishing *see Upholsterer*

Although furniture is rarely hand made any more and is no longer made solely from timber, but from a variety of materials and with the help of a wide range of machines, a craft-based industry, using skilled workmen at all stages of the production process, still exists. The sawyer stacks wood for seasoning, and cuts it into suitable lengths for the machinist who shapes it into furniture parts. These may be made more attractive by the application of a veneer and are then assembled by the cabinet maker and finally stained and polished either by hand or with sprays. Skilled frame makers provide frames to be filled, sprung and covered by upholsterers; much of this work is done by hand and is similar in many ways to that of the clothing and textile industries.

There are opportunities in this industry for people to work on a freelance or self-employed basis or for one of the many manufacturing units which may specialise in particular items, or materials, or in certain types of furniture such as school, office or domestic furniture. In the design of furniture, carpets, fabrics, curtaining and wall coverings, opportunities exist to work freelance, in studios and in the retail trade. There are also a number of openings for teachers – craft design and technology teachers are in short supply.

Qualifications and Training

Craft training is generally gained through a three- to four-year apprenticeship with part-time study on a day or block release basis to obtain the City and Guilds certificate or BTEC certificate and diploma. The City and Guilds first-year course covers all aspects of the furniture trade with specialisation in the second and subsequent years. A general education to GCSE level standard is required for these courses; woodwork, maths and English, though not essential, are an advantage. NVQs, level 2, are available in various aspects of furniture production.

For those wishing to follow a career in design, training usually begins at 16 with education to GCSE level standard being followed by attendance on a two-year foundation course covering all aspects of art and design. This is reduced to one year for older students with five GCSEs and one A level or equivalents.

Full-time and sandwich degree courses lasting three and four years respectively and leading to BA (Hons) in art and design are available at various universities and colleges of higher education. For entry, applicants should be 18 and have either five GCSEs and two A levels or equivalents, or have successfully completed a foundation course and have five GCSEs and one A level or equivalents.

Personal Qualities

Furniture craftsmen must be neat, accurate and able to follow drawings exactly. They must be interested in practical work which requires great precision, have care and patience, and strength sufficient to lift heavy furniture. Good eyesight is an advantage. Designers are required to work as part of a team to a busy schedule and present their work well; a sound knowledge of how furniture is made is most valuable.

Starting Salary

Apprentices at 16 earn £70+ a week, and when qualified from £170. Individual craftsmen working for themselves set their own rates. Designers start at £7500–£8000+ upwards.

Further Information

Rural Development Commission, 141 Castle Street, Salisbury, Wiltshire SP1 3TP; 01722 336255

G

Gamekeeper

Gamekeepers work on large country estates for private landlords, management firms and for private syndicates who wish to organise a shoot. They rear the game-birds and fish, and protect them from poachers and predators. They must ensure that the proper environment for the game is maintained and, on shooting days, organise the beaters.

Qualifications and Training

No formal qualifications are necessary, though a keeper should be able to use a gun, handle a dog and be able to drive. Training is usually on the job, but there is a one-year full-time course available at Hampshire Agricultural College. There is an NVQ award available in gamekeeping, levels 1 and 2. A number of other agricultural colleges run courses on keeping and allied subjects.

Personal Qualities

Gamekeepers should love the outdoor life, be self-reliant and independent.

Starting Salary

Based on agricultural wage, but generally a house is provided.

Further Information

The Game Conservancy Trust, Fordingbridge, Hampshire SP6 1EF; 01425 652381

Garage Work

This work involves the selling and buying of cars, the supplying of parts, the selling of petrol, the repair and maintenance of cars and other vehicles and the overall management of the garage.

Qualifications and Training

No specific educational qualifications are necessary for people working on a petrol forecourt as training is given on the job. Mechanics are not required to have qualifications but GCSEs (grade D or above) in maths and science are advantageous. Training is usually through Network leading to a level 2 NVQ. Apprenticeships are increasingly available but relate to the achievement of standards and not time. Preferred qualifications for salesmen/women are four GCSEs, grade C. Courses available are a City and Guilds craft course followed by a course in car salesmanship. Partsmen/women need no formal qualification but GCSEs (grade D and above) are helpful. Network is the usual course leading to a level 2 NVQ. Managers are recruited with varying qualifications but it is becoming usual for them to hold GCSEs, A or B grades and sometimes a degree. Membership of the industry's professional institute is encouraged.

Personal Qualities

Petrol pump attendants must be polite, enjoy being outdoors, and able to work quickly. Mechanics must have a high degree of responsibility and take pride in doing a good job. Sales people should be confident, friendly and polite; partsmen/women need to be well organised with good administrative skills. Managers need the latter qualities and also the ability to inspire confidence and gain respect.

Starting Salary

Approximate wages are: Partsmen/women and apprentice mechanics at 16, £70, and at 20, £140, petrol pump attendants £130 (all for 39-hour weeks). A manager's starting salary is variable and negotiable and often includes a car.

Further Information

Local Jobcentres and Careers Offices

Retail Motor Industry Training, 210 Great Portland Street, London W1N 6AB; 0171 580 9122

Gardener *see Horticulturist, Landscape Architect*

Gardening involves not only planting and caring for flowers, trees and shrubs, but also routine jobs of cleaning out beds, sweeping leaves and, in the winter, shovelling snow.

Gardeners may be employed by local authorities to care for parks, school and hospital grounds, work for a garden centre, landscape contractor, or be self-employed. If the latter, they may run their own business or work for a variety of people.

Landscape Gardening
This involves either renovating an old garden for a client or creating an entirely new one. Landscape gardeners, using their own ideas and the customer's design, make a plan of the 'new' garden. Such items as drainage systems, rockeries, garden paths and plants are all shown.

Qualifications and Training
It is not necessary to have formal qualifications to become a gardener. Training is given on the job, often as part of an apprenticeship. However, day-release courses are available leading to City and Guilds, NVQ, levels 1, 2 and 3, and Royal Horticultural Society qualifications. Education and training courses are available at many colleges throughout the country with varying entry qualifications up to GCE A level.

Personal Qualities
Gardeners should be prepared to be outdoors in all weathers and be patient and caring. The ability to drive is useful.

Starting Salary
£120–£160 a week when trained.

Further Information
Local Jobcentres and Careers Offices
Institute of Horticulture, Careers Officer, Askham Bryan College of Agriculture and Horticulture, Askham Bryan, York YO2 3PR; 01904 702121
Royal Horticultural Society, 14–15 Belgrave Square, London SW1X 8PS; 0171 245 6943
Careers Working Outdoors, Kogan Page

Gas Fitter

The work involves fitting and repairing appliances such as cookers, boilers, water heaters, the installation, maintenance and replacement of gas appliances, and inspecting for the source of reported leaks. Most fitters are employed by the area gas boards.

Qualifications and Training
No formal qualifications are necessary but a good general education with some knowledge of maths and physics is advantageous. Training is by a four-year apprenticeship; apprentices learn on the job and are

given time off to attend courses leading to a City and Guilds qualification.

Personal Qualities
As much of the work takes place in private houses, fitters must be friendly, polite and honest. It is necessary too to be able to drive.

Starting Salary
About £75 a week at 16, £175+ when qualified.

Further Information
Area Gas Boards

Construction Industry Training Board, Bircham Newton, King's Lynn, Norfolk PE31 6RH; 01553 776677 (ext 2466)

Genealogist

Genealogists trace lines of descent from ancestor to ancestor and also study pedigrees. Their work is useful to the legal profession in cases of intestacy or disputed claims and, sometimes, to doctors when trying to establish the origins of a disease. However, the vast majority of genealogists work for private clients who are interested in tracing their family trees. There are some firms of genealogists, and other individuals who work from home.

Qualifications and Training
Genealogists must have knowledge of history, Latin and legal terminology. The Institute of Heraldic and Genealogical Studies provides training leading to professional qualifications. Preference is given to graduates. There are also short courses on ancestry available for beginners provided by the Institute, certain local authorities and the Society of Genealogists.

Personal Qualities
Curiosity, historical integrity and attention to detail are all useful attributes.

Starting Salary
Salaries vary depending on whether full- or part-time work is undertaken, for a firm or on one's own behalf. The hourly rate is around £12.

Further Information

The Association of Genealogists and Record Agents, The Secretary, 15 Dover Close, Hill Head, Fareham PO14 3SV; 01329 662512

The Institute of Heraldic and Genealogical Studies, 79–82 Northgate, Canterbury, Kent CT1 1BA; 01227 768664

The Society of Genealogists, 14 Charterhouse Buildings, Goswell Road, London EC1M 7BA; 0171 251 8799

General Practitioner, see *Medicine*

Geologist

Geologists study the earth's crust, the materials which comprise it, their origin, formation and composition. The work involves the examination of rocks and mineral deposits; some deposits (for example, coal) are assessed for their value. Specimens of rock, soil, water, fossils and minerals are collected for laboratory analysis and preservation for future reference. Geology not only includes field work but much laboratory work, testing and analysing, often involving the use of computers. Findings are then compiled into reports. Geologists work mainly for oil, mining, quarrying or engineering firms and government establishments, and are becoming increasingly involved in environmental issues.

Closely allied to the work of the geologist is that of the geophysicist, geochemist and hydrogeologist, who use field and laboratory-based techniques to better understand the earth's physical and chemical properties and its underground water supplies. Hence, most of their work is related to the resources and the environment.

Qualifications and Training

An honours degree in geoscience (geology, geophysics, geochemistry) is necessary. Training is given on the job or on a further course. Specialist one-year postgraduate courses are available covering particular aspects of geoscience.

Personal Qualities

Geologists must be fit as many of them work in difficult climatic conditions or even underground. They must be able to work both as team members and as team organisers when required. Relevant foreign languages are useful.

Starting Salary
£12,000+ to £16,000+, higher abroad.

Further Information
The British Geological Survey, Nicker Hill, Keyworth, Nottingham NG12 5GG
London: Natural History Museum Earth Galleries, Exhibition Road, London SW7 2DE; 0171 589 4090
The Geological Society, Burlington House, Piccadilly, London W1V 9AG; 0171 434 9944

Geophysicist*, see *Oil/Gas Rig Work

Glazier

Glaziers fit glass into window frames for domestic use and also for commercial buildings, some of which require the use of enormous sheets. They work for private contractors, local authorities and independently, in private homes and on building sites.

Qualifications and Training
No formal educational requirements are necessary. Training is on the job by three-year apprenticeship. It is usual for time off to be allowed to attend classes leading to NVQs, levels 1 and 2, awarded jointly by the City and Guilds and the Construction Industry Training Board.

Personal Qualities
Useful attributes are strength, a liking for being outdoors, a steady hand, neatness and agility.

Starting Salary
Recommended rates are: £73.90 at 16; £103.46 at 17; £147.81 at 18; and, when qualified, the Craftsman rate is £178.62.

Further Information
Construction Industry Training Board, Bircham Newton, King's Lynn, Norfolk PE31 6RH; 01553 776677 (ext 2466)

Groom

Grooms look after all aspects of the horse's welfare. Their duties include: grooming and strapping, mucking out, feeding, cleaning tack, saddling up, exercising and leading both mounted and dismounted, elementary veterinary care and sick nursing, preparation for and travelling with horses by road, sea and air and care of the horse when at grass. Grooms work in racing stables, hunting establishments, private stables, studs and breeding concerns, riding schools and occasionally (seasonally) with polo ponies and at trekking centres.

Qualifications and Training

No formal qualifications are necessary but it is recommended that grooms take the British Horse Society examinations stages 1, 2 and 3, horse knowledge and care, which comprise the Grooms Certificate. Alternative options are NVQs in horse care levels 1, 2 and 3.

Training is usually on the job and should be sufficient to prepare students for examinations. There are also courses of varying lengths to prepare students for particular examinations; however, the fees are often high. Further Education Funding Council assistance may be available for the achievement of British Horse Society qualifications providing that the person is not eligible for any other type of funding. Details may be obtained from a local further education college.

Personal Qualities

A love of horses is essential, plus patience and the willingness to work long hours and perform many routine tasks. A heavy goods vehicle driving licence may be an advantage.

Starting Salary

Stable staff at 20 years of age earn around £135–£140 a week. In some cases food and accommodation may be free, and in others deducted from the wage. The hours may be long.

Further Information

The British Horse Society, Stoneleigh Park, Kenilworth, Warwickshire CV8 2LR; 01203 696697

Groundsmen/women

Groundsmen and women prepare, maintain and care for the various types of sports surfaces, both natural and synthetic turf – cricket and football pitches, bowling greens, athletic tracks and tennis courts.

Nowadays groundsmen/women have to be familiar with the developments in science and technology both in machinery and materials used in the maintenance of grounds. Employment can be found in both the private and public sectors with local authorities, sports clubs and schools.

Qualifications and Training

Training can take place either on the job, or through colleges on residential or day release courses. The Institute of Groundsmanship (IOG) also organises courses and has its own examination structure. There are a number of routes to gain qualifications including NVQs, HNCs and HNDs.

Personal Qualities

A groundsman/woman is a resourceful person who prefers working outdoors regardless of the weather. An enjoyment of the physical challenge plus an interest in sport are an advantage.

Starting Salary

This ranges from about £6000 at 16, £9,000 at 18 and over, to £14,500 for a head groundsman.

Further Information

Institute of Groundmanship, 19–23 Church Street, The Agora, Wolverton, Milton Keynes MK12 5LG; 01908 312511

Hairdresser

Hairdressers not only wash, cut and set hair, but must be familiar with the more specialised techniques of permanent waving, tinting, streaking and colouring. They work in individual salons; salons in department stores, hotels, airports and passenger liners, hospitals and prisons; and from home. There are also opportunities to work in television and films.

Qualifications and Training

Although no GCSEs are required for an apprenticeship, a good general knowledge of English, chemistry and art is useful. A traditional apprenticeship with a reputable salon lasts for three years. A few modern apprenticeships are available within the industry, with training to NVQ level 3. Normally, applicants will enter hairdressing at the foundation level, this is the NVQ/SVQ level 2 in Hairdressing, accredited by the National Council for Vocational Qualifications. This certificate is jointly awarded by the Hairdressing Training Board and City and Guilds (NVQs) and SCOTVEC (SVQs). Hairdressers can then go on to NVQ/SVQ level 3 in hairdressing and eventually NVQ/SVQ level 4, the management side of the industry. Training also may take place on a full-time course at a further education college or private school.

Personal Qualities

Applicants should be friendly, polite and have a calm unflappable nature. As hairdressers spend a lot of time on their feet, they must have stamina. Good grooming is essential.

Starting Salary

Initial earnings are low. When trained, hairdressers' earnings will reflect their skills, artistic talents and personality.

Further Information

Hairdressing Training Board, 3 Chequer Road, Doncaster DN1 2AA; 01302 342837 (career packs, publications and general information)

National Hairdressers' Federation, 11 Goldington Road, Bedford MK40 3JY; 01234 360332 (*Professional Hairdressing* – the official guide to level 3)

Careers in Hairdressing and Beauty Therapy, Kogan Page

Running Your Own Hairdressing Salon, Kogan Page

Health Care Assistant* see *Nursing Auxiliary

Health Service

There are many non-medical jobs within the health service, employing a wide range of skills, but services are increasingly being provided by private contractors, especially for laundry and cleaning.

Management

Management is concerned with efficiency and cost effectiveness at all levels of the health service. General management within a hospital, where the managers will be in contact with professional staff, patients and the public, will involve forward planning, finance, personnel management, purchasing and supply, building maintenance, and the organisation of laundry, catering and cleaning. At district and regional health authority levels the responsibilities are for ascertaining the health needs of the local population and for an overall monitoring role.

Catering

In hospitals, ordinary meals are provided for both patients and staff, as well as special diets. The catering officer supervises the kitchen, plans menus in consultation with the dietitian, and is in control of ordering the food as well as its preparation.

Domestic Services

This covers all grades, from basic domestic cleaner level, through domestic supervisors and housekeepers. This section is responsible for cleaning groups of beds and areas within the hospital, under the charge of the domestic superintendent. It includes district and area domestic managers, who coordinate the hospital domestic services.

Laundry
This department deals with the supply of sterilised sheets, towels, blankets and overalls; the number of items handled weekly within one hospital may run into millions.

Medical Records (patient services)
Clerks arrange appointments, patients' registration, maintain waiting lists and filing systems, keep patients' records and maintain statistical data. The medical records officer may work within the hospital, in charge of the clerks and medical secretaries, or may work at regional or district authority level.

Ancillary Staff
Includes porters, who move supplies and people around the hospital, general building maintenance staff, and ambulance services.

Qualifications and Training

Staff are recruited and trained by the hospitals and health authorities. Some health care staff may work towards NVQs, levels 1 and 2. The Institute of Health Services Management accredits courses leading to professional management qualifications. Entry to courses is not restricted to those in management but is open to a wide range of staff from clerical staff to doctors. Entry qualifications vary and are set by individual colleges.

There is also a General Management Training Scheme run by the NHS Training Division which is open to graduates and lasts for 22 months. Those already employed in the health service and over 21 and with two A levels may also apply.

Personal Qualities

Working for the health service requires a real and sympathetic concern for people, and management calls for a sense of responsibility as well as a capacity for organisation.

Starting Salary

Approximate salaries are: Clerical grades £5500+ at 16, £6000+ at 17, £7000+ at 18 upwards; administrative grades £10,000–£12,500+.

Further Information

The Institute of Health Services Management, 39 Chalton Street, London NW1 1JD; 0171 388 2626

NHS Training Division, St Bartholomew Court, 18 Christmas Street, Bristol BS1 5BT

Local Jobcentres and Careers Offices

Health Visitor

Health visitors promote health and contribute towards the prevention of mental, physical and social ill-health in the community. This involves educating people in ways of healthy living and also making positive changes in the environment. Education may be achieved by teaching individuals or families in their own homes, in health centres, clinics or in informal groups, or through campaigns for the promotion of good health practices through local or national mass media.

The health visitor may work with people who are registered with a general medical practitioner or who live within a defined geographical area. The work includes collaboration with a wide range of voluntary and statutory organisations.

Qualifications and Training

Applicants must be registered general or adult nurses with post-registration experience. Health visitor courses of one year's duration are provided at institutions of higher education.

By October 1998 all approved programmes will lead to the award of Specialist Practitioner (public health visiting/health visiting). These new programmes are at a minimum of first degree level.

Personal Qualities

Health visitors must have a desire to help people. They should be friendly and able to respond tactfully. An ability to communicate with all types of people and to speak in public is useful.

Starting Salary

£18,156–£21,007 approximately.

Further Information

ENB Careers, PO Box 2EN, London W1A 2EN; 0171 391 6200/6205
Health Visitors Association, 50 Southwark Street, London SE1 1UN; 0171 378 7255

Home Economist

Home economics covers a variety of subjects connected with the home and family life. They include nutrition and health, the preparation of food, equipment used in the home, home management, budgeting; and may extend further into textiles, consumer affairs, family problems and community work. A trained home economist may be able to work abroad. There are several levels of training, from certificate courses to a full degree course.

Demonstrator

Home economists may demonstrate products for manufacturers in shops or exhibitions, organise exhibitions themselves and train demonstrators, or give talks to institutions or in the home on products or services, or give advice on home management.

In Industry

Many home economists are employed in the food industry in marketing and/or the research and development of new products to supply retailers. Their counterparts in retailing are the home economists who, as buyers/selectors, choose the products to be stocked. Home economists are similarly employed in the domestic appliance manufacturing industry and with those retailers.

Local Authorities

Home economists are used by local authorities in the social services, housing departments, consumer services and health promotion units.

In the Media

There are opportunities on magazines, newspapers, in broadcasting, advertising and in public relations.

Teaching

A knowledge of science, particularly chemistry, is advisable for teaching, which necessitates a degree course. There are openings for teachers in colleges and universities, as well as in schools. Food and textiles are taught under technology.

Qualifications and Training

Standard entry requirements for degree courses are a minimum of two A levels or three H grades, preferably including home economics, and three other GCSEs/S grades (A–C/1–3) or equivalent qualifications such as BTEC ND/GNVQ – advanced/NVQ level 2 for GCSE. (No specific A levels but maths, English language and a science are usually required at GCSE level.) Three GCSEs to include a subject showing the use of English are needed for the BTEC national diploma for students of 17 and over; this is a two-year course. NVQs offer five levels of attainment from level 1 for those at the start of their career to level 5, senior management level.

Personal Qualities

Home economists care about people and the quality of life and need therefore to have an interest in the quality, performance and safety of goods and services related to the people who use these products. Much of the work involves communicating with the general public on the one hand and specialists on the other. Thus home economists must be confident and have the ability to express themselves in both oral and written work. Good self-management and good interpersonal skills are needed.

Starting Salary

In the region of £12,000 or over £13,000 for those with a degree or diploma, maybe a little more in London.

Further Information

Institute of Home Economics, 21 Portland Place, London W1N 3AF; 0171 436 5677

National Association of Teachers of Home Economics and Technology, Hamilton House, Mabledon Place, London WC1H 9BJ; 0171 387 1441

College Courses Guide, NATFHE

Homoeopath

Homoeopathy is a method of treating the whole person to create a healthy whole individual. There are three main principles of homoeopathy. First, treating like with like – what produces the symptoms of a disease may also cure it; the patient is treated by a small amount of the substance causing the symptoms and the natural defences are stimulated. Second, the lower the dose the better the result. Third, the remedy should be unique to the particular patient at a particular time. Homoeopathic remedies may be used to treat almost any reversible illness in adults, children or animals.

Many newly qualified homoeopaths set up in partnership in a clinic with other homoeopaths and some now work with GPs in fundholding practices.

Homoeopathic patients may come privately or be referred by GPs.

Qualifications and Training

Qualified medical doctors who have been qualified for a minimum of two and a half years may take a six-month postgraduate course at the Faculty of Homoeopathy. A part-time course is also available.

Non-medically qualified candidates have a choice of institutions of which the following are examples: The British School of Homoeopathy has a four-year part-time training course. Two A levels are required but this may be waived for students over 25. The London College of Classical Homoeopathy offers both a four-year full-time and part-time course. Candidates under 21 should offer five GCSEs or three A levels. Those over 21 should have a GCSE in human biology.

Personal Qualities
Homoeopaths must have an interest in people, an ability to consider and interpret information and be good listeners and communicators.

Starting Salary
Varies greatly, depending on hours worked and number of patients.

Further Information
British School of Homoeopathy, 23 Sarum Avenue, Melksham, Wiltshire SN12 6BN; 01225 790051

Faculty of Homoeopathy, The Royal London Homoeopathic Hospital, Gt Ormond Street, London WC1N 3HR; 0171 837 9469

London College of Classical Homoeopathy, Morley College, 61 Westminster Bridge Road, London SE1 7HT; 0171 928 6199

London School of Classical Homoeopathy, 94 Green Dragon Lane, Winchmore Hill, London N21 2NJ; 0181 360 8757

Society of Homoeopaths, 2 Artizan Road, Northampton NN1 4HU; 01604 21400

Working in Complementary and Alternative Medicine, Kogan Page (*contains details of courses*)

Horticulturist *see Gardener*

Commercial Horticulture

This is concerned with growing crops: vegetables on open land, and glasshouse crops such as tomatoes, lettuce and cucumbers. Both orchard and soft fruits account for over one-fifth of the value of all horticultural production. Commercial horticulture also covers the growing of flowers, including chrysanthemums, roses and carnations under glass and, for the gardening market, nurseries and seedsmen.

Amenity Horticulture

Landscape architects, parks directors, landscape gardeners and groundsmen maintain public and private gardens and parks, sport and recreational facilities, industrial and residential areas, and the landscaping and planting of roadsides. Employers may be local authority public parks and recreation departments or commercial landscaping or contract garden maintenance firms.

Arboriculturists, who care for and maintain trees, are mainly employed by local authorities, though there are some opportunities in private firms. The term 'tree surgeon' is often used for a commercial arboriculturist.

Research
Scientists work on pest and disease and general cultural problems to produce better and healthier plants, in industrial and government organisations and in universities and colleges. There is a wide range of prospects for graduates.

Advisory Work
The adviser provides a link between research workers and the grower, to pass on the result of experimental work. The Agricultural Developments and Advisory Service, a department of the Ministry of Agriculture, Fisheries and Food, is one employer, but commercial firms and producer organisations also provide opportunities for advisers. A degree plus practical experience are necessary.

Teaching
Opportunities for teaching occur in universities, colleges and schools. A degree or diploma is required.

Qualifications and Training

There are openings in horticulture for all standards of education. No GCSEs are required for part-time or full-time initial training courses, although beginners should be competent in biology, chemistry and maths. Applicants may work towards NVQs, levels 1 to 4. The Royal Horticultural Society offers the prestigious qualification of Master of Horticulture; entry qualifications are five GCSEs or equivalent to include maths and science. All candidates must have spent at least five years in horticultural employment or education.

Those with five GCSEs, including science and maths plus one A level pass in a science subject, or SCE passes with two at H grade and one year's experience can study for the higher national diploma, specialising in commercial or amenity horticulture.

Two GCE A levels or three SCE H grades, including chemistry and biology, plus maths and chemistry at GCSE level, are necessary to study for a degree in horticulture at university, or as a postgraduate course.

Personal Qualities
As machinery is now used a great deal in horticulture it is essential to be able to work with it, as well as being interested in growing plants. For commercial horticulture, business acumen is essential, and artistic ability is important in the field of landscape gardening.

Starting Salary
Unqualified staff when trained, £120–£160 per week; qualified technical staff from £11,000, and graduates after two years' training £15,000 upwards.

Further Information
Institute of Horticulture, 14–15 Belgrave Square, London SW1X 8PS; 0171 245 6943
'Come into Horticulture' (*address as above, free*)

Hotel Work *see Catering and Accommodation Management*

Cooking
Depending on the type and size of hotel, cooking may involve traditional British and French cookery, large-scale kitchen production or the reheating of pre-cooked meals. It may entail working under pressure in hot and noisy kitchens, but leads to good career opportunities as a chef.

Food and Drink Service
Food, beverage and alcoholic drinks service requires social skills, a pleasant personality, alertness and a good memory for customers; working hours may entail early or late shifts and weekend duty, but there will be compensating time off.

Housekeeping
Room staff, cleaners and other support staff keep the hotel clean and comfortable. The head housekeeper is in charge of this side of hotel life.

Reception
Receptionists receive guests and handle reservations, and also perform bookkeeping duties, so it is important to be good at figures, and be able to handle cash and use computers. Languages are an advantage. Working hours are arranged to deal with early and late arrivals and departures, and may entail shift and weekend work.

Management

Large hotels have a general manager, food and beverage manager, personnel and training manager and house manager, and there are also heads of departments or sections. There are specialised opportunities in the fields of finance, administration, food and beverage operations, accommodation services, sales and marketing product development, public relations, personnel and training.

Qualifications and Training

Qualifications are the same as for Catering and Accommodation Management (see page 61).

Personal Qualities

Depending on which aspect of hotel work is undertaken, candidates need an understanding of food and drink, good social skills and an ability to establish good relationships with staff and colleagues, and with customers and guests, a good head for figures and grasp of statistics.

Starting Salary

Salaries vary according to the field of work and degree of responsibility. Many employees live in hotel accommodation and have food provided. Salaries are similar to those given for Catering and Accommodation Management (see page 61).

Further Information

Careers Information Service, Hotel and Catering Training Company, International House, High Street, London W5 5DB; 0181 579 2400

Hotel and Catering International Management Association, 191 Trinity Road, London SW17 7HN; 0181 672 4251

Springboard Careers Advice Centre, 1 Denmark Street, London WC2H 8LP; 0171 497 8654.

Careers in Catering and Hotel Management, Kogan Page

Housing Officer

Housing officers work mainly for local authorities and housing associations but there are also opportunities in voluntary and private housing concerns. The work covers a broad range of areas that will vary by organisation and sector. In catering for the demand for rented accommodation, the housing officer will manage and maintain properties which includes dealing with rent arrears, reporting repairs, applications, allocations and arranging property exchanges and transfers. Housing officers often work with social and welfare agencies and need to have a basic understanding of the different welfare benefits.

Qualifications and Training

The basic qualifications needed to commence your professional training in housing are three GCSE or five Standard grade passes, including English language and one GCSE at A level or three H grade passes or BTEC/SCOTVEC equivalents. Students over the age of 21 who do not meet these requirements but have relevant work experience may be considered as exceptional entrants. You should contact your local college to discuss this in more detail.

Usually, people who work in housing undertake a day-release or distance learning course to do the Chartered Institute of Housing's professional qualification (PQ). In addition to the course, candidates also need to do the work-based test of professional practice (TPP) which comes in two parts. The PQ can take three or four years to complete, depending on whether you take the graduate or non-graduate route.

Graduates or mature entrant candidates are required to study a one-year graduate foundation course followed by a two-year professional diploma. Non-graduates are required to complete a BTEC/SCOTVEC HNC in housing studies followed by a two-year professional diploma.

Also, there are full-time degree courses, and full and part-time post-graduate diplomas. The test of professional practice will still need to be undertaken with these alternative routes.

In 1993, N/SVQs in housing were introduced (levels 2, 3 and 4). Anyone working in housing is eligible to do an N/SVQ. Currently, a level 4 N/SVQ will allow candidates to proceed to stage 2 of the Chartered Institute of Housing's PQ (ie the professional diploma).

Personal Qualities

An interest in improving people's living conditions, good interpersonal skills, effective organisation skills, sensitivity to an individual's needs, flexibility.

Starting Salary

Salaries vary from area to area, job to job. However, trainee posts are offered in the range of £8500 to £12,000. A standard housing officer/manager post (which requires one to five years' experience) will have a salary of £11,000 to £19,000 (the higher figure includes London weighting).

Further Information

Chartered Institute of Housing, Octavia House, Westwood Business Park, Westwood Way, Coventry CV4 8JP; 01203 694433

Chartered Institute of Housing in Scotland, 6 Palmerston Place, Edinburgh EH12 5AA; 0131 225 4544

Institute of Housing in Wales, 4th Floor, Dominions House North, Dominions Arcade, Queen Street, Cardiff; 01222 397402

I

Illustrator, see *Artist, Medical Illustrator, Technical Illustrator*

Indexer

Indexers provide a systematic arrangement of the terms appearing in a book or journal together with the page numbers where they appear in order to aid location of information. They are employed by publishers or authors. Indexers are generally freelances and work from home.

Qualifications and Training

No formal qualifications are required but a good education is necessary plus subject knowledge in the case of specialist books. Training is by open-learning course.

Personal Qualities

Meticulous attention to detail is essential, plus the ability to work to set requirements and time limits.

Starting Salary

Payment may be by lump sum or by the hour. The minimum rate recommended by the Society is £12 per hour (1997 rate).

Further Information

Society of Indexers, Secretary: Mrs C Shuttleworth, Mermaid House, 1 Mermaid Court, London SE1 1HR; 0171 403 4947; Fax: 0171 357 0903

Industrial Designer

Art school and college trained designers work within industry with the engineers who have created a product; they are concerned with designing products that look attractive, and are efficient and convenient in use. The competition for the sale of new goods, from suitcases or spectacles to cassette players or cars, has resulted in an increased demand for the services of industrial designers.

Qualifications and Training

16 year olds with GCSE or H grade passes may take a two-year foundation course which gives an introduction to art subjects, including drawing, painting and photography. 17 year old students with at least five GCSEs or H grades and one AS level may take a one-year foundation course. Students may then enter more specialised art or design training.

Students aged 18, preferably having completed a foundation course as above *or* any other passes accepted by the Council for National Academic Awards (NB all qualifications must include English), may apply for courses at schools of art and design, universities and colleges of higher education for full-time courses lasting three years, or four-year sandwich courses. Students should show a portfolio of their art work when they are interviewed.

Students aged 21 or over may be able to enter college without the normal qualifications required if the college is satisfied with their work and motivation.

Personal Qualities

As well as artistic ability, an understanding of mass production processes is necessary; the industrial designer should also be able to work as part of a team and to schedule, and recognise the needs of the consumer.

Starting Salary

£10,000–£11,000.

Further Information

Local Jobcentres and Careers Offices

Information Scientist *see Librarian/Information Manager*

The work is akin to that of a librarian and involves collecting, indexing and classifying information for experts such as scientists, engineers or economists. However, in information science more emphasis is placed on current technology (IT) eg online, CD-ROM and other electronic media. Information scientists work for industrial concerns and research organisations in their information departments or 'special libraries'. The information scientist often needs to have specialist knowledge, and must be able to keep up to date with technical information, reading journals and papers, and making a summary of the information in them, indexing and researching for information in other sources, such as other libraries, so that the knowledge can be passed on.

Qualifications and Training

Five GCSE/SCE passes are needed plus two A levels, or three SCEs including English at H grade; passes must also include maths, a foreign language and a science subject. These can give entry to the three-year full-time course at Leeds Metropolitan University for first degrees in information science.

In Scotland there are HND courses in information studies at Kirkcaldy College of Technology, Scottish College of Textiles at Heriot Watt University, Queen Margaret College and Bell College of Technology.

Those with a relevant first degree can take a postgraduate course in information science. Full-or part-time courses leading to diplomas or MScs are available. Non-graduates with qualifications equal to a pass degree may enter the City University (London) course.

Personal Qualities

A methodical approach and accuracy, the ability to retain information, and an interest in the appropriate field of research, plus a desire to help people to find the information they want, are all important attributes.

Starting Salary

£10,000–£14,000.

Further Information

ASLIB (Association of Information Management), Information House, 20–24 Old Street, London ECIV 9AP; 0171 253 4488

Institute of Information Scientists, 44 Museum Street, London WC1A 1LY; 0171 831 8003/8633

The Library Association, 7 Ridgmount Street, London WC1E 7AE; 0171 636 7543

'Information Work as a Career' (ASLIB)

Information Technology

Information technology (IT) is concerned with all aspects of the handling of information. It is the acquiring, processing, storing and disseminating of textual, numerical, vocal and pictorial information by means of computers and telecommunications.

Qualifications and Training

There are jobs in IT at many different levels. There are openings for those with good GCSE results or equivalents, English being particularly important. Other useful subjects are business studies, commerce, accounting, office practice and physics. For those taking A levels or going on to further study at degree level, subjects such as economics, statistics, electrical or mechanical engineering and electronics should be considered. The City and Guilds offers a course in IT, 'Basic Competence in Information Technology', aimed at sixth-formers. One of the most useful skills for working in IT is the ability to operate a typewriter keyboard. NVQs level 4 are available in software systems development and software systems design.

Personal Qualities

Workers in IT should be accurate, clear thinking, practical and have the ability to work on their own.

Starting Salary

Typical salaries are: data preparation £8500–£13,000; data preparation management £11,500+; word-processing £8500–£15,000+; word processing management £17,250+.

Further Information

The British Computer Society, 1 Sanford Street, Swindon SN1 1HJ; 01793 417424

Institute for the Management of Information Systems, IDPM House, Edgington Way, Ruxley Corner, Sidcup, Kent DA14 5HR; 0181 308 0747

Insurance *see Actuary*

Apart from statutory obligations, insurance is a way of covering the costs arising from disasters of various kinds: many people pay into a common pool, and those who incur losses can draw money from the pool. The four main areas are personal lines (motor, household, travel), commercial lines (fire, liability, goods in transit), life assurance and marine insurance. Work undertaken in the office includes assessing risks, policy drafting, underwriting (the acceptance and rating of business), claims settling, and often involves computers. Sales staff work outside the office, as do surveyors and claims inspectors who assess losses on site. Other aspects of insurance include investment, legal and accountancy work. Insurance companies also operate pension funds for businesses. Lloyd's is a group of private insurers and is traditionally connected with marine insurance, although they offer all types of cover.

Broker
As the link between client and insurer, brokers advise on and arrange policies, for a wide range of businesses.

Loss Adjuster
They work independently, and are appointed by insurers to negotiate settlement of insurance claims.

Agents and Inspectors
Agents call on people in their homes, selling insurance and collecting premiums; inspectors are sales people and may also supervise agents and areas.

Qualifications and Training

Those with three GCSEs at grade C or above, including English and maths, may enter a company and at the same time study part time at a college for a BTEC/SCOTVEC national certificate or diploma. Most insurance employers run a minimum basic training scheme, and candidates can also attend courses run by the employer or at the College of Insurance, leading to the examinations of the Chartered Insurance Institute. To take the initial qualifying exam of the Institute, candidates need three GCE A level or four SCE H grade passes; *or* two subjects at grade C, GCSE and two A levels or five SCE passes, including three at H level, both including certain specified subjects; *or* the BTEC/SCOTVEC national certificate or diploma; *or* NC/ND or SNC/SND in business studies or public administration. Other routes to professional qualifications are available for those entrants without A levels or equivalents. There is the Chartered Insurance Institute's certificate of insurance practice (CIP). This can be taken by applicants over 21 without specific qualifications or by those under 21 with four GCSEs grades A to C or BTEC equivalent. National and Scottish vocational qualifications (N/SVQs) are available at levels 2, 3 and 4 for general or life insurance and intermediaries. The CII's certificate of proficiency (COP) provides the insurance knowledge base for the level 2 NVQs, which then require individuals to prove their competence in insurance disciplines.

Personal Qualities
Absolute integrity is necessary, as well as some mathematical ability and an interest in people. Communication skills in speech and writing are also necessary.

Starting Salary
Salaries vary from employer to employer depending on qualifications and location. Some examples are: at 16 clerks earn from £6700–£8500 as do claims officials; insurance salespeople earn £10,000+; loss adjusters, underwriters and brokers earn from £7000–£10,000 to start, but later are highly paid.

Further Information
The British Insurance and Investment Brokers Association, 14 Bevis Marks, London EC3A 7NT; 0171 623 9043

The Chartered Institute of Loss Adjusters, Manfield House, 376 Strand, London WC2R 0LR; 0171 240 1496

The Chartered Insurance Institute, Careers Information Service, 20 Aldermanbury, London EC2V 7HY; 0171 606 3835

Interior Decorator *see Interior Designer, Painter and Decorator*

Decorators may be the craftsmen who do the work of papering and painting in private homes, or larger buildings, or they may give advice on interior decoration – the colour schemes, including carpets and curtains, as well as the paint, wall coverings and fittings. In this context they may be employed by large stores, manufacturers, architects or specialist shops, and also private individuals and companies.

Qualifications and Training
Craftsmen decorators can learn the trade without formal educational qualifications through apprenticeships, whereby they work towards NVQs awarded jointly by City and Guilds and the Construction Industry Training Board. Advisory decorators can learn by working in a workroom or studio of a store, specialist shop or architect's office as a junior, and taking suitable evening classes and City and Guilds courses. Unlike interior designers, interior decorators do not need to hold art and design qualifications.

Personal Qualities
Manual dexterity is necessary for craftsman decorators; artistic sense is imperative for advisers and useful for craftsmen too.

Starting Salary
£65–£75 a week at 16; £165+ for craftsmen.

Further Information
IDDA, 1–4 Chelsea Harbour Design Centre, Lots Road, London SW10 0XE; 0171 349 0800

Interior Designer *see Interior Decorator*

Interior designers work for commercial organisations, as well as undertaking private commissions. They are responsible for the interiors of buildings, whereas an architect is responsible for its shell. Interior design can cover materials for floors and ceilings, fitments and fittings and colour schemes along with electrical and spatial planning. The commercial organisations may be offices, a chain of hotels or pubs, stores or banks. Interior designers may work with architects, have their own consultancies, or work in design units within large organisations, or have their own business.

Qualifications and Training
Entry to art school and college via a foundation course is the same as for an industrial designer (see page 177). Once at art college, the student may specialise in interior design.

Personal Qualities
A natural aptitude for art is necessary, and the ability to work as part of a design team, and to present work to customers.

Starting Salary
About £11,000 according to experience and ability.

Further Information
IDDA, 1–4 Chelsea Harbour Design Centre, Lots Road, London SW10 0XE; 0171 349 0800
Careers in Art and Design, Kogan Page

Interpreter *see Translator*

Interpreters communicate between people who do not share a common language. Very few openings are available for interpreters, even worldwide. Conference interpreters work at international conferences at UNO and the EC and at the International Court of Justice by simultaneous or consecutive interpreting. Some work for international agencies; others are freelance. Demand for conference interpreters in particular languages may fluctuate depending on the political requirements of the day. Interpreters with specialist knowledge, such as engineering or economics, may have the chance to work at conferences on their subject.

Interpreters may also work as guides in tourist centres, and to do this must usually be accredited and trained as guides. Demand for interpreting in the public services (police, courts, public health and local government) has led to the creation of the National Register of Public Service Interpreters covering a wide range of African, Asian, European and Far Eastern languages. This Register is supported by the Home Office and the UK legal agencies.

Qualifications and Training

To take a degree course, two GCE A levels or three SCE H grade passes, including a foreign language, are normally required. At the newer universities and colleges, training in interpreting and translating is offered, combined with regional studies or technological or business studies, aimed at industry, commerce and international organisations. A list of these courses is offered by the Institute of Linguists. Such degree courses usually involve work or study abroad.

Those with a BTEC national award or one A level and three GCSEs may enter for the BTEC higher national diploma course. Those with SNC/SND with a language pass or three H grade passes including English and at least one foreign language and two Standard grade passes can apply for SCOTVEC courses at levels up to postgraduate.

Personal Qualities

Fluency in languages should be allied with a natural feeling for words and phrases and a good ear. It is necessary to be able to think quickly, to remain alert for long periods, and to be socially confident. Subject knowledge is essential, especially for simultaneous interpreting which requires a degree of understanding and anticipation of subject matter and context.

Starting Salary

Interpreters earn £200 per day and £25 per hour on average.

Further Information

Institute of Linguists, 24A Highbury Grove, London N5 2DQ; 0171 359 7445

Institute of Translation and Interpreting, 377 City Road, London EC1V 1NA; 0171 713 7600

Average rates for translation 1994 (Institute of Linguists)
Careers Using Languages, Kogan Page
Languages and Your Career (1994);
Schedule of Courses for Translators and Interpreters (Institute of Linguists)

Investment Analyst

Investment analysts analyse the financial markets in order to advise on the best investments for clients. Investment managers rely on their information.

There are two main types of investment analyst: first, those who work for stockbrokers and undertake their own analysis to provide information for fund manager clients. The aim is to generate 'buy and sell' orders for the stockbrokers for whom they work. This is known as the 'sell side'. Second, there are those who work for investment management institutions. They provide ideas and information to enable their in-house fund managers to make the best decisions for their clients. This is known as the 'buy side'. The majority of investment analysts work on the 'sell side'.

Qualifications and Training

Entrants generally have a degree and often a professional qualification. The most useful degrees are economics, accountancy or statistics. Training is on the job and during this time entrants study for a professional qualification by an examination set by the Institute of Investment Management and Research.

Personal Qualities

Entrants must be able to work as part of a team as well as on their own initiative. Considerable time is spent on the telephone, so communication skills are important. Naturally, a keen interest in world financial and current affairs is essential.

Starting Salary

Trainees in investment analysis work draw a fairly modest salary but with experience may earn £35,000+.

Further Information

The Institute of Investment Management and Research, 21 Ironmonger Lane, London EC2V 8EY; 0171 796 3000

Investment Fund Manager

Investment fund managers invest the funds of other people: private clients and institutions, such as insurance companies, charities, independent schools and specialised research institutions. Managers must keep their clients' interests continually under review, offering advice on how to retain their clients' income and when to change investments. Investment fund managers may be employed by the larger institutions or work in specialist firms that tend to serve smaller clients.

Qualifications and Training

Entrants generally should have a degree; the most useful being economics, accountancy or statistics. The regulatory authorities now have rigorous training requirements including the passing of a basic competence examination, the Investment Management Certificate (IMC), which is operated by the Institute of Investment Management and Research. The Associate examination of the Institute is the formally recognised qualification for investment fund managers.

Personal Qualities

Investment managers must have a keen interest in world financial and current affairs, be logical and trustworthy.

Starting Salary

Trainees in investment work draw a fairly modest salary but with experience may earn £35,000+.

Further Information

The Institute of Investment Management and Research, 21 Ironmonger Lane, London EC2V 8EY; 0171 796 3000

J

Jewellery Trade

Design
Jewellery designers craft a wide variety of items either by hand or through methods of large-scale production. These may be very expensive traditionally styled pieces, using gold or platinum, cheaper costume jewellery using synthetic stones and base metals, or fashion accessories made from beads, plastic, wood etc.

Although there are a few openings for designers of expensive jewellery, the more costly costume jewellery, and mass-produced jewellery, there is more scope for original designers on either a freelance or artist/craftsman basis, making fashionable ranges with semi-precious stones.

Manufacture
The jewellery, silverware and allied industries encompass a vast range of specialist skills. Apart from mounting and silversmithing, other skills are also needed to support these occupations, such as gem setting, engraving (hand and machine), enamelling, chasing, engine turning, spinning, electro-plating, polishing. Each skill may usually be learnt at specialist companies or within larger companies' departments.

Qualifications and Training
It is advisable for those wishing to follow a career in jewellery design to have had full-time specialist training before looking for employment. Full-time three-year, and some sandwich-based, degree courses in three-dimensional design, with main options in jewellery, silver, metal etc are available at a number of colleges and universities.

The minimum entrance requirements are usually two A levels and three GCSEs or equivalents, or satisfactory completion of a one- or two-year foundation course at a college of art and design, together with one A level and four GCSEs or equivalents.

Manufacturing training can be by traditional trade apprenticeships, lasting between three and five years, or Youth Training Credit programmes lasting two years and with competency linked to NVQ/SVQ level 2 – manufacturing jewellery and allied products. The diploma examination of the National Association of Goldsmiths may be studied over a period of two years by correspondence. The Gemmological Association and Gem Testing Laboratory have two diploma qualifications, the first of which is the diploma in gemmology. This two-year course may be studied by correspondence or as a college course. The second is the gem diamond diploma, a one-year course which can be studied by correspondence, as a college course or as an evening class at GAGTL. There are also two examinations conducted by the British Horological Institute: the certificate for clockmakers and the diploma for salesmen.

Personal Qualities

People in the jewellery trade must have a sense of design and an appreciation of quality.

Designers must be prepared to work hard and keep to a busy schedule. Self-employed or independent designers will need determination to keep going and unflagging enthusiasm to sell their products. Manufacturing employees and craftspeople must possess good manual dexterity, creativity, integrity, attention to detail, initiative and self-motivation.

Starting Salary

Shopworkers earn about £170 a week. Individual craftsmen set their own rates. Apprentice craftsmen earn £70+ a week.

Further Information

British Jewellers' Association, 10 Vyse Street, Birmingham B18 6LT; 0121 237 1109

Gemmological Association and Gem Testing Laboratory of Great Britain, 27 Greville Street, London EC1N 8SU; 0171 404 3334

National Association of Goldsmiths, 78a Luke Street, London EC2A 4PY; 0171 613 4445

Jobber*, see *Market Maker

Jockey

Jockeys are employed by trainers of flat racing and National Hunt racehorses to ride horses at race meetings. They may ride for one trainer or for several. To become a jockey it is necessary first to work in a racing stable as an apprentice jockey or stablehand.

Only those showing most talent, about one out of every ten, are chosen to ride in a race; for the others, who remain as stablehands, promotion to head lad is possible (this title applies to boys and girls).

Stable Lad

Stable lads do much labouring work: mucking out, fetching straw, filling haynets and sweeping. They must also learn to groom and exercise the horses, and usually become responsible for a certain number of their 'own'. On race days a stable lad will accompany his horse, groom him, walk him round before the race and lead him into the winner's enclosure if he wins.

Qualifications and Training

No specific educational qualifications are needed to become a jockey; some experience of riding is useful but serious training is given by the stable. The racing industry has recently introduced NVQs, levels 1, 2 and 3 in racehorse care and management. Flat racing apprenticeships start at 16 and last until the age of 24, National Hunt apprenticeships start at 17–18 and last until the age of 25.

There is a nine-week training course available at the British Racing School in Newmarket, funded by racing, and open to school-leavers who wish to work in a racing yard; pupils are taught to ride, look after horses and carry out elementary stable management. The Northern Racing School at Doncaster runs a 12-week course for those coming into the industry to train as stable staff. Both schools run a Youth Training scheme.

Personal Qualities

Apprentice jockeys must be prepared to work long hours in all weather conditions. At 16, flat race apprentices should weigh 7–8 stone (44–51kg), girls 8–9 stone (51–57kg); National Hunt jockeys may be heavier. Jockeys need strong hands and arms and must be able to deal with nervous horses in a calm, confident and unemotional way. Jockeys must also be able to work within the strict, rather conservative traditions of the racing world.

Starting Salary

Apprentice jockeys and stablehands over 19 and with a year's experience earn about £140 a week. Apprentice and conditional jockeys receive their normal wage plus half the riding fee when racing. Racing jockeys' salaries vary according to their success: there is a rate per ride plus a percentage of the prize money.

Further Information

British Racing School, Snailwell Road, Newmarket, Suffolk CB8 7NU; 01638 665103

National Trainers' Federation, 42 Portman Square, London W1H 0AP; 0171 935 2055

Racing and Thoroughbred Breeding Training Board (RTBTB), Careers and Recruiting Officer, PO Box 21, Newmarket CB8 9BL; 01638 560743

Stable Lads' Association (SLA), 4 Dunsmore Way, Midway, Swadlincote, Derbyshire DE11 7LA; 01283 211522

The Northern Racing School, The Stables, Rossington Hall, Great North Road, Doncaster DN11 0HN; 01302 865462

Joiner*, see *Carpenter and Bench Joiner

Journalist

This covers a variety of jobs.

Reporter

Journalists find, research and write news articles and features for newspapers, magazines, special interest periodicals, news agencies, radio and television. They work irregular hours to meet deadlines and must be able to produce accurate, interesting and readable copy quickly, often in noisy offices or even public places. Reporters cover all kinds of stories, from weddings and council meetings (at local level) to world events and sensational murder cases (for the national papers). Some opportunities exist for foreign correspondents and freelance journalists.

Sub-editor

Sub-editors reduce or, if necessary, re-write articles to an appropriate size depending upon importance and position in the paper. They also deal with continuing stories which come in a bit at a time. The sub-editor also writes the headlines and, in between editions, may amend stories to accommodate sudden developments or change the page layout if required. Sub-editors may specialise, for example, dealing only with the sports page.

Fashion Editor

The fashion editor is responsible for researching and anticipating the latest fashion trends and presenting them in articles which will appeal to readers.

Feature Writer and Columnist
Feature writers suggest subjects for research and produce longer than average articles dealing with topics not necessarily of current news value but of general interest, such as an interview with a public figure or an article about tax relief, motoring etc. Columnists write about subjects from their own personal point of view.

The Editor
The editor is responsible for the policy of the publication, its content and the appointment and organisation of the staff.

Qualifications and Training

Most journalists begin their career by serving for two or three years on a provincial newspaper. Each year approximately 800 school-leaver entrants, with at least five GCSEs and two A level passes, and from the one-year National Council for the Training of Journalists (NCTJ) pre-entry course, find positions. Direct entrants undertake a qualifying period of two years, pre-entry trainees 18 months, of on-the-job training and experience in full-time employment. Part of the learning process is spent on block-release courses at colleges approved by the NCTJ or tuition on in-house schemes, the rest of the time being taken up with work as junior reporters. Preliminary exams lead finally to the examination for the certificate awarded by the NCTJ. (This equates to level 4 NVQ.) There are also a number of postgraduate courses available, usually lasting for one year, plus two 18-week NCTJ postgraduate courses.

Personal Qualities

Journalists must possess powers of self-expression, observation, accuracy, patience and tact. They must take pride in their work, be resourceful, willing to travel and to work under pressure and irregular hours; stamina is required, as is confidence, great curiosity and the ability to put people at their ease. One must be able to write fast in longhand, and learn shorthand and word-processing skills.

Starting Salary

Salaries vary greatly. Trainees on a small weekly paper earn about £7000+. In London trainees start at about £12,000+. Generally, journalists' salaries are higher than average.

Further Information

Chartered Institute of Journalists, 2 Dock Offices, Surrey Quays Road, London SE16 2XU; 0171 252 1187

National Council for the Training of Journalists, Latton Bush Centre, Southern Way, Harlow, Essex CM18 7BL; 01279 430009

Careers in Journalism, Kogan Page

Kennel Work *see Dog Groomer*

Kennel staff ensure that the animals in their care have clean accommodation, are fed a regular and nutritious diet, that they are clean, well groomed and given sufficient exercise. Where animals are sick or recovering from an operation, they must also be able to provide adequate nursing care.

There are a number of different types of kennel: greyhound kennels train dogs for racing, hunt kennels for hunting, and both of these involve a lot of outdoor work, exercising the dogs, and some travelling to meetings. There are quarantine kennels licensed by the Ministry of Agriculture, Fisheries and Food and breeding kennels where duties will also include weaning and training puppies, preparing dogs for, and possibly handling them at, shows. Boarding kennels look after animals while their owners are away. Some of the racing and quarantine kennels are large operations situated near racing stadia, airports and ports but others may be smaller, family-run concerns.

Qualifications and Training

No formal qualifications are needed to work in kennels, and most employers prefer school-leavers to train on the job – this is best done via a Youth Training course. Indeed a good entry route is via work experience while still at school. The NVQ level 2 qualification in animal care is nationally recognised by the industry and this is a good base for further study. Many training organisations throughout the country offer this qualification. Entry requirements vary depending on the institution.

Personal Qualities

Good health, general fitness and stamina are required for this manual, physically demanding, outdoor work. Kennel staff must be unsentimental about animals but at the same time have a genuine concern for their well-being; they require patience and a placid but firm nature. A willingness to work long days, weekends and public holidays is also required.

Starting Salary
£70–£100+ a week.

Further Information

Animal Care College, Ascot House, High Street, Ascot, Berkshire SL5 7JG; 01344 28269

Bellmead Kennel Staff Training College, Priest Hill, Old Windsor, Berkshire SL4 2JN; 01784 432929 (*Approved Training Organisation*)

Our Dogs, 5 Oxford Road, Station Approach, Manchester M60 1SX; 0161 228 1984 (*Weekly magazine featuring job offers and advertisements from kennels. Also publishes* Cats)

Universities Federation for Animal Welfare (UFAW), 8 Hamilton Close, South Mimms, Potters Bar, Hertfordshire EN6 3QD; 01707 658202

Local Jobcentres and Careers Offices

Careers Working with Animals, Kogan Page

Running Your Own Boarding Kennels, Kogan Page

L

Laboratory Technician *see Biomedical Scientist*

Laboratory technicians assist scientists, engineers, lecturers and doctors by carrying out the practical work to be done in laboratories. The work includes: preparation, and in some cases cultivation, of specimens for testing, caring for small animals and insects, maintaining apparatus, preparing solutions and experiments, projecting films etc. Highly sophisticated equipment is used for some of this work and the results may be analysed by computer. Some technicians go out to offices and factories and either take away samples for testing or do tests on site. Laboratory technicians work in industry, schools, hospitals and universities, for the government and research establishments.

Qualifications and Training

GCSEs or equivalent are preferred for this work, and some of the courses available specify four passes. Science and maths subjects plus English language are generally required. Training is on the job with time off to attend courses leading to BTEC and SCOTVEC qualifications.

Personal Qualities

Laboratory technicians must be practical, numerate, methodical, conscientious and accurate. Good colour vision is essential.

Starting Salary

£6500–£8500+ depending on age and qualifications.

Further Information

Institute of Science Technology, Mansell House, 22 Bore Street, Lichfield, Staffordshire WS13 6TJ; 01543 251346

Working as a Laboratory Technician, Batsford

Land Agent *see Surveyor/Surveying Technician*

Land agents work for estate owners and sometimes for large institutional owners. Their work overlaps to some extent with that of agricultural surveyors in that they are both concerned with the use and development of land and may advise owners on agricultural methods, forestry, accountancy and the building or improving of farm buildings. In addition the land agent may be responsible for stocking and for employing estate staff, as well as attending to the owner's personal business matters.

Qualifications and Training

Formal qualifications are not always necessary for a land agent who is employed by a private owner. However, it is advisable to become professionally qualified as a Surveyor. See Surveyor/Surveying Technician, page 335.

Personal Qualities

Necessary requirements include a love of the land and being out of doors, a practical approach and the ability to direct one's own work.

Starting Salary

A school-leaver could expect about £8000, whereas a newly qualified surveyor with professional competence would receive about £15,000–£20,000.

Further Information

The Royal Institution of Chartered Surveyors, 12 Great George Street, London SW1P 5AD; 0171 222 7000

Landscape Architect

Landscape architects are trained in the planning and design of all types of outdoor spaces. They use design techniques based on their knowledge of the functional and aesthetic characteristics of landscape materials, and of the organisation of landscape elements, external spaces and activities. Their work ranges from large-scale landscape planning to the preparation of schemes for the short- and long-term development of individual sites. It also includes the preparation of detailed designs, specifications, contract drawings and the letting and supervision of contracts.

Some practitioners are also qualified in other disciplines such as planning and architecture, and the landscape architect draws on many fields in order to promote new, and sustain existing, landscapes.

Qualifications and Training

In order to become a landscape architect it is necessary to complete an accredited course in landscape architecture, become a graduate member of the Landscape Institute and take the Institute's professional practice examination. A list of accredited courses can be obtained from the Landscape Institute. Entry requirements for landscape architecture courses are usually two A levels in related subjects (eg art, biology, geography, botany). After completing their course, graduate members must complete two years' experience before taking the professional practice examination and becoming an associate member of the Institute (ALI).

Personal Qualities

Necessary requirements are creativity, imagination, a practical outlook, interest in the landscape and an enthusiasm for being out of doors.

Starting Salary

A graduate just out of college could expect between £9000 and £15,000. An associate who has just taken the professional practice examination could expect to start on £15,000–£17,000.

Further Information

The Landscape Institute, 6–7 Barnard Mews, London SW11 1QU; 0171 738 9166

Careers Working Outdoors, Kogan Page

'Landscape Architecture as a Career' (The Landscape Institute)

Landscape Manager

Landscape managers employ management techniques in the long-term care and development of new and existing landscapes and also in determining policy and planning for future landscape management and use. They have particular expertise in the management and maintenance of landscape materials, both hard and soft, based on established principles of construction, horticulture and ecology. In addition, the landscape manager will have a thorough knowledge of budgetary control procedures, property and resource management, especially related to manpower and machinery, and of the letting and administration of contracts. Landscape managers are usually educated in horticulture, forestry, agriculture or other natural sciences and have further training in land management or related disciplines.

Qualifications and Training

The Landscape Institute is the professional body for landscape managers. There is one accredited course in landscape management – the MA in landscape management at the University of Manchester. Successful completion of the MA leads directly to graduate membership at the Landscape Institute. Otherwise, qualification as a graduate member of the Institute's landscape management division relies on a combination of academic degrees and relevant practical experience, although it is possible to be accepted on the basis of academic qualifications alone, eg an appropriate degree in horticulture followed by the postgraduate courses at either the University of Manchester or Wye College, University of London. The BSc in land management at the University of Reading can also provide a similar academic route to membership.

A more common route for entry is via a natural sciences-based first degree with between two and four years' experience (depending on relevance of degree). Candidates with less relevant degrees will almost certainly need a postgraduate relevant qualification, with up to a maximum of four years' experience, again depending on the relevance of both degrees and the overall candidate profile. In order to become an associate member of the Institute (ALI) candidates must complete the professional practice examination.

Current degree courses that concentrate on landscape management are: BSc in land management at the University of Reading; MSc in landscape ecology, design and maintenance at Wye College (University of London); MA(LM) at the Victoria University of Manchester. Details are available from the relevant establishments.

Personal Qualities

Desirable qualities are an interest in the landscape, good organisational and interpersonal skills, consistent application and a practical outlook.

Starting Salary

A graduate just out of college could expect between £9000 and £15,000. An associate who has just passed the professional practice examination could expect to start on £15,000–£17,000.

Further Information

The Landscape Institute, 6–7 Barnard Mews, London SW11 1QU; 0171 738 9166

Landscape Scientist

Landscape scientists have a specific understanding of the principles and processes of natural biological and physical systems. They relate their environmental training and experience to the solution of practical landscape problems, providing both traditional and innovative input to landscape design, planning and management work. Their scientific training in subjects such as ecology, conservation, biology, soil science, botany or related disciplines, together with the ability to apply these skills to a variety of landscape issues, make them key participants in the field of environmental impact analysis. Evaluation of the significance, effects and possible amelioration of major and minor planning proposals, along with creating new habitats and environments in association with mineral workings, forestry and agriculture, are significant roles of the landscape scientist. Smaller scale ecological and habitat surveys, species assessments, wildlife management plans and the appraisal and preparation of conservation schemes are frequent tasks. Some are involved in research and teaching, but this work is directly applied to real landscape situations and the practical training of landscape architects, managers and scientists.

Qualifications and Training

The Landscape Institute is the professional body for landscape scientists. Qualification as a graduate member of the Institute's science division is achieved by means of an appropriate first degree, followed by a higher degree or some relevant experience or a combination of both. The required duration of the experience depends on the standing and relevance of the individual candidate's academic qualifications. More experience, up to a total maximum of four years, is demanded for the less well-qualified candidates. Exceptionally, scientists who are particularly well qualified at both first degree and postgraduate levels may be admitted to graduate membership of the Institute on academic grounds alone.

Within this division there is scope for a range of specialisms. The first degree should be scientific in emphasis and an ecology or natural sciences course would be a good start. Similarly, a course with options or units has attractions, as long as care is taken throughout to develop depth in science. 'Environmental studies' or similar broad-based courses need to have a substantial and rigorous scientific content to be satisfactory. Graduate membership does not follow immediately on completion of a first degree course. The needs at that stage are to develop skills and experience in applying scientific knowledge to practical problems together with an awareness of other areas such as design, management, planning, contracts and legislation, which are unlikely to have been covered in an initial science course.

The MSc courses at University College London (conservation) and University of Aberdeen (ecology) are examples of appropriate higher degree courses and PhD research on topics relevant to landscape work is acceptable. Some research can also be valuable experience, although many potential members will gain their practical experience in a local authority, central government agency or private consultancy. All graduate members must complete two years' experience and take the Institute's professional practice examination before they can become associate members, ie full professional members of the Institute.

Personal Qualities

Desirable qualities are enthusiasm for the subject, technical commitment, a practical and realistic outlook and good communication skills.

Starting Salary

A graduate member just out of college could expect between £9000 and £15,000. An associate who has just taken the professional practice examination could expect to start on £15,000–£17,000.

Further Information

The Landscape Institute, 6–7 Barnard Mews, London SW11 1QU; 0171 738 9166

Laundry and Dry Cleaning Work

Laundries vary from those that have shops where customers may take their clothes, and those that collect, to those that supply and launder linen for hotels, factories etc. The work includes the care of delicate garments and the removal of stains, as well as washing and pressing.

Dry cleaning staff operate dry cleaning machines and presses, in addition to receiving and returning goods to the public. There are opportunities within the laundry and dry cleaning industry for trainee managers.

Qualifications and Training

No formal educational qualifications are required for general staff and training is on the job. Entrants may also take NVQs in laundry and dry cleaning at levels 1 and 2.

Qualifications for supervisors and dry cleaning managers at level 3 are under development. Senior managers are able to take Management Charter Initiative (MCI) qualifications, together with other general management qualifications.

Personal Qualities

General workers must have a careful, responsible attitude to their work, and shop workers must be numerate. Managers need good organisational skills and the ability to cope with crises.

Starting Salary

A rate of around £3.00 an hour is paid, with £4.50 for overtime; trainee managers' and dry cleaning staff's salaries are negotiable.

Further Information

Local Jobcentres and Careers Offices

Law Commission (Research Assistant)

The statutory government advisory body on law reform, the Law Commission is currently working on projects in a variety of fields including common law, company and commercial law, crime and property law, and on general revision of statute law. The work is carried out in small teams, each under the direction of a commissioner, consisting of qualified lawyers and research assistants. Draft Bills are prepared by Parliamentary Counsel on loan to the Commission. Extensive consultation and investigation takes place before proposals are formulated; a sizeable proportion result in legislation. Projects range from major investigations of controversial areas of law to the consideration of a specific problem.

Qualifications and Training

Law graduates (upper second class honours minimum), and graduates of other disciplines who have completed the Legal Practice Course or the Bar Vocational Course, are recruited annually to work as research assistants. The work offers a unique opportunity of taking part in the creation of new legislative measures, as well as the in-depth development of skills in a particular area of law. Former research assistants have found their experience a valuable asset in their subsequent legal careers, whether in practice or in academic posts. The initial appointment is for one year with the possibility of extension for a further period up to a maximum of three years in all.

Personal Qualities

Entrants should have a good knowledge of and genuine interest in the law, and should be able to think and write clearly.

Starting Salary
About £13,500.

Further Information
The Law Commission, Conquest House, 37–38 John Street, Theobalds Road, London WC1N 2BQ; 0171 453 1210

Law Costs Draftsman

The way a solicitor's bill is drawn up is complicated: different fees are charged depending on the experience and seniority of the solicitor involved, the solicitor may have had to pay travelling expenses and court fees, a barrister might have been engaged. Some bills are paid by clients direct, others out of public funds if the client is entitled to legal aid.

To save time, some solicitors are now employing law costs draftsmen to prepare their bills for them. Some law costs draftsmen work in solicitors' offices, others in independent firms of law costs draftsmen and others work at home, going into a legal office to pick up the files.

Qualifications and Training
No formal educational requirements are necessary but four GCSEs or equivalent, to include English, would be beneficial. A good head for figures and a good standard of written and spoken English are necessary. No particular training is required but some begin the work with a background in accounts and others have previously worked as legal executives.

Personal Qualities
Law costs draftsmen need to be patient, able to cope with detail and be methodical and careful in their work.

Starting Salary
From £11,000–£16,000, but in this work there is a range of payments and some people may earn much more than these figures.

Further Information
Association of Law Costs Draftsmen, c/o S A Chapman, Church Cottage, Church Lane, Stuston, Diss, Norfolk IP21 4AG; 01379 741404

Leather Production

Leather is produced from skins and hides to make shoes, bags, gloves, clothes, upholstery and saddlery. Staff are needed to tan and dress the leather to produce different grades and weights for different uses. Because of new technology, the nature of the product and the waste product resulting, there is a need for a considerable number of technologists. In addition to a knowledge of leather, they must be familiar with different dyeing agents and materials used to bring a finish to the leather.

Qualifications and Training

Training for operators is on the job, and City and Guilds qualifications are available for operatives and craftsmen through block release or open learning. NVQ/SVQ level 2 are available for leather production. Qualifications vary for technologists from a good general education necessary for City and Guilds courses, subjects studied to GCSE level to include a science, maths and a subject showing the use of English for a BTEC certificate taken by block release, or four GCSEs or equivalent to include chemistry for a one-year full-time course, to an A level in chemistry and GCSEs in biology or physics for the degree course, BSc Hons Leather Technology.

Personal Qualities

Operatives and craftsmen must be physically fit and possess stamina. Technologists must have a practical, responsible approach to their work and be prepared to travel abroad if required.

Starting Salary

Manual workers £130, rising with expertise to £175–£300 (40-hour week); a BSc leather technologist could expect £12,500.

Further Information

BLC, The Leather Technology Centre, Leather Trade House, Kings Park Road, Moulton Park, Northampton NN3 6JD; 01604 494131; Fax: 01604 648220

British School of Leather Technology, Nene College, Moulton Park, Northampton NN2 7AL; 01604 735500 (*education and training*)

Lecturer

Higher Education
Lecturers in universities, and other higher education institutions (HEIs) teach mainly undergraduates. As well as teaching, many carry out their own research, write articles and books, give outside lectures and, in some cases, broadcasts. Competition is fierce and it is unlikely that a new graduate will be able to enter higher education as a first job.

Further Education
Lecturers in this field may teach 16–18 year olds who may be re-sitting examinations, students on block release, day-release and sandwich courses and adults studying academic or leisure pursuits.

Qualifications and Training

Higher education lecturers in HEIs must have first or upper second class degrees; many have postgraduate qualifications, and some further degrees. In the new universities lecturers may be drawn from industry or commerce.

Qualifications for lecturers in further education vary, depending on the subject taught. A degree, a professional qualification, BTEC/SCOTVEC higher certificate or diploma, or City and Guilds qualifications, plus a teaching qualification are all acceptable and desirable. There are one-year full-time and two-year part-time courses available for those intending to teach in further education.

Personal Qualities

All teachers/lecturers must have a high level of knowledge of, and enthusiasm for, their subject combined with a desire to communicate this to others. They must have the ability to organise and deliver their material in a way that is understandable to their students.

Starting Salary

Starting salaries in higher education are from £14,600 upwards; salaries in the new universities are comparable for similar levels of work. Full-time lecturers in further education can expect a starting salary of about £12,000.

Further Information

Department for Education, Sanctuary Buildings, Great Smith Street, London SW1P 3BT; 0171 925 5000

Department of Education for Northern Ireland, Rathgael House, Balloo Road, Bangor, Co Down BT19 7PR; 01247 279279

NATFHE – The University and College Lecturers' Union, 27 Britannia Street, London WC1X 9JP. Written enquiries only.
Scottish Community Education Council, Roseberry House, 9 Haymarket Terrace, Edinburgh EH12 5EZ; 0131 313 2488
The Scottish Office Education Department, Victoria Quay, Edinburgh EH6 6QQ; 0131 556 8400

Legal Cashier/Administrator

Legal cashiers and administrators work in solicitors' offices and are responsible for dealing with the accounts and administration. Legal cashiers may work as the sole bookkeeper, administrator or manager, or, in a big firm, be responsible for a large number of staff.

The Institute of Legal Cashiers & Administrators keeps a register of vacancies, providing a free service to solicitors and members.

Qualifications and Training

The Institute of Legal Cashiers & Administrators has three levels of qualification: Diploma, Associateship and Fellowship. It offers correspondence courses leading to the Diploma and Associateship examinations. Formal academic qualifications are not required to take these exams. The Diploma is a qualification in its own right and covers the maintenance of solicitors' internal financial records. It is particularly aimed at those without bookkeeping knowledge. The Associateship is for those who wish to make a career as a legal cashier or administrator and enables them to advise and manage financial and administrative affairs in any solicitor's office. The Fellowship, available to associates, is the highest qualification, offering a deeper insight into the profession.

Most students are in employment before embarking on the examinations, although it is possible to qualify or partly qualify first. NVQ status is under consideration.

Personal Qualities

Entrants must have a high standard of integrity and reliability and be very discreet.

Starting Salary

£10,000–£16,000.

Further Information

The Institute of Legal Cashiers & Administrators, 2nd Floor, 146–148 Eltham Hill, Eltham, London SE9 5DX; 0181 294 2887

Legal Executive

Legal executives are professional lawyers employed in solicitor's offices and the legal departments of commerce and central local government. The training and academic requirements in a specified area of law are at the same level as those required of a solicitor. Consequently, with few exceptions, legal executives are able to carry out tasks which are similar to those undertaken by solicitors. The main areas of specialisation are conveyancing; civil litigation; criminal law; family law and probate. In addition to providing a worthwhile career in its own right, the legal executive qualification provides access to those wishing to qualify as solicitors via the 'Institute route'.

In Scotland, the term legal executive is not used, but solicitors engage assistants to do similar work.

Qualifications and Training

The minimum entry requirement is four GCSEs to include English, but A level students and graduates are welcome. As an alternative, the Institute accepts a qualification in vocational legal studies and has special arrangements for students who are over 21 years of age. In the main, training is on a part-time basis so that there is potential for trainees to 'learn while they earn'. An NVQ in law is expected to be available during 1997, and ILEX will be an awarding body.

Personal Qualities

An ability to communicate, both verbally and in writing, with people at all levels. Absolute discretion and trustworthiness, together with a meticulous attention to detail, are essential.

Starting Salary

Varies according to age and qualification, and the type of work undertaken. Currently, the commencing salary is likely to be in the order of £9500, rising to £20,000–£30,000 when qualified. Many established legal executives receive salaries in excess of £50,000.

Further Information

The Institute of Legal Executives, Kempston Manor, Kempston, Bedford MK42 7AB; 01234 841000

Careers in the Law, Kogan Page

Leisure and Amenity Management *see Sport and Recreation Facility Management*

People employed in this field may work in leisure sports centres, outward bound centres, theatre and arts centres, historic houses and ancient monuments, country areas offering nature trails, fishing and camping facilities to the public or even be in charge of bingo or dance halls. Managers, as well as being interested in their particular leisure activity, must be responsible for the administrative and financial running of the enterprise. Many in this field are employed in local government, but there are also opportunities in private sports centres, health and fitness clubs and tourist attractions.

Qualifications and Training

The Institute of Leisure and Amenity Management (ILAM) offers four levels of qualification based upon the completion of work-based projects: the ILAM first award for candidates who are new to the industry and who hold junior positions within leisure organisations; the ILAM certificate in leisure operations for candidates who have a working knowledge of the industry and hold junior supervisory positions; the ILAM certificate in leisure management for candidates with a good understanding of the industry and who hold junior or middle management jobs; the ILAM diploma in leisure management for candidates who have successfully demonstrated their managerial ability at a senior level.

HND courses are available and a range of degree courses in leisure studies/recreation management and sports sciences.

GNVQs/GSVQs are available in leisure and tourism at levels 2 and 3. GNVQs differ from NVQs in that they measure attainment whereas NVQs are based upon a statement of competence. They are also more broadly based than NVQs.

Personal Qualities

A strong interest in one's particular area of leisure is necessary, as too is the ability to organise, administer and manage people.

Starting Salary

An assistant manager would probably receive £15,000–£20,000 depending on the size and type of establishment.

Further Information

Institute of Leisure and Amenity Management, ILAM House, Lower Basildon, Reading, Berkshire RG8 9NE; 01491 874222

Librarian/Information Manager

Librarians and information managers anticipate the information needs of their clients, acquire that information by the most efficient means possible on behalf of their clients, and may well analyse it and repackage it for the client. Information may come in the form of a book or journal, or may be extracted from databases in house, on CD-ROM or online. Ideally they are skilled navigators and facilitators on the Internet.

They organise the information to make it accessible to users by indexing, cataloguing and classifying it. They promote and exploit the library's collection to the library or information source users and assist them with any enquiries. Library and information services managers work in public libraries and schools, universities and colleges, in government, in the law, in hospitals, business and industry, and also in accountancy and engineering, professional and learned societies, and in virtually all areas of economic activity.

Qualifications and Training

Library assistants are usually required to have four to five GCSEs or equivalent, to include English language; training is on the job. Part-time or distance learning vocational courses leading to City and Guilds and SCOTVEC qualifications are available to library assistants in post. S/NVQs levels 2–4 in information and library services are also available. To qualify as a professional librarian or information officer and gain chartered membership of The Library Association, a degree or postgraduate qualification accredited by the Association is necessary. Degree courses in library and information studies lasting three years full time, five to six years part time, are available for those with A levels or equivalents. Graduates of other disciplines may take a one-year full-time or two-year part-time postgraduate course. Mature entrants without the usual entry qualifications can gain admission to degree courses.

Personal Qualities

Librarians and information managers need to be well educated, with outgoing personalities, and be able to communicate with people at all levels with clarity, accuracy and tact. They need intellectual curiosity and breadth of knowledge and a logical and methodical approach to organising and subsequently seeking out and presenting information. A good memory is also useful. Management skills and an interest in working with computers are important assets.

Starting Salary

Depending on age and experience, library assistants' salaries range from £8000 to £16,500; newly qualified librarians earn from £11,900 to £16,500 and middle managers from about £17,000–£27,000. The most senior qualified library managers of large services can earn above £32,000.

Further Information

Information Services, The Library Association, 7 Ridgmount Street, London WC1E 7AE; 0171 636 7543; Fax: 0171 436 7218

Linguist*, see *Interpreter, Translator

Literary Agent

Literary agents act as middlemen between authors and publishers, film producers and theatre managements. Initially they read authors' manuscripts and decide whether or not to accept an author as a client. Once accepted, an author may be guided by his agent about ideas for books and changes to existing manuscripts. The agent then finds a publisher or producer for the author's work and negotiates the best possible terms for his client. He deals with the publisher on all matters that will affect the client, including the contract, manuscript delivery, follow-up titles, advertising, publicity, paperback, television and film rights, and obtaining payments when due.

Some literary agents also act for foreign publishers attempting to find British publishers who will bring out an English edition of a book already published abroad. Like publishers, agents tend to specialise in such areas as fiction, general non-fiction and specialist publishing.

Qualifications and Training

No particular educational qualifications are necessary. Experience of the book trade is the most important factor, and most literary agents have gained this by working in a publishing house. Foreign languages are an asset, particularly in the international field.

Personal Qualities

Agents need shrewd literary judgement and a knowledge of world-wide market conditions, negotiating and legal skills, business and financial ability. They must be hardworking, persistent, adaptable and sympathetic towards their authors.

Starting Salary

Agents receive a percentage of the money earned by the author – usually in the 10–20 per cent range.

Further Information
The Writers and Artists Handbook, Barry Turner, Macmillan (*annual publication*)

Local Government

Local authorities provide a range of services to the community. They organise the facilities that affect the daily lives of people living in their area, from sports centres to refuse collection; schools to homes for the elderly; bus services to libraries. They also have responsibility for ensuring that food sold in shops and restaurants is fit to eat; that streets are lit; and that land is developed with environmental considerations and the needs of the local population in mind. Consequently there are many varied areas of work to consider and over 500 different careers to choose from.

Local government employs many staff, approximately 1.8 million in England and Wales, some of whom are administrators who supervise, coordinate and organise the provision of services to the community. They also employ professional and technical staff, for instance, architects, accountants, engineers and electricians.

At present the emphasis is moving away from employing large numbers of staff, to buying in help when needed.

Qualifications and Training
There are a variety of paths to follow to obtain a position in local government. GCSE and A level passes may be necessary, or a degree, and some posts require professional qualifications. Work experience and appropriate NVQs are recognised as equivalent in value.

Training is seen as an important commodity in local government and as such is available in abundance in the form of internal and external courses.

Personal Qualities
These vary according to the job to be performed, but in general local government employees should be able to communicate effectively both with colleagues and the community at large, work well in a team and be professional in their approach.

Starting Salary
Salaries in local government can be competitive. There may also be a variety of benefits including relocation packages available as well as many flexible working arrangements.

Further Information

Local Government Opportunities, The Local Government Management Board (LGMB), Layden House, 76–86 Turnmill Street, London EC1 5QU; 0171 296 6600
Chief executive of Scottish regions
Personnel officer of individual counties, metropolitan counties and London boroughs
Careers in Local Government, Kogan Page

Lorry Driver

This work ranges from driving conventional flat-bodied lorries that can carry a variety of loads to driving lorries such as car and animal transporters and milk tankers that are designed for one purpose. Drivers who work for large firms may often take a load from A to B then carry one back from B to A in the UK or across Europe. As well as driving, lorry drivers may have to help with the loading and unloading of goods. Drivers of potentially dangerous products must know how to handle them safely, and special training is required.

Qualifications and Training

No formal educational requirements are necessary, but drivers must have a good enough education to be able to do simple sums, read maps, follow instructions and handle documents concerned with the delivery of goods. An LGV licence is essential. Some firms will not take on drivers until they are 25, when the cost of insurance is reduced. Some companies, particularly those with specialised loads, run short training courses. NVQs have been developed.

Personal Qualities

It is unusual for drivers to have a mate, so much of their time is spent on their own. They must be self-reliant, physically strong, responsible, and careful drivers. The job involves nights spent away from home.

Starting Salary

£150–£230 a week. Travelling outside Europe or with a dangerous load merits an extra payment of about £250 a week.

Further Information

Centrex Training and Conference Centre, Highercall, Telford, Shropshire TF6 6RB; 01952 770441

Loss Adjuster*, see *Insurance

M

Maintenance Person, see *Electrician*

Make-up Artist, see *Broadcasting, Film Production*

Management Consultant

Management has been defined as the art of getting results through other people, and consultancy as giving professional advice. Management consultants are employed to provide a higher degree of expertise than is available in a particular company; to give objective appraisals (it is often easier for an outsider to adopt a broader view); to recommend solutions and assist in their implementation; and to provide assistance when there is a temporary increase in the management's workload.

There is specialisation among firms of management consultants and they tend to divide their activities into the following areas: organisation development and policy formation – long-range planning and re-organisation of the company's structure; production management – production control arrangements; marketing, sales and distribution; finance and administration – installation of budgetary control systems etc; personnel management selection; management of information systems – the provision of software, systems analysis; economic and environmental studies – urban and regional development planning, work for overseas organisations.

Qualifications and Training

Management consultants tend to have qualifications in at least one of the following: accountancy, engineering, marketing, industrial relations, social sciences, and operating experience in one of these fields.

On joining a firm, a new entrant will receive training and after six months is eligible to join the Institute of Management Consultants (IMC) as an associate. Associates are entitled to become members after three years' continuous work as an associate.

Personal Qualities
Management consultants must have the integrity to put their clients' interests first, the ability to communicate, an enquiring mind, clarity of expression and the ability to get on with people at all levels.

Starting Salary
Varies from practice to practice depending on the number and type of clients, but generally is at a level commensurate with qualifications and experience.

Further Information
AP Information Services, Roman House, 296 Golders Green Road, London NW11 9PZ; 0181 455 4550

Directory of Management Consultants in the UK (*directory of member firms and their services to clients*)

Institute of Management Consultants, 5th Floor, 32–33 Hatton Garden, London EC1N 8DL; 0171 242 2140

Management Consultants Association, 11 West Halkin Street, London SW1X 8JL; 0171 235 3897

Mapping,* see *Cartography, Ordnance Survey Work

Marine Biologist

Although marine biology is a relatively new and expanding area of biology, as yet there are not many job opportunities in this field. It is a science that studies the ecology of the sea and coastal waters and is particularly concerned with food stocks and the effects of pollution. Marine biologists are employed by the Ministry of Agriculture, Fisheries and Food, the Natural Environment Research Council and in the marine laboratories of some private organisations.

Qualifications and Training
Two or three A level or three H grade passes in biology, chemistry and maths or another science (or similar suitable subjects), plus GCSE level or equivalent in maths and physics are necessary for entry to a first degree course in biology at university or college of higher education. Some universities offer first degree courses in marine biology, but it may be advisable to take a broader degree in applied biology first.

Personal Qualities

Biologists need the same characteristics as all scientists: patience and the willingness to repeat experimental work and measurements to check results, a methodical way of working, good observation and accuracy.

Starting Salary

£10,000+.

Further Information

Institute of Biology, 20–22 Queensberry Place, London SW7 2DZ; 0171 581 8333 (*Please enclose an sae*)

Plymouth Marine Laboratory, Prospect Place, West Hoe, Plymouth PL1 3DH; 01752 633100

The Scottish Association for Marine Science, PO Box 3, Oban, Argyll PA34 4AD; 01631 562244

'Careers in Biology' (Institute of Biology, *address above; send £3.90*)

Marine Engineering*, see *Engineering

Market Gardening *see Horticulturist*

Crops grown in market gardens are vegetables, salad crops – including tomatoes – and flowers. The work consists of using machinery, such as tractor ploughs, to prepare the soil, and also of working by hand on such jobs as transplanting young plants and thinning seedlings, and grading, washing and packing the produce after harvesting so that it can be sold.

Qualifications and Training

No special qualifications are needed to work in a market garden; training is on the job. Further training programmes are provided through apprenticeship, and it is possible to gain City and Guilds qualifications. Those with A levels and/or NVQ practical work experience can apply for entry to an agricultural college, which will provide a full training in horticulture.

Personal Qualities

An ability to use the necessary machinery is essential, plus physical strength, and a willingness to work outdoors, whatever the weather. The ability to drive is useful.

Starting Salary
£115–£150 a week for trained staff.

Further Information
Institute of Horticulture, 14–15 Belgrave Square, London SW1X 8PS; 0171 245 6943
'Come into Horticulture' (*address as above, free*)

Market Maker

Jobbers, now known as market makers, conduct their business on the Stock Exchange, the market where industrial and commercial organisations raise finance through the sale of stocks and shares to individuals or institutions willing to invest their capital. Formerly they operated from the floor of the Stock Exchange. Now they work from their own offices, the prices quoted being shown on computer. Market makers aim to make their profits by buying and selling securities to other market makers and stockbrokers, and now some market makers deal direct with the public. It is usual for firms to employ individual market makers with specialist knowledge of all the factors which may influence prices, and who have the ability to judge and predict the performance of companies within that particular field.

Qualifications and Training
Firms of market makers recruit at GCSE, A and degree level and it is usual to start in a clerical position and progress to working alongside a senior member and then alone on the floor of the Exchange. To become a partner in a firm it is necessary to be elected as a member of the Stock Exchange. Candidates for election must be aged at least 21, have three years' experience or more with a member firm, and have passed the Stock Exchange examination. This may only be taken by employees of member firms or firms allied to stock broking. Candidates must have five GCSEs or appropriate professional qualifications such as a national certificate in business studies with four individual credits or a BTEC national award in order to take the exam.

Market maker is a new title and the structure of the career, qualifications and training may change over the next few years.

Personal Qualities
Market makers must have the ability to keep abreast of current affairs and any factors that may affect the price of shares, be able to make decisions very quickly and be willing to take calculated risks. They must have the ability to work hard and to conduct business verbally. A good memory and a flair for dealing with people are helpful.

Starting Salary
Salaries are low initially, but there are eventual opportunities to earn a salary from £60,000 upwards.

Further Information
Stock Exchange Employment and Careers Office, Stock Exchange, London EC2N 1HP; 0171 588 2355

Marketing *see Advertising, Events Officer and Retailing*

Marketing is concerned with undertaking market research, identifying consumer needs and demands relative to product or service, price, place and time, organising their production and promoting them to the appropriate customer segment. It includes new product development, packaging, advertising, pricing, sales, distribution and after-sales service.

Direct Marketing
More and more companies are finding that direct selling – by post or by telephone – is more cost-effective than sending fleets of salespeople out on the road. Direct selling is part of a company's marketing activities, and can provide opportunities for copywriters (eg compiling brochures and catalogues, writing accompanying letters and advertisements etc) and telephone salespeople, who will either follow up by phone the leads produced by the responses to the company's catalogues, brochures and advertisements or call other prospective customers who may or may not have otherwise been approached.

Qualifications and Training
Entry qualifications can vary considerably, depending on the products or services being sold. Good GCSEs would probably be the minimum but employers are more and more demanding an appropriate degree or diploma such as the Chartered Institute of Marketing's internationally recognised graduate diploma in marketing. There is a wide range of marketing courses, or courses including marketing options, available from colleges and universities. Additionally, most companies give some sort of in-house training in product knowledge, selling techniques, customer relations, order processing procedures etc. A wide range of marketing courses, or courses including marketing options, is available from education and training organisations such as the Chartered Institute of Marketing and colleges and universities.

Personal Qualities

All types of skills and abilities can be usefully employed in marketing; however, outgoing personality, good appearance, resilience, tact and a certain toughness are required in all selling jobs.

Starting Salary

Many salespeople have the added financial incentive of commission paid on sales made, and marketing people can command a rewarding remuneration package, but the hours are often long.

Market Research

Market research is essential in the early stages for obtaining data on what customers want, with the object of avoiding losses on unwanted and unpopular products. Market research can be desk or field research. Market researchers carry out sample surveys in which potential customers are personally interviewed, or the necessary information is gained through postal questionnaires, analysis of manufacturers' records and research into statistics. The interviewers are known as field workers, and their work, and that of the analysis personnel, is organised by the research executive, who is in overall charge of the project for a marketing executive or client, and is responsible for interpreting the results.

People usually come into marketing either from being a salesperson or from the market research side, or they may have worked for an advertising agency before joining the marketing team of a manufacturing company.

Qualifications and Training

A degree, preferably in social science (such as economics, mathematics, business studies, statistics, psychology and sociology), or BTEC/SCOTVEC higher national diplomas or equivalent is normally required by companies for training research executives. A science or technological degree or diploma is also of value. Training is usually on the job, or through training courses.

The Market Research Society offers training through lectures, weekend courses and summer and winter schools, and awards its own diploma. Courses in market research are also available through further education centres.

No special qualifications are required by field workers, and companies themselves will give training. Those with several GCSEs, or equivalents, including maths, can apply for training as analysis personnel, who may be trained as punch operators, tabulating machine operators or computer programmers.

Personal Qualities
Field workers must be good at getting on with people of all types. Analysis personnel should be able to work with figures and maintain accuracy. The research executives need to understand figures as well as being capable of setting up a survey to cater for the client's or marketing executive's needs, administering it and reporting on the results.

Starting Salary
£10,000+ for permanent staff, analysis personnel and for trainee executives. Field workers are paid a day rate of £30+ for a six- to seven-hour day; from £3 per hour for market research.

Further Information
Chartered Institute of Marketing, Moor Hall, Cookham, Maidenhead, Berkshire SL6 9QH; 01628 427500
Market Research Society, 15 Northburgh Street, London EC1V 0AH; 0171 490 4911 (*send A4 sae*)
Careers in Marketing, Advertising and Public Relations, Kogan Page
How to Get On in Marketing, Advertising and Public Relations, Kogan Page

Market Research*, see *Advertising, Marketing

Masseur

Massage is a way of kneading and rubbing the body in order to relieve aches, tone muscles and give relaxation. Sportspeople, in particular, find it relaxing and therapeutic. Masseurs work on their own, with a number of other masseurs, or in a centre offering a range of treatments, eg beauty treatment, sauna.

Qualifications and Training
The Northern Institute of Massage offers part-time and open-learning courses leading to the diploma in massage therapy. A diploma in remedial massage is also available, plus higher grade diplomas in advanced remedial massage and manipulative therapy. There are postgraduate courses in: sports therapy, electrotherapy, manual lympatic drainage and remedial exercise.

Personal Qualities
Masseurs must be physically capable, able to get on with people and put them at their ease.

Starting Salary
Varies according to whether self-employed or employee, and number of clients.

Further Information
The Northern Institute of Massage, 100 Waterloo Road, Blackpool FY4 1AW; 01253 403548

Materials Manager*, see *Purchasing Officer

Materials Scientist

Materials science is the study of a wide variety of materials, including plastics, glass, ceramics, natural materials and metals, that are used in modern technology. The scientist or technologist is responsible for selecting materials for a specific job, or for finding uses for materials. There are opportunities in many industries, including the car and electronics industries, and in nuclear power, research, development and production work.

Qualifications and Training
Technicians should have a good education to GCSE level to include studies in maths, a science and English in order to take the technician's certificate in metal finishing. A BTEC certificate and diploma are available in metals technology with the technician's certificate counting towards the units.

Two GCE A level or three SCE H grade passes in maths, physics or chemistry; or BTEC or SCOTVEC awards, or equivalents, are necessary for entry to the universities that offer courses leading to degrees in: metallurgy, science and engineering of metals, and metallurgy and materials science. The necessary practical experience is gained through apprenticeships or trainee posts by both technicians and scientists.

Personal Qualities
An interest in the scientific and technological problems posed, and the ability to find constructive solutions, must be allied to the scientific qualities of orderly and logical thought.

Starting Salary
This varies, depending on the level of employment and its nature, but around £12,000–£13,000.

Further Information

The Institute of Materials, 1 Carlton House Terrace, London SW1Y 5DB; 0171 839 4071

The Institution of Mining and Metallurgy, 44 Portland Place, London W1N 4BR; 0171 580 3802

Meat Industry *see Butcher*

As well as retail and supermarket work as a butcher, or working for large organisations such as hotels, there are other openings in the meat industry. Some wholesale establishments selling prepacked meat need teams of butchers for boning, cutting and packing the meat, or processing it into pies. Wholesale butchers do not meet the general public but deal with other butchers and retailers.

Workers are also needed in abattoirs, to handle and kill the animals, and to inspect and deal with the meat.

Qualifications and Training

A good general education is necessary but there are no formal educational requirements. Training is on the job and courses are available at further education establishments and approved training organisations, leading to NVQs, levels 1 to 4, and examinations of the Meat Training Council, formerly of the Institute of Meat. Some modern apprenticeships are available; details from the Meat Training Council.

Personal Qualities

An above-average attitude to hygiene is vital. In addition, workers in the meat industry must be strong enough to cope with heavy lifting and fit enough to work in cold conditions.

Starting Salary

About £60 a week at 16; £250 when trained.

Further Information

The Meat Training Council, PO Box 141, Winterhill House, Snowdon Drive, Milton Keynes MK6 1YY; 01908 231062

National Federation of Meat & Food Traders, 1 Belgrove, Tunbridge Wells, Kent TN1 1YW; 01892 541412

Scottish Federation of Meat Traders, 8 Needless Road, Perth PH2 0JW; 01738 637472

Mechanical Engineer*, see *Engineering

Medical Illustrator

The work done by the medical illustrator is used both as a record for doctors and other medical staff and to illustrate medical journals and textbooks for teaching purposes. Both photographers and artists are classed as medical illustrators, and they normally work in hospitals, though there is also some freelance work. The field is very small, however, and competition strong.

Qualifications and Training

The basic entry qualification to the degree in medical illustration is an HND or equivalent in photography, art or graphics. Candidates without the HND but with prior experience may be able to have their experience accredited. The BSc in medical illustration is a part-time work-based course offered by Caledonian University, Glasgow.

To become a medical photographer, four GCSEs at grades A to C including English and a science are necessary for entry into the profession as a trainee medical photographer. However, if entrants prefer to obtain qualifications at a college, A levels may be necessary. There are many courses in photography available that lead to a BTEC professional qualification, or a degree in photographic science, photography or media studies (photography).

It is also possible to take a course directly in medical photography which includes on-the-job training in hospitals. This latter course is offered by the School of Medical Photography, Institute of Health Care Studies, Cardiff; Glasgow College of Building and Printing; and Berkshire College of Art and Design.

Personal Qualities

As well as having a natural artistic ability, the medical illustrator must be prepared to draw, or photograph, any part of the body in any condition.

Starting Salary

About £8500.

Further Information

British Institute of Professional Photography, Fox Talbot House, Amwell End, Ware, Hertfordshire SG12 9HN; 01920 464011

Institute of Medical Illustrators, Bank Chambers, 48 Onslow Gardens, London SW7 3AH

Medical Technical Officer (Cardiology) (Cardiac Clinical Scientific Officer)

They set up, operate and are responsible for the application of increasingly specialised equipment used to diagnose, monitor and treat various heart conditions; for example, measuring blood flow in a specific part of the heart or reprogramming a cardiac pacemaker. Their work ranges from out-patient clinics to operating theatres, cardiac catheterisation laboratories and intensive/coronary care units. The more routine procedures are often handled by a cardiographer, who is less qualified.

Qualifications and Training

Four GCSEs or equivalent passes (English language, mathematics, double science) are necessary from candidates just leaving school. Training involves a minimum period of two, but typically four, years taking block or day release leading towards BTEC national and higher national certificate qualification in medical physics and physiological measurement. Alternatively an increasing number of trainees are registering for a four year part-time BSc (Hons) clinical science (cardiology) degree or 'topping-up' BTEC qualifications with degree courses post HNC. A number of trainees are recruited alreading holding relevant BTEC qualifications or university degrees.

Personal Qualities

Candidates need technical skills and interest as well as a high sense of responsibility and an ability to communicate sympathetically with the patients.

Starting Salary

Trainee: £6693–£8179; once qualified: depending on grade £9064–£25,908

Further Information

Public Relations Officer, Society for Cardiological Science and Technology, c/o British Cardiac Society, 9 Fitzroy Square, London W1P 5AH

Medicine

A newly qualified doctor must work for a year in a hospital as a pre-registration house officer and will then either remain in hospital practice, work as a general practitioner, or in one of the other fields open to him/her. Some doctors specialise within the hospital service in subjects such as geriatrics, mental illness and handicap, radiology, anaesthetics or general surgery.

General Practitioner (GP)

Family doctors may form a longstanding relationship with their patients. They must be able to diagnose and deal with a broad spectrum of illnesses and disorders, mainly those common within the community, but also be able to recognise those that are rare. Increasingly doctors are asked to help their patients to cope with personal and emotional problems. About 90 per cent of GPs now work together in group practices, giving both better working conditions and allowing some specialisation.

Public Health and Community Health

Public health doctors are mainly concerned with preventive medicine and environmental health. They may have overall management over paramedical services, eg health promotion. Community health doctors deal with child health, family planning, social services, special hostels and day centres and other roles as advisers to the authority. The career structure is similar to that within a hospital.

Hospital

A hospital doctor begins as a senior house officer (about three to four years), registrar (about three years), senior registrar (three or more years) and finally (usually) to consultant in a particular specialty. The choice of specialty must be made early; the main groups are surgical specialties, medical specialties (ie patients who do not need operations), pathology (concerned with disease and its effect on the body) and psychiatry. Other large specialties are obstetrics and gynaecology; anaesthetics and radiology.

Research and Teaching

Research work is carried on in universities, hospitals, public health laboratories, and other research establishments and pharmaceutical manufacturing companies. There are opportunities too for teaching in universities. Teaching may involve very little or no contact with patients, or it may be similar in content to hospital doctors' work.

Occupational

This aspect of medicine is one in which part-time work is possible. Medical check-ups are given to people at their place of work. In addition, doctors may also research the effects of occupational and environmental conditions on the health of staff.

Qualifications and Training

A minimum age of 18 and good A level/H grade passes in chemistry and two other subjects, from biology, physics or maths, or suitable alternatives, are necessary for entry to medical school. Competition is keen. Most universities prefer school-leavers, but older people (up to 20, or 30 in some cases) can also apply, though relevant experience or a first degree in a related subject may also be required. Undergraduate training lasts for five years.

Students who do not have the necessary science subjects may, in certain circumstances, be able to study during a preliminary year for the first professional examination, and then continue with the five-year course.

Students who have already completed part of their training at medical school and wish to serve with HM forces may apply for medical cadetships with the Ministry of Defence.

After obtaining medical qualifications, some graduates may go on to take a specialist diploma in subjects such as genetics, endocrinology and haematology.

Personal Qualities

Those who want to become members of the medical profession must have a caring and responsible attitude to other people, as well as ability in scientific subjects.

Starting Salary

Salary scales are: senior house officer earns £24,114, a registrar £25,772, a senior registrar from £30,971, a consultant from £55,709 and GPs receive a basic salary of about £45,822 plus certain allowances.

Further Information

British Medical Association, BMA House, Tavistock Square, London WC1H 9JP

Careers in Medicine, Dentistry and Mental Health, Kogan Page

Learning Medicine 1997, Peter Richards BMA

Member of Parliament*, see *Politics

Merchant Navy

The Merchant Navy carries passengers and cargoes of all kinds and is made up of a large number of independent organisations. Some operate exclusively in UK coastal waters, others around Europe and the Baltic ports, while the deep-sea trade sends ships round the world, including the Far East and South America. Crews on these ships can be away from home for several months at a time, with long periods of leave. Most shipping organisations belong to the The Chamber of Shipping which has set up the National Sea Training College at Gravesend where school-leavers are trained as deck, engineering or catering ratings. Only a small number of shippers offer their own training. There are limited opportunities for entry at present as the size of the merchant fleet has been reduced.

Although the three main areas of deck, engine room and catering are still important, there is now, as regards ratings, a move towards less specialisation. Currently (1995) the Merchant Navy is looking for deck and engineering officer cadets only. Ratings are not being recruited.

Deck

Ratings work on the securing of cargo, making the ship ready for sea, handling the mooring ropes and anchors and doing maintenance jobs when the ship is at sea, all under the supervision of the deck officers. In addition to these tasks, deck officers are also responsible for navigation and watch-keeping. Ratings may train to become officers.

Engine Room

Ratings may share the work of cleaning, maintenance and lubrication with deck ratings; the bulk of the work in the engine rooms of modern ships is done by officers, who are responsible not only for the ship's engines, but also for the electrical system, air-conditioning, refrigeration and safety systems.

Purser

Pursers look after the comfort of passengers on passenger liners. They arrange entertainments for them and provide banking services. In addition they deal with accounts and clerical work and handle customs and immigration.

Radio and Electronics Officers

Some ships carry a radio officer, responsible for the radio communication equipment and often other electronic equipment, including radar, navigational aids and closed circuit television. Competition for jobs is strong, even among qualified radio officers.

Catering

The two sides to catering are cooking and stewarding, with promotion possible in both, and the opportunity to switch from one to the other.

Qualifications and Training

No formal qualifications are required for deck, engineering or catering ratings at the National Sea Training College at Gravesend but education to GCSE standard with particular reference to maths and English is expected; candidates should be aged 16 to 18, boys or girls, who must be sponsored by a shipping company. Courses are 13 weeks for deck ratings, 11 weeks for catering ratings. On completion, the trainees will have been assessed for City and Guilds certificate Part I. Part II may be taken after service at sea.

Candidates with four GCSEs to include maths, science (preferably physics) and an English subject can apply for a sponsored training scheme for deck officers combining training at the National Sea Training College at Gravesend (where the course starts) and at sea, leading to master mariner certificates. The same requirements apply for trainee engineering officers but they spend one year less at sea than the trainee deck officers.

Those holding A level, H grade or equivalent qualifications including maths or a suitable science subject with a strong element of physics can enter accelerated training schemes which can be completed within three years.

For those interested in a career in the European Trading Area, three GCSEs or equivalent in maths, a science and preferably a language are necessary.

For radio/electronics officers GCSEs or equivalents in maths, physics and English allow entry to colleges offering courses leading to the maritime radio communication general certificate and the Department of Trade radar maintenance certificate for radio/electronics officers.

Gradually NVQs will be introduced ranging from level 1 for a junior rating to level 5 for the most senior officer.

There are cadetship schemes available for deck and engineer entrants. These combine periods at sea with courses of training in a nautical college.

Personal Qualities

Physical fitness is very important, and candidates who have to wear glasses or contact lenses are not acceptable as deck officers or ratings. Colour blindness is also unacceptable for engineer officers and ratings, and radio officers. A ship carries an enclosed, isolated community, and so the ability to get on well with other people and the ability to adapt to new conditions are also important.

Starting Salary

Salary details may be obtained from the Chamber of Shipping. They are commensurate with those paid for 'similar' work in other fields.

Further Information

The Marine Society, 202 Lambeth Road, London SE1 7JW; 0171 261 9535 (*information on careers at sea and on grants and loans*)
The Chamber of Shipping, Carthusian Court, 12 Carthusian Street, London EC1M 6EB; 0171 417 8400
National Sea Training Centre, North West Kent College, Dering Way, Gravesend, Kent DA12 2JJ

Metallurgist

Metallurgists are involved with the extraction of metals from ores, and their purification, and often nowadays with reclaiming them from scrap. They are also concerned with the development of new alloys and with the processing of metals during manufacture.

Qualifications and Training

GCSE passes in a science subject, maths and English, or an English subject, or SCE Standard grade passes in chemistry, physics or maths are required for entry to BTEC and SCOTVEC two-year courses for a certificate or diploma in metallurgical studies.

Candidates who have successfully completed the two-year course and those with GCE A level or SCE H grade passes in maths, physics or chemistry may study for the BTEC/SCOTVEC higher certificates and diplomas.

Two or three (preferably) GCE A level or three SCE H grade passes in maths, physics or chemistry qualify for entry to full-time, sandwich or part-time courses leading to degrees in metallurgy. Those with BTEC/SCOTVEC higher awards may also gain admission to degree courses.

Graduates with two years' supervised training and two years' professional experience can apply for corporate membership of the Institute of Materials. BTEC or SCOTVEC awards plus at least three years' training and practical experience qualify for associate membership of the Institute of Materials.

Personal Qualities

Metallurgy demands an interest in scientific and technological subjects, and an ability to solve practical problems and work with other people on specific projects.

Starting Salary

Salaries vary, but are about £9000–£13,000+ with a degree.

Further Information

The Institute of Materials, 1 Carlton House Terrace, London SW1Y 5DB; 0171 839 4071

The Institution of Mining and Metallurgy, 44 Portland Place, London W1N 4BR; 0171 580 3802

Meteorologist

The Meteorological Office (Met) is an executive agency within the Ministry of Defence. It is a centre of excellence for the production of numerical weather forecasts, climate prediction and related studies. It serves the different and varying needs of defence, other areas of government, civil aviation, industry, commerce and the general public.

Qualifications and Training

From time to time there are vacancies in administration for which a minimum of five GCSEs to include English language are required. Most vacancies arise in the forecasting, research and IT areas for which a first or upper second degree is necessary in maths, one of the physical disciplines, computer science or meterology.

Personal Qualities

Candidates need to be adaptable and prepared to work in more than one specialist area. Good communication and computing skills are necessary.

Starting Salary

Graduates' salaries range from £14,834–£15,950.

Further Information

Local Jobcentres and Careers Offices

Meteorological Office College, Shinfield Park, Reading, Berkshire RG2 9AU; 01344 855205

Microbiologist *see Bacteriologist*

Microbiology, which includes the sciences of bacteriology, mycology and virology, is the study of microscopic living organisms which not only cause diseases in humans, animals and plant life, but also have beneficial uses. Microbiology has a place in medicine, agriculture and industrial biotechnology – in fermentation technology, treatment of industrial products and wastes, and the food and pharmaceutical industries. Microbiologists are also employed by government scientific establishments. New opportunities are opening up for microbiologists in molecular biology and recombinant DNA technology.

Qualifications and Training

Five GCSE level/Standard grade passes at grades A–C plus two or three (preferably) A levels or three H grade passes in suitable subjects, such as biology, chemistry and maths or another science, are required for entry to universities and colleges of higher education offering full-time first degree courses in biological subjects. Some universities run courses in special subjects, such as bacteriology, immunology and parasitology. It is also possible to obtain technical qualifications by part-time study whilst working in a laboratory.

Personal Qualities

Scientific subjects require a high degree of accuracy and patience and a methodical way of working, as well as initiative in those engaged in research work.

Starting Salary

£12,000–£14,000+.

Further Information

Society for General Microbiology, Marlborough House, Basingstoke Road, Spencers Wood, Reading, Berkshire RG7 1AE

'Careers in Microbiology' (*free from above*)

Midwifery *see Nurse*

Midwives (female or male) deliver babies at home and in hospitals and maternity homes and give care and advice to mothers before and after the birth. The midwife takes responsibility for all normal births and for 28 days afterwards.

Qualifications and Training

A three-year programme of midwifery education is available at various centres. Candidates need to have five GCSEs (grade A–C), including English and a science, and be at least 17½ years old (17 in Scotland). Otherwise, training is available only to registered general nurses. This course lasts 18 months and leads to the qualification of registered midwife (RM).

Personal Qualities

An understanding of people, kindness, practical ability, common sense and an ability to get on well and cheerfully with people of all kinds are essential.

Starting Salary

Staff midwife starts at £13,877–£16,075, midwifery sisters and community midwives earn from £18,156–£21,007.

Further Information

English National Board for Nursing, Midwifery and Health Visiting, Careers Service, 170 Tottenham Court Road, London W1P 0HA; 0171 388 3131

The Chief Nursing Officer, The Welsh National Board for Nursing, Midwifery and Health Visiting, Floor 13, Pearl Assurance House, Greyfriars Road, Cardiff CF1 3AG; 01222 395535

Nursing Careers Information Service, National Board for Nursing, Midwifery and Health Visiting for Scotland, 22 Queen Street, Edinburgh EH2 1JX

The Recruitment Officer, National Board for Nursing, Midwifery and Health Visiting for Northern Ireland, RAC House, 79 Chichester Street, Belfast BT1 4JE

Careers in Nursing and Related Professions, Kogan Page

Milkman

A milkman delivers milk and other products such as fruit juice, eggs and bread to his customers. He must keep an account for each customer and take payment for goods delivered once a week. The work involves beginning early in the morning but, with experience, a milkman may finish his work just after lunch.

Qualifications and Training

Formal academic qualifications are not necessary but applicants are tested as to numeracy. Applicants must be able, or learn, to drive. Training is on the job. NVQs are now available in dairy retailing.

Personal Qualities

Milkmen must be physically strong, prepared to be out of doors and ready to drive in all weather conditions, honest, friendly and reliable.

Starting Salary

About £145 a week. London weighting is £22.55 a week.

Further Information

National Dairy Council, 5–7 John Prince's Street, London W1M 0AP; 0171 499 7822

National Dairymen's Association, 19 Cornwall Terrace, London NW1 4QP; 0171 935 4562

Milliner

Expensive 'model' hats are designed by a milliner and made up by the workers in a small retail workroom or factory attached to a boutique or fashion house. Hats for the wholesale trade are mass produced by machine, though some may be hand finished. The designs used are bought from model milliners and passed on to copyists, who work out how the hat can be adapted to machine production.

Qualifications and Training

Training may be obtained as a junior in a retail workroom or factory, supplemented, if possible, by evening classes. Academic qualifications are not necessary, except for those who wish to design millinery, when a full fashion training is required. Full-time courses are also available that include instruction in hat making, among other topics.

Personal Qualities

Those making hats in a retail millinery workroom need manual skill and patience – a hat may take up to three days to complete. The production side of wholesale hat making requires an understanding of technology in the senior posts. Designers and copyists should have fashion sense and artistic creativity.

Starting Salary

Rates of pay are generally low.

Further Information

CAPITB Trust, 80 Richardshaw Lane, Pudsey, Leeds LS28 6BN; 0113 239 3355

Minicab Driver

Minicabs are private hire vehicles, which means that instead of being able to ply for hire in the streets, the drivers can operate only if they have first been contacted by the customer, by telephone. Owner-drivers of private hire vehicles often obtain their business through a taxi firm, which passes on enquiries from customers, and charges the owner-driver for the service. Drivers often stay on the taxi firm's premises waiting for calls, or receive them on their radio. Their outgoings include the taxi firm's charge plus bills for servicing and repairs to the vehicle.

Qualifications and Training

Not all areas require hire vehicles or their drivers to be licensed. In areas where a licence is necessary, the vehicle has to undergo testing and the driver must be over 21, with at least a year's driving experience and a group A licence. (Normally people under 25 do not apply, because of the high cost of insurance for the under-25 age group.) A character reference and medical test are also necessary.

Personal Qualities

Minicab drivers must be able to cope with long and unsocial hours, and get on with a wide range of passengers, dealing with difficult ones as necessary.

Starting Salary

Dependent on the number of hours worked, rates paid and passengers carried.

Further Information

Local minicab firms and local newspapers.

Mining Engineer*, see *Engineering

Model

Models work as 'live' or photographic models, generally showing clothes or accessories. Photographic and advertising models rely on an agent to get them work and handle the fees.

Fashion

Models employed full time by couturiers, wholesalers or fashion stores are 'live' models. They have the garments draped and pinned on them during the design stages, and show the garments to the public. Live models must be particularly tall, about 5ft 10in (178 cm).

Photographic modelling involves posing in garments chosen to be illustrated in magazines, newspapers, catalogues or on advertising posters. This work is often out of season for the type of garments being modelled – furs in August, for example. However, there can also be trips abroad. Expenses include the provision of accessories, a good basic wardrobe and hairdressing.

Qualifications and Training

Private model schools run training courses for live and photographic modelling. Reputable schools will only take entrants whom they think will succeed, and will introduce them to agencies at the end of the training period (four to six weeks).

Those who have received education to GCSE level, and preferably have three passes, are at least 16, and are not less than 5ft 8in (173 cm) (female) or 6ft (180 cm) (male), may apply for the one-year full-time course at the London College of Fashion.

Personal Qualities

A model must be able to work hard, be punctual, get on well with people, and have a good fashion sense. Competition is intense, and only the more intelligent, who can interpret what the stylist and photographer want, will get to the top. A female model should be at least 5ft 8in tall and more or less 34–24–34. A male model should be at least 6ft tall, chest 38/40, waist 30/32, inside leg 33 in. They should have clear skin, good hands, nails and teeth, healthy hair and attractive features.

Starting Salary

Starting salaries are low; with experience, in the region of £25,000 a year, and the sky's the limit for top models. The highest salaries are often earned abroad.

Further Information

Association of Model Agents, The Clockhouse, St Catherine's Mews, Milner Street, London SW3 2PQ; 0891 517644

London College of Fashion, 20 John Prince's Street, London W1M 0BJ; 0171 629 9401

Careers in Fashion, Kogan Page

Modelmaker

Models can be made to represent almost anything: towns, office blocks, oil terminals, shopping centres, motorways, houses, cars and planes. Models are often scaled down versions of the real thing, but sometimes they can be enlargements. They are used to show what the real thing will look like and, if they are working models, may be used as testers. Models are often used too in television and films. Modelmakers work for firms specialising in such work, or sometimes branch out on their own.

Qualifications and Training

Formal academic qualifications are not necessary. Modelmakers may teach themselves or learn at evening class; some large firms offer apprenticeships. BTEC courses are available on modelmaking at Kingsway College, Hertfordshire College of Art and Design, University of Sunderland, Rycote Wood College, Barking College of Technology, Kent Institute of Art and Design, and South Devon College of Arts and Technology.

Personal Qualities

Patience, manual dexterity, a good sense of design, shape and colour are necessary. Modelmakers must be prepared to do one job for a considerable length of time: a project such as a model town could take up to a year to complete.

Starting Salary

Low when training, and with experience £170+ a week; good modelmakers may earn much more.

Further Information

Local Jobcentres and Careers Offices

Motor Body Repairer *see Vehicle Technician*

The motor body repairer works in a highly mechanised industry where most of the body parts are pressings, forgings or castings. Body building and repairing are allied to the other specialist skills of painting and industrial finishing, and trimming. Often a motor mechanic will specialise in several areas of work.

Qualifications and Training

No formal educational qualifications are necessary, but GCSEs or equivalent in maths, English and a science are advantageous. Mechanics and body repairers usually take part in a training scheme whereby different skills are learnt and tested. When an employer deems that a sufficient standard has been reached, trainees may apply for the national craft certificate awarded by the Road Transport Industry Training Board. An NVQ is available in vehicle body repair, level 3.

Personal Qualities
A good standard of physical fitness, a sense of responsibility (since the safety of drivers and passengers is involved) and an aptitude for dealing with machinery and tools are required.

Starting Salary
£70+ per week to start with, £160+ with experience.

Further Information
Local Jobcentres and Careers Offices

Moulder

Moulders or coremakers work in the foundry industry making the mould or core later to be used to make a variety of other objects. If there is any damage to the mould, the moulder will be required to repair it using various handtools. This is a highly skilled job offering variety – no two moulds or cores are exactly the same.

Qualifications and Training
Formal academic qualifications are not required. Training lasts for three and a half years during which, depending on the employer, time will be spent at a training centre and day or block release allowed for study leading to a City and Guilds or regional examining body qualification.

Personal Qualities
Care, patience, manual dexterity and some initiative are all required. An understanding of the casting process and the properties of sands and metals is also useful.

Starting Salary
£70+ per week to start with, £180+ when trained.

Further Information
Local Jobcentres and Careers Offices

Museum and Art Gallery Work

Art galleries and museums of various kinds (general, archaeology, social history, natural history, transport, science, local history) are administered by the government, local authorities, universities, private organisations or individuals. The director (or keeper, or curator) is responsible for running the museum. In large museums there are many staff with a curator at the head of each department. Curators are involved in all aspects of running the museum or department: display, cataloguing, advising on new acquisitions, and even lecturing. In addition they must involve themselves in education work and marketing.

Qualifications and Training

No special qualifications are required for attendants and wardens. There are different levels of entry for curators or conservation officers: four GCSEs including English, or, in Scotland, three Standard grade passes or equivalent including English. Relevant work experience is helpful. Curators may also join after obtaining a degree, and for those applying for higher grades, a degree plus relevant postgraduate experience are necessary.

Training courses at different levels, including postgraduate, are available as in-service training schemes for museum and art gallery work. Postgraduate courses are also available at some universities and colleges. A postgraduate qualification improves a person's chances of finding museum work.

Personal Qualities

Staff must have an interest in the objects under their care and they should have the ability to make the information they offer interesting and clearly understood.

Starting Salary

Graduates without experience £5000–£8000, graduates with some voluntary experience and a postgraduate qualification £8000–£10,500, with one to two years' experience £10,500–£15,000.

Further Information

The Museums Association, 42 Clerkenwell Close, London ECIR 0PA; 0171 608 2933

Museum Training Institute, Glyde House, Glydegate, Bradford BD5 0UP; 01274 391056/391087/391092

'Careers in Museums', The Museum Training Institute (*available free on request*)

Musical Instrument Technologist *see Piano Tuner*

The instrument technologist is concerned with making and repairing instruments of all kinds, from pianos to guitars. Good training and practical skill are essential, and ensure plenty of work for the technologist.

Qualifications and Training
Manufacturers of musical instruments will train technologists through apprenticeship schemes.

Three GCSEs or equivalent are required for entry to the three-year full-time course at the London Guildhall University, leading to a college certificate. There is a BTEC national diploma in musical instrument technology, entry requirements being GCSEs in maths, physics and English. Holders of the diploma or those with five GCSEs plus one A level may take the BTEC HND in musical instrument technology. Practical ability is required for candidates for full-time courses in instrument manufacture, repair and maintenance offered by Newark and Sherwood Technical College, leading to City and Guilds or college certificates. There are also courses at: the London Guildhall University; Merton Technical College, Morden; Stevenson College of Further Education, Edinburgh; City of Leeds College of Music; and Anniesland College, Glasgow.

Personal Qualities
Practical skills are necessary for this work, but special ability in music is not important.

Starting Salary
Salaries vary, £170+ a week when trained, but are low without experience.

Further Information
Crafts Council, 44a Pentonville Road, London N1 9BY; 0171 278 7700
Institute of Musical Instrument Technology, 8 Chester Court, Albany Street, London NW1 4BU

Musician

Although many qualified musicians become performers, there are also many other areas open to them in teaching, administration, broadcasting, recording, journalism, publishing, promotion, library work and the retail trade.

Composer

Although there are a few thousand composers, very few earn even a substantial part of their income from composition. The most lucrative area is writing for TV programmes, films and videos, although competition for this work, even among established composers, is very tough. Professional advice on copyright (from a solicitor or professional association) is essential.

Performer

Most professional musicians work on a freelance basis, even if they play instruments with large orchestras. Work is not plentiful, and classical musicians may also play at recording sessions for lighter music for commercial television or radio jingles. Professional musicians also play in chamber music ensembles, sometimes in rock, dance and jazz groups. Most performers also teach privately.

Hours can be long and unsocial, with long periods of practice in addition. Some musicians arrange their own engagements, others have agents. For all performers, membership of a professional association or union is desirable.

There are opportunities, particularly for those who already play an instrument, to join the Army, the RAF or Royal Marines as bandsmen.

Teacher

There is a demand for music teachers, both within mainstream education and privately.

Music is one of the foundation subjects in the National Curriculum. Class teachers (and some visiting instrumental teachers) in maintained schools need qualified teacher status.

Private teachers have to set up their own business. They need to develop business skills as well as having musical and teaching ability.

Qualifications and Training

Qualifications for entry vary but five GCSEs are usually required, with one or more A levels being necessary for some courses provided by music colleges, universities and colleges of higher education. These provide full-time training courses of three to four years with possible further study for professional musicians. The age limits for candidates are 16 to 25. Singers take longer for their voices to develop and therefore longer to train. Most music colleges offer appropriate postgraduate courses.

To teach music in a maintained school, a teaching qualification is also necessary.

Personal Qualities

As music standards are high and there is keen competition, only very talented musicians can make a career as a performer, and very few of these get to the top. Physical and mental stamina is needed to cope with the irregular lifestyle and setbacks. An ability to get on well with other people helps to ensure bookings. Good hearing is essential, and singers are helped by attractive looks and personality.

Music teachers must have a genuine interest in their pupils' development, and the ability to make music stimulating and exciting.

Starting Salary

Salaries depend on the type and amount of work. Music teachers in maintained schools earn from £12,711 without a degree and from £13,473 with a degree.

Further Information

Incorporated Society of Musicians, 10 Stratford Place, London W1N 9AE; 0171 629 4413

Musicians' Union, 60–62 Clapham Road, London SW9 0JJ; 0171 582 5566

Careers in Music (Trotman)

'Careers with Music' (Incorporated Society of Musicians)

The Rock File, Oxford University Press

Music Therapist

Music can be of great help to physically and mentally disabled and maladjusted people, who can benefit from listening to music, and from making it. Both music teachers and performers, who are interested in helping these people, may work in this field.

Qualifications and Training

Those who have completed a three-year course in music, or are experienced professional musicians, may take a one-year full-time course in music therapy. There is also a part-time training course available.

Personal Qualities

Working with handicapped people requires patience and sympathy, and a genuine desire to help them. Music therapists also need good keyboard and improvisatory skills.

Starting Salary

Salaries are in the region of £12,000–£13,000.

Further Information

British Society for Music Therapy, 25 Rosslyn Avenue, East Barnet, Hertfordshire EN4 8DH; 0181 368 8879

Incorporated Society of Musicians, 10 Stratford Place, London W1N 9AE; 0171 629 4413

N

Nanny *see Nursery Nurse*

A nanny's job today is generally much less formal than it used to be. Instead of being confined to nursery quarters, a nanny now often lives as part of the family; and she rarely has to wear neatly starched uniforms. A nanny is often employed by a working mother who is out for most of the day and so she is in sole charge of feeding, changing and generally supervising the children. Frequently she has to accompany the elder children to school or playgroup or on social outings. As a rule domestic work is not a nanny's responsibility, although sometimes she is asked to keep the children's rooms tidy and care for their clothes as well as preparing simple meals.

Some posts are residential – in which case a nanny may be 'on call' for late or night feeds but employers are expected to provide adequate private accommodation and a reasonable number of free evenings. Other nannies are employed on a daily basis, working set hours and returning to their own homes at night. A nanny may often remain in one family for a number of years while the children grow up; others are taken on as a temporary measure – to take charge during a mother's illness or for the birth of a new baby, for instance.

Qualifications and Training

A nanny is generally expected to hold the Diploma in Nursery Nursing of the NNEB (the National Nursery Examination Board award) or be registered with the Scottish Nursery Nurses Board, the Scottish equivalent. There are no minimum academic standards laid down for entry to this course which can be followed at most colleges of further education. A good standard of English is usually required, however, and candidates who have no formal GCSE qualifications may have to take a written test before admission. This course aims to equip students to work with children from birth to the age of seven and much emphasis is laid on practical experience and observation. It can be followed full time or on a day-release basis. In addition there are a number of private, fee-paying colleges which specialise in preparing students for private employment. These have their own individual entrance requirements.

Personal Qualities
A nanny, naturally, has to love children and be able to gain their confidence and encourage their development. Competence in all the basic tasks of looking after children is crucial and employers generally ask for references to prove reliability. Tact and consideration are important too, since a nanny has to live in intimate contact with the whole family. Patience, common sense and a sense of humour are invaluable when dealing with children. Knowing how to drive is frequently an advantage.

Starting Salary
Salaries vary according to the type of post involved. A live-in nanny receives board and lodging as well as a salary. Daily nannies earn from £75 to £250 a week and live-in nannies from £60 to £230; larger sums are paid for work in London and abroad.

Further Information
Local Jobcentres and Careers Offices
CACHE, 8 Chequer Street, St Albans, Hertfordshire AL1 3XZ; 01727 47636 (*enclose sae*)
Careers Working with Children and Young People, Kogan Page

Naturopath

Naturopathy does not form part of the National Health Service and so naturopaths work in private practice. Naturopaths believe in treating the whole patient, and in encouraging the body to cure itself. They do not believe in giving drugs which, they feel, treat local infections or one set of symptoms without dealing with the actual cause of a problem. A naturopath uses treatments designed to correct total body chemistry; diet is seen as a major factor and patients are encouraged to eat more natural and unspoilt food. Fasting, or partial fasting, may sometimes be recommended to eliminate toxic substances. Hydrotherapy is used to stimulate the blood to a specific area of the body or to draw it away from another (by applying cold packs to combat throbbing headaches, for example).

Naturopaths also need to be skilled in psychology since they recognise that physiological complaints may frequently be caused by psychological problems. Such medicaments as they use are virtually confined to those used by herbalists, and naturopaths frequently study herbalism itself. Naturopathy is also closely linked to osteopathy and many naturopaths are qualified osteopaths and use these skills in treating their patients.

Qualifications and Training

Entry requirements are *one* of the following: a minimum of two A levels in biology and chemistry; a science access or foundation course; mature students with other qualifications; equivalent qualifications from European and overseas applicants. Training, which is full time and lasts four years, is provided by the British College of Naturopathy and Osteopathy. This course leads to a BSc (Hons) Osteopathic Medicine validated by the University of Westminster.

Personal Qualities

Professional skills must be combined with a sympathetic and caring manner.

Starting Salary

Salaries vary depending on hours worked, number of patients and fee scales.

Further Information

The British College of Naturopathy and Osteopathy, Frazer House, 6 Netherhall Gardens, London NW3 5RR; 0171 435 6464

Naval Architect

Naval architects are engineers who play a key role as project leaders and specialists in the design, building and marketing of all systems which have to move just above, on or under the sea including merchant ships, warships, offshore structures, submarines, hovercraft, yachts and other small craft. They work for ship and repair yards, offshore rig fabricators and operators, government departments, classification societies, consultants, equipment manufacturers, small craft and yacht builders, research organisations, educational establishments and shipping companies.

Qualifications and Training

Fully qualified and informed naval architects may become members of the Royal Institution of Naval Architects if they meet the education, training and experience requirements. They need to have had an aggregate of seven years' engineering education, training and responsible experience, and have passed an exam of the standard of an accredited honours degree in engineering.

Personal Qualities
Any young man or woman who has a keen interest in engineering and the sea and who wants to play an important part in society will find a career as a naval architect challenging and satisfying.

A naval architect needs precision and attention to detail as well as an interest in and a sound knowledge of the sea. An ability to work as part of a team is essential.

Starting Salary
£20,000 per year with five years of responsible experience after qualifying.

Further Information
The Royal Institution of Naval Architects, 10 Upper Belgrave Street, London SW1X 8BQ; 0171 235 4622

Neurophysiology Technologist

A more familiar name for the neurophysiology technologist is the EEG (electro-encephalography) technologist, who is responsible for setting up and operating electronic equipment which records electrical activity in the brain and nervous system. These tests often include visual or auditory or other types of evoked potentials (EPs) which are the response of the brain to specific stimuli. The EEG and EP tests are performed to help in the diagnosis of patients with, for example, epilepsy, cerebral tumours, strokes, dementias, multiple sclerosis etc. In many departments the technologist is also required to assist the clinician with electromyography (EMG) and nerve conduction studies (NCS). These tests look at the way in which nerves and muscles in the body are working, and help in the diagnosis of diseases such as dystrophies, nerve dysfunction etc. All these procedures are carried out either in the department or in the wards, intensive care units or operating theatres. Both out-patients and in-patients come to the department and the tests are performed on all ages (babies, children, adults). Heart rate and respiration may also be recorded. The neurophysiology technologist works as part of the hospital team in the surgical, neurological or psychiatric department.

Qualifications and Training
Five GCSEs, grade C or above, are normally required, including maths, English and combined science. There are two main ways of entering the profession: (a) as a student technologist employed by a hospital in an EEG clinical neurophysiology department; (b) as a

student supernumerary technologist employed by a regional health authority. Training takes place mostly on the job with day release facilities to study for a BTEC qualification/NVQ award, level 3.

Personal Qualities
A medical technologist needs to be willing to take responsibility, able to keep calm under pressure and must be meticulous in his/her work. In addition a pleasant manner to put patients at their ease is essential.

Starting Salary
Trainee £6693–£8719, once qualified: £9064–£25,908.

Further Information
Electrophysiological Technologists' Association, EEG Department, St Bartholomew's Hospital, West Smithfield, London EC1A 7BE (*please enclose sae*)

Notary Public

A notary public is an international officer of the law whose duty is to prepare and authenticate legal documents intended to take effect abroad. There are two classes of notaries: 1. general notaries who are allowed to practise throughout England and Wales apart from the area reserved exclusively to scrivener notaries; 2. scrivener notaries who have an exclusive right to practise in the City of London, the City of Westminster, the Borough of Southwark and within a radius of three miles of the boundary of the City of London. Scrivener notaries may also practise throughout England and Wales.

Qualifications and Training
Most general notaries are also solicitors and, if they are not solicitors, they must have a legal background. They have to take an examination set by the Faculty Office of the Archbishop of Canterbury.

Scrivener notaries have to serve a five-year apprenticeship with a practising scrivener notary and take two sets of examinations. There are only 20 or so of these notaries and there are few openings.

Personal Qualities
In addition to having a basic legal knowledge, a notary must be a person of discretion and integrity.

Starting Salary

A general notary will only receive the remuneration he earns as a notary. This will, of course, be in addition to his income arising from his position as a solicitor. A scrivener notary upon admission may expect to earn about £24,000 per annum.

Further Information

The Notaries' Society, 7 Lower Brook Street, Ipswich, Suffolk IP4 1AT; 01473 214762

The Society of Public Notaries of London, 10 Philpot Lane, London EC3M 8AA; 0171 623 9477

Nurse

Nurses are employed in a wide variety of situations in hospitals, institutions (such as prisons), the armed forces and in private organisations. Once qualified, a nurse may choose to specialise in a number of different fields – adult nursing, maternity, geriatrics, children's nursing, orthopaedic, surgical, psychiatric, mentally handicapped, ophthalmic and so on. Nurses may work in National Health or private hospitals or in the community (as midwives, district nurses, health visitors or health centre nurses). There are increasing opportunities to work for a practice of doctors as a nurse practitioner. Here the nurse sees patients with minor ailments, and is often responsible for giving inoculations. In addition nurses are in demand for posts abroad, in private houses and within education and commerce. Many organisations employ occupational health nurses whose primary task is to promote health and prevent mental or physical illness by screening, health education and counselling.

A nurse's work is almost always physically and emotionally demanding.

Qualifications and Training

A new system of nurse education called Project 2000 (P2000) has been introduced. Courses are offered at degree and diploma level. Entry to degree courses is through the university entrance system. For the diploma, entry is directly to the Colleges of Nursing and Midwifery in Northern Ireland and Wales and through central clearing houses in England and Scotland. A minimum of five GCSEs or equivalent are required but candidates without such qualifications may sit an education test known as the DC test. The minimum age of entry to programmes is 17½ years (17 in Scotland).

The diploma course lasts three years. Courses are offered in colleges of nursing and midwifery which may be linked with a university or college of higher education. Eighteen months is spent on the Common Foundation Programme gaining a general introduction to nursing and then eighteen months in one of four branches, chosen before the course begins: adult nursing, mental health nursing, nursing people with a mental handicap or children's nursing. The focus of the course will be equally split between theory and practice. Students will spend time in the hospital and the community gaining experience. They will have full student status. This means they will not be employed as part of the workforce and not included on duty rotas until the later part of training.

Once registered, nurses practise in a wide variety of settings. Some take further courses to gain specialist knowledge in meeting the needs of patients in differing clinical specialties. Others may choose nurse teaching or management within the health services. Whatever the area chosen, the initial nursing qualification will be the first step in a lifetime of professional education.

Personal Qualities

Nursing is always about people: patients, their families, their friends and the team of colleagues working to deliver nursing care. So the ability to get on with others and good communication skills are essential. As nursing is physically demanding, candidates will need to be fit. Nurses must be committed to developing their knowledge and skills throughout their careers, enhancing their ability to care.

Starting Salary

Nurses under 26 on the Project 2000 scheme receive £4450, £5010 if over 26. London weighting is £780. (Additional allowances may be available for dependants.) Traditional course nurses start at £7635 (more in London). The minimum salary scale for a registered nurse is £12,133–£13,877.

Further Information

English National Board for Nursing, Midwifery and Health Visiting, Careers Service, Victory House, 170 Tottenham Court Road, London W1P 0HA; 0171 388 3131

The Chief Nursing Officer, The Welsh National Board for Nursing, Midwifery and Health Visiting, Floor 13, Pearl Assurance House, Greyfriars Road, Cardiff CF1 3AG

Nursing Careers Information Service, National Board for Nursing, Midwifery and Health Visiting for Scotland, 22 Queen Street, Edinburgh EH2 1JX

The Recruitment Officer, National Board for Nursing, Midwifery and Health Visiting for Northern Ireland, RAC House, 79 Chichester Street, Belfast BT1 4JE

Health Service Careers, PO Box 204, London SE5 7ES
The nursing officer of local regional health authorities (area health boards in Scotland)
Careers in Nursing and Related Professions, Kogan Page

Nursery Nurse

A nursery nurse works with babies and children under eight in the public, private and voluntary sector. This can include schools, nurseries and hospitals. In schools, nursery nurses work in nursery, reception and infant classes alongside the teacher, providing and supervising educational and play activities. Nursery nurses in hospitals can work in maternity and special care units, and on children's wards. Day nurseries, both private and local authority, employ nursery nurses to care for children under five whose parents are unable to care for them during the day. Nursery nurses can also be employed in clinics, residential homes, the community, family centres and in private homes as nannies.

Qualifications and Training

There is a variety of recognised training courses for nursery nurses; these normally run for two years and lead to a diploma in nursery nursing. The courses are a combination of theory and practical placements in schools, nurseries, etc. The minimum age for entry to a course is usually 16, with individual colleges setting entry qualifications. Private colleges may set a minimum age for entry at 18 years.

Personal Qualities

A genuine love of children is essential, with the ability to work with patience, tolerance, imagination and energy. Good motivation skills and a sense of fun are important.

Starting Salary

£8000–£10,000 as a Nursery Assistant, £10,000–£13,000 as a Nursery Nurse/Officer.

Further Information

National Association of Nursery Nurses, 10 Meriden Court, Great Clacton, Essex CO15 4XH (*please enclose sae*)
Council for Awards in Children's Care and Education (CACHE), 8 Chequer Street, St Albans, Hertfordshire AL1 3XZ; 01727 847636
The Scottish Nursery Nurses' Board (SNNB), 6 Kilnford Crescent, Dundonald, Kilmarnock, Ayrshire KA2 9DW; 01563 850440

Nursing Auxiliary

Auxiliaries work on the wards assisting qualified nursing staff with routine tasks (such as taking temperatures, making beds, sterilising equipment and so on). They may work full or part time but generally have to put in a set number of hours each week. (In psychiatric hospitals the term nursing assistant is used.)

In time the title of nursing auxiliary will be changed to that of healthcare assistant. Healthcare assistants will be able to take NVQs and undertake more tasks than nursing auxiliaries do at present.

Qualifications and Training

No special qualifications are demanded. Candidates are interviewed by the hospital concerned and, if found suitable, are sent on an internal training course (generally about two weeks) and then continue training on the job.

Personal Qualities

Like qualified nurses, auxiliaries must have patience, tact, tolerance and an ability to communicate with the patients in their charge. Physical fitness is essential as the job sometimes involves heavy work (such as lifting and turning patients).

Starting Salary

Grade A: £7171–£9603; Grade B: £9297–£10,583

Further Information

Local Jobcentres and Careers offices
Personnel departments of local hospitals

Occupational Therapist

Occupational therapists are concerned with assessing and treating people with a wide range of physical and psychological problems. The aim of occupational therapy is to enable people to be as independent as possible in their work, leisure and daily living, despite illness, disability or old age. Occupational therapists begin by establishing the reasons why people have difficulty with a particular task and then, together with the patient, devise a programme of activity to solve that problem. People of all age groups with a wide variety of permanent or temporary disability can be helped by occupational therapy.

Occupational therapists work in hospitals, social service departments, schools, in voluntary organisations, in private practice and in people's own homes. As patients now spend less time in hospital and there is an increasing emphasis on caring for people in the community, the skills of occupational therapists are more in demand than ever before.

Qualifications and Training

Candidates must be 18 years of age (17½ in Scotland). Five GCE/GCSE/SCE passes (including English language and a science); a minimum of two A levels, or three Highers, are also required. Most schools will now accept alternative entry qualifications, particularly for mature students. Most courses are full time and last for three years, leading to the award of a degree, the BSc in Occupational Therapy. There are accelerated courses for those who already have a degree in a related subject. Although courses vary, all include the principles and practice of occupational therapy, behavioural, biological and medical sciences, and periods of clinical practice in a variety of hospital and community settings.

Personal Qualities

In addition to academic ability, potential occupational therapists require good communication skills, an interest in people and problem-solving ability. Occupational therapy attracts students from a wide variety of backgrounds and more men are choosing to enter the profession.

Starting Salary
£12,500 for the newly qualified, rising to over £20,000 for occupational therapy managers. Therapists working in London receive London weighting.

Further Information
College of Occupational Therapists, 6–8 Marshalsea Road, London SE1 1HL; 0171 357 6480
Careers in Nursing and Related Professions, Kogan Page

Oceanographer

Oceanography is the study of the seas, the organisms within them and the sea floor and its sediments. Scientific and commercial interest in this field has increased considerably over the past few decades and researchers are investigating the possibilities of deriving energy sources, minerals and food from the sea. Oceanographers are also concerned with the study of pollution and erosion, navigation and underwater work.

Qualifications and Training
An honours degree in one of the sciences is usually essential. There are only a few universities (Liverpool, Plymouth, Southampton and the University of Wales at Bangor) which run first degree courses in oceanography itself.

Personal Qualities
Candidates should have a scientific aptitude and training together with an enquiring mind.

Starting Salary
£11,500 (scientific officer level).

Further Information
The Society for Underwater Technology, 76 Mark Lane, London EC3R 7JN; 0171 481 0750; Fax: 0171 481 40001

Oil/Gas Rig Work *see Diver, Geologist*

There are various openings for personnel working on oil or gas drilling rigs, both onshore (on land) and offshore (such as those in the North Sea). Opportunities in all fields are generally limited to experienced and/or highly qualified applicants. An offshore rig has to be self-sufficient and is virtually a combination of a factory, a hotel and heliport. The catering and accommodation side is similar to that onshore. Many of the routine factory tasks (such as cleaning and maintenance) are carried out by outside contractors and service companies. The oil companies themselves employ certain technical experts, including geologists, geophysicists and drilling and petroleum engineers.

Geologist

Geologists collect and analyse data from a variety of sources in an effort to determine whether drilling might prove successful at a particular site and to optimise production from existing oilfields. There are opportunities at home and overseas.

Qualifications and Training

A good honours degree is the minimum required; some companies prefer postgraduate training. Training courses cover areas not touched on in sufficient detail at university, including essential links to geophysics, and petroleum engineering can be offered.

Geophysicist

Geophysicists use remote sensing to study the composition and structure of the sub-surface. A major element of this is computer-aided analysis of seismic data.

Qualifications and Training

An honours degree in geology or geophysics is a standard qualification but companies also employ graduates in other numerate disciplines, such as maths or physics. Postgraduate training may be an advantage. Companies arrange courses to cover specific technical areas, and to build essential links to petroleum geology and engineering.

Personal Qualities

Scientific aptitude, numeracy, a good eye for detail and an enquiring mind are essential, as is the ability to work in a team under pressure.

Drilling Crew

The drilling crew are responsible for the drilling of wells, and the operation and maintenance of a variety of heavy machinery. The crew consists of a toolpusher who manages the team and is responsible for the safety and integrity of the operation, and a team of people including a driller, assistant driller, derrickman, roughnecks and roustabouts. A typical drill crew will number around 10 people. Progression to the role of driller is hierarchical, with people working through general labouring jobs (roustabouts), working on the drill floor (roughnecks) or at the top of the derrick (derrickman). The work is physical, from the operation of the drilling equipment to the cleaning and maintenance of pumps and equipment. A graduate drilling engineer and a range of other specialists such as logging engineers, directional drilling specialists and mudloggers will also work with the drill crew.

Qualifications and Training

Traditionally experience and 'rise up the ladder' were the main criteria; however, there are now a variety of courses at all levels. Generally applicants are sponsored by drilling companies. Roughneck courses last four weeks. Drillers, toolpushers and drilling engineers will receive further training including statutory well-control and emergency response training.

Personal Qualities

All drilling crew must be physically fit as the work is arduous, and must be prepared to work as part of a team for long periods of time.

Divers

Divers are employed in exploration and production work, as well as underwater repair work such as welding. See *Diver*.

Qualifications and Training

All divers must be trained on courses approved by the Health and Safety Executive. Training is expensive and courses are few. Most candidates are sponsored by employers such as service companies.

Personal Qualities

Physical fitness and the ability to stay calm in a crisis are essential.

Engineers

Engineers are also employed in the rig work or petroleum, drilling or facilities engineering. Their work is generally split between the office and the production site. The production engineer supervises activities ranging from production and storage, gas compression and injection (to assist in the recovery of the oil), and tanker loading. The reservoir engineer is concerned with the behaviour of the oil accumulation or reservoir, and has to attempt to discover how much oil remains below ground and what are the most effective methods of recovery. Economics plays an important role. The maintenance engineer must ensure that all equipment is functioning properly, selecting and monitoring the companies under contract.

Qualifications and Training

Oil companies recruit graduates for engineering posts, normally with an engineering degree. Specialist postgraduate training may be an advantage. Training courses then supplement the knowledge gained at university and build links to allied areas such as petroleum geology.

Starting Salary

Salaries vary depending on position, but are often high.

Further Information

The British Geological Survey, Keyworth, Nottingham NG12 5GG; 0115 936 3100
The Engineering Careers Information Service, 41 Clarendon Road, Watford, Hertfordshire WD1 1LB; 01923 238441
The Geological Society, Burlington House, Piccadilly, London W1V 9AG; 071 434 9944
Aberdeenshire Council, Woodhill House, Westbury Road, Aberdeen AB16 5GB; 01224 664634

Operating Department Assistant

This is a relatively new job in the health service and involves assisting in a hospital operating theatre. The assistant works as a member of a team which includes the surgeon, anaesthetist and a trained nurse. One of the assistant's tasks is to provide extra support in the management of the complicated equipment now used in operating theatres.

Qualifications and Training

Candidates must be over 18, have four GCSEs or equivalent, or sit an entrance test. An aptitude for dealing with equipment is useful. Training is on the job and by attendance at classes and training courses. Training lasts for two years and leads to City and Guilds examinations. There is an NVQ award, level 3, available in operating department practice.

Personal Qualities

Operating department assistants must be physically fit, quick and competent, and able to work as part of a team.

Starting Salary
Trainees: £6693; £9064 when qualified.

Further Information
British Association of Operating Department Assistants, 70a Crayford High Street, Dartford, Kent DA1 4EF

Optician *see Orthoptist*

Opticians are classified in two categories, ophthalmic and dispensing. Both must be registered in accordance with the Opticians Act in order to practise.

Ophthalmic Optician/Optometrist
They are trained to examine eyes and test sight, to detect and measure defects in healthy eyes and, if necessary, to prescribe spectacles, contact lenses or other appliances to correct or improve vision. They do not treat actual eye diseases; patients with these are referred to medical practitioners. Most optometrists work in general practice in a variety of arrangements including independent businesses, partnership, as an employee of corporate bodies or as a franchisee. There are also job opportunities in research organisations, academic departments, ophthalmic hospitals and clinics.

Dispensing Optician
They do not examine eyes or test sight, but are concerned only with supplying and fitting spectacles, lenses and other aids prescribed by the ophthalmic optician. Most dispensing opticians work in general practice in a variety of arrangements including independent businesses, partnership, as an employee of corporate bodies or as a franchisee. There are also job opportunities in ophthalmic hospitals and clinics.

Qualifications and Training
An optometrist must be registered with the General Optical Council before being permitted to practise in the United Kingdom. To obtain registration an optometrist must pass the professional qualifying examination of the College of Optometrists. The examination is in two parts: part 1, the award of a BSc honours degree in optometry after three years of study at an accredited institution or four years in the case of Glasgow Caledonian University; part 2, the candidate must complete a pre-registration year of supervised practice and pass part 2 of the professional qualifying examination.

For acceptance onto a university course the student will normally need three A levels, two of which must be mathematics or science, or four/five Scottish higher certificates, two of which must be mathematics or science. GCSE/Scottish Standard Grades should include English and physics if not gained at A or H level. Average entry grades vary but are usually between 20–22 A level points. The professional qualifying examination combines practical and oral assessment of the candidate's ability to manage patients and practise safely as an independent optometrist.

Dispensing opticians need to be Fellows of the Association of British Dispensing Opticians. Minimum educational standards required for training are five GCSEs/SCEs (including English, maths or physics plus a third science-based subject). Training takes three years and may be by means of a two-year, full-time course followed by a year of practical experience, or three years' practical experience coupled with part-time courses. Students of the Association of British Dispensing Opticians may follow a three-year correspondence course with short residential college courses each year.

Personal Qualities

Opticians need mathematical and scientific skills to make accurate observations and calculations. They also need an ability to get on with patients of all ages and backgrounds and to be able to put them at their ease.

Starting Salary

Salaries are from £21,000+ for ophthalmic opticians and £14,000+ for dispensing opticians.

Further Information

Association of British Dispensing Opticians, 6 Hurlingham Business Park, Sulivan Road, London SW6 3DU; 0171 736 0088

College of Optometrists, 10 Knaresborough Place, London SW5 0TG; 0171 373 7765

The General Optical Council, 41 Harley Street, London W1N 2DJ; 0171 580 3898

Scottish Committee of Optometrists, 3 Castleton Crescent, Newton Mearns, Glasgow G77 5JX; 0141 639 6483

Ordnance Survey Work *see Cartography*

The Ordnance Survey is part of the Civil Service and is responsible for producing all kinds of official maps covering the whole of Great

Britain. There are, for example, large-scale plans used by local authorities, estate agents, solicitors, architects, civil engineers and government departments; the popular 'one-inch' map (now replaced by the 1:50000 metric equivalent) beloved of ramblers, riders, motorists and cyclists; and maps showing historical detail (such as Roman Britain) or statistical data (population density, for instance). Most of these are regularly revised and updated. There are limited opportunities in the Ordnance Survey for cartographic draughtsmen, cartographic assistants and field surveyors. Field surveyors go out checking detail – drawing in new features such as buildings, hedges, fences, roads etc and making a note of alterations that have occurred since the last map was printed.

The Ordnance Survey headquarters are in Southampton and most employees are based there; field surveyors, however, may be posted virtually anywhere in England, Scotland or Wales.

Qualifications and Training

Mapping and charting technicians grade 1 must have a minimum of three GCSE passes or equivalent, including at least three of the following subjects – English language, geography, maths, art, technical drawing, surveying, a modern or classical language and a science subject. Mapping and charting technicians grade 2 (aged 16 to 18) need two GCSEs or equivalent, including at least one of the subjects already listed. Training is by means of internal courses with regular tests and a final examination.

There are also opportunities for graduate cartographers with a geography A level, a degree in cartography, GIS, topographic science, surveying and mapping science, or a relevant postgraduate qualification.

Personal Qualities

Map-making requires great attention to detail, neatness and some mathematical/drawing skills, and increasingly a willingness to work with computers. Surveyors should also enjoy working out of doors.

Starting Salary

Mapping and charting technicians grade 2 start at £8000+; grade 1 from £11,000. Graduates are paid from £13,000.

Further Information

The British Cartographic Society, c/o R W Anson, Oxford Brookes University, Headington, Oxford OX3 0BP; 01865 483346

Personnel Division, Ordnance Survey, Romsey Road, Maybush, Southampton SO9 4DH; 01703 792639/40 (*enquiries only from those who already have the minimum entry qualifications*)

Organisation and Methods Work *see Work Study Practitioner*

Organisation and methods staff usually work as a team studying how a job is done at present and what could be done to improve its efficiency. They make detailed analyses of office work, including systems of paperwork, and then devise new methods (such as installing computer systems for filing, ordering and invoicing, for instance) to handle these. Clerical jobs may be assessed by work measurement techniques similar to those used by work study staff to measure manual work. Personnel in this field usually belong to the IMS – the Institute of Management Services – and are mainly employed in manufacturing industries or in the public sector.

Qualifications and Training

Professional examinations are set by the Institute of Management Services. Entry to the certificate course (for those under 21) requires a BTEC national award in business studies, or alternatively A levels or extremely good GCSEs. (Older candidates without these qualifications may be considered.) To enter direct into the diploma course, the certificate must have been completed. The certificate course lasts for one year (part time) and the diploma course a further two years.

The Institute of Administrative Management also sets examinations directly relevant to students of organisation and methods work. Because of the nature of the job, few school-leavers are accepted direct but it is quite possible to gain suitable background experience in commerce or industry prior to training (starting in a clerical post, for instance, or by gaining a technical qualification).

Personal Qualities

O and M staff must be able to get on with people of all ages and at all levels within an organisation. They need tact, self-confidence and analytical minds, as well as an ability to communicate.

Starting Salary

Trainees earn £11,000+ depending on qualifications and experience.

Further Information

Institute of Administrative Management, 40 Chatsworth Parade, Petts Wood, Orpington, Kent BR5 1RW; 01689 875555

The Institute of Management Consultants, 32–33 Hatton Garden, London EC1N 8DL; 0171 242 2140

Institute of Management Services, 1 Cecil Court, London Road, Enfield, Middlesex EN2 6DD; 0181 366 1261

Orthoptist

Orthoptists diagnose and treat various abnormalities and weaknesses in the eye – squints, for instance, or double vision. Many patients are children and special equipment and exercises are used to help correct any defects while young. Orthoptists work closely with medical eye specialists and, where operations are necessary, with ophthalmic surgeons. Most orthoptists work within the National Health Service, in hospitals and clinics (including school clinics). There are also opportunities in private practice and in teaching.

Qualifications and Training

The minimum age limit for training is 17 (although most schools require candidates to be at least 18 years of age). Applicants must have five GCSEs (plus three A levels) and subjects must include at least one science, English language and maths. Scottish students must hold SCEs in six subjects, including four at H level (again at least one science, English and maths are specified). Qualification is by a degree in orthoptics. Orthoptic degree courses are based at Glasgow Caledonian University, University of Sheffield and University of Liverpool.

Personal Qualities

Orthoptists have to be able to win the confidence of their patients (who are often very young) and so need a sympathetic manner and a good deal of patience. Some mathematical and scientific ability is also called for.

Starting Salary

From £12,635 in the health service, generally slightly more in private practice.

Further Information

The British Orthoptic Society, Tavistock House North, Tavistock Square, London WC1H 9HX; 0171 387 7992

Osteopath

Osteopathy is a system of diagnosis and treatment whose main emphasis is on conditions affecting the musculo-skeletal system. Osteopaths use predominantly gentle manual and manipulative methods of treatment to restore and maintain proper body function.

Osteopaths work in private practice and are increasingly being asked to work as part of mainstream medicine.

Qualifications and Training

Entry requirements are one of the following: a minimum of two A levels in biology and chemistry; a science Access or Foundation course; mature students with other qualifications; equivalent qualifications from European and overseas applicants. The course includes the study of anatomy, physiology and biochemistry, followed by a clinical course in the principles, diagnoses and techniques of osteopathy, under the leadership of a senior practitioner. In 1995 the school launched the Extended Pathway, which allows students to work full time while training for the first three years of a five-year course. In addition BSO offers a Conversion Pathway for healthcare professionals, eg doctors, dentists, physiotherapists.

Personal Qualities

Osteopaths require good manual dexterity and a genuine desire to help and care for people. An ability to get on with and gain the confidence of their patients is also important.

Starting Salary

Within the first five years of practice new graduates can earn approximately £25,000–£30,000 per annum.

Further Information

The British College of Naturopathy and Osteopathy, Frazer House, 6 Netherhall Gardens, London NW3 5RR; 0171 435 6464

The British School of Osteopathy, 1–4 Suffolk Street, London SW1Y 4HS; 0171 930 9655

Working in Complementary and Alternative Medicine, Kogan Page

Packaging Technologist

The purpose of packaging is to protect, preserve, contain and present its contents. It may also have a selling function. Opportunities for work exist with manufacturers of raw materials which may be converted into packaging, with companies that carry out the converting, and with companies that have a product to be packed. Many small firms will not have their own packaging adviser/technologist and will hire a consultant when the need arises.

There are work opportunities in actually designing and making the packaging material – sample making, cutting, folding, glueing – and for scientists and technologists.

Qualifications and Training

Many firms insist on formal qualifications. The internationally recognised standard is the Institute of Packaging diploma. There are also opportunities to take packaging as an optional module with some first degrees and for progression to an MSc in packaging technology.

There are various courses (part time, residential and correspondence) for those wishing to take the Institute of Packaging's membership exam. Candidates should have four GCSEs including English and maths, or, if they are over 25, have an equivalent standard of education and three years' experience.

Personal Qualities

Manufacturing workers must be able to work neatly and with dexterity. Technologists and scientists must be able to look at problems in a practical way and have the ability to communicate their ideas to others both verbally and on paper.

Starting Salary

Apprentices in manufacturing about £70–£80 a week at 16, technicians £5000+ a year and graduates £12,500+.

Further Information

The Head of Training, Institute of Packaging, Sysonby Lodge, Nottingham Road, Melton Mowbray, Leicestershire LE13 0NU; 01664 250 0055; Fax: 01664 64164 *(for details of available training and careers advice)*

Painter and Decorator *see Interior Decorator*

Painting and decorating involves much more than just hanging paper and applying paint. Appropriate paint for different surfaces must be chosen, surfaces must be prepared and holes and cracks in walls filled in; scaffolding may have to be erected. Specialist skills, such as graining – using paint to give the effect of wood; marbling – doing the same for marble; and gilding – the application of gold and silver leaf to wood, glass and other surfaces may be needed. Painters and decorators work for large firms, building contractors, local authorities and as self-employed craftsmen.

Qualifications and Training

No formal educational requirements are necessary, but good mathematical ability is useful. Training is on the job by three-year apprenticeship. During this time apprentices may work towards NVQs, awarded jointly by City and Guilds and the Construction Industry Training Board.

Personal Qualities

As well as the necessary practical skills, painters and decorators must have an artistic sense, be neat in their work, able to get on with people and be prepared to work out of doors, standing most of the time.

Starting Salary

Recommended weekly rates are: £73.90 at 16; £103.46 at 17; £147.81 at 18; and, when qualified, the Craftsman rate is £178.62.

Further Information

Construction Industry Training Board, Bircham Newton, King's Lynn, Norfolk PE31 6RH; 01553 776677 (ext 2466)

Patent Agent/Patent Examiner

Patent agents advise individual clients and companies on matters relating to patent law and act on their behalf if they wish to patent an invention, or to register a trademark or a design in this country or abroad. First, records are searched to gauge the likelihood of a patent being granted. The agent then draws up the particulars of his client's invention in as clear and concise a way as possible and ensures that it neither infringes another patent nor is liable to be copied without infringing the patent. In cases where a client's patent has been infringed, the agent advises as to the best course of action.

Patent agents are employed by private practice firms of patent agencies, industrial companies with a patent department and the government.

Patent Examiner

They are civil servants and examine the applications for patents submitted by patent agents and others. The principal task is to establish the originality or otherwise of the invention, and whether or not the applicant is entitled to the protection he claims. There is some opportunity to work abroad in the European patent office.

Patent Officer

They are civil servants employed in protecting Crown rights in new inventions and developments, compensating the owners of patents used by the Crown and generally advising government departments on matters relating to patents.

Qualifications and Training

The minimum educational requirements for an agent are five GCSEs/Standard grade passes and two A levels/three H grades including either physics or chemistry. Training is on the job and involves passing the examinations of the Chartered Institute of Patent Agents. Nowadays it is becoming more important to hold a degree in a science subject as it is usually necessary to register as a patent agent both in the UK and Europe. This involves taking the European qualifying examinations for which a degree is necessary.

Patent examiners and officers need a first or second class honours degree in engineering, physics, chemistry, mathematics or an equivalent professional qualification.

Personal Qualities

Necessary qualities are curiosity, the ability to assimilate new ideas, good analytical and critical skills, clear and concise thinking and the ability to express oneself logically and clearly both in speech and writing.

Starting Salary
About £13,000 for trainee patent agents; newly registered agents earn about £20,000; examiners begin at £13,651 and progress to about £43,000.

Further Information
Chartered Institute of Patent Agents, Staple Inn Buildings, High Holborn, London WC1V 7PZ; 0171 405 9450

The Patent Office, Cardiff Road, Newport, Gwent NP9 1RH; 01633 814544 (*patent examiners*)

Pattern Cutter*, see *Clothing Industry, Fashion

Personal Assistant *see Secretary*

A senior secretary/personal assistant (PA) may work with one or more senior executives. He or she must have accurate skills (ie shorthand or audio typewriting, word processing, information management) and may act as: administrator, information centre, organiser of the boss(es)' day, progress chaser, arranger of travel and meetings, receptionist, communicator (oral and written) internally and externally. A senior secretary or PA assumes responsibility without direct supervision and takes decisions within the scope of assigned authority.

Qualifications and Training
GCSEs (including English), A levels or a degree are all acceptable qualifications. (Numeracy and a second language are very useful.) An NVQ award in administration (secretarial), level 3, is available. A secretary usually gains experience as a member of a management team, although some find jobs at a senior level following a postgraduate secretarial or secretarial/linguist course. Some secretaries progress to management through further study in personnel, administration, public relations, marketing, information technology etc.

Personal Qualities
Good secretaries are judged by what they do, but qualities such as self-motivation, discretion, tact, loyalty, personality, flexibility, communication skills and smart appearance are expected.

Starting Salary
£12,000–£20,000 or more in London.

Further Information

Institute of Qualified Private Secretaries (IQPS Ltd), First Floor, 6 Bridge Avenue, Maidenhead FL6 1RR; 01628 25007 *(from 1998 625007)*

Careers in Secretarial and Office Work, Kogan Page

Personnel Officer

Personnel management is all about the effective use and development of people's skills, knowledge and experience to achieve the goals of an organisation – in other words, getting the best out of people at work. A major part of personnel work is concerned with the staffing of businesses and ensuring that jobs are filled by people with the required abilities, and that people are employed where their abilities can best be used. To do this, the personnel officer undertakes job analysis, observing the work done and asking questions. The information so obtained enables a job specification to be completed, detailing the skills, knowledge and qualifications the job requires. The personnel officer may then undertake recruitment and follow this with a programme of training.

Another of the personnel officer's tasks is to ensure that in a big firm young qualified staff gain experience in a wide range of departments. The personnel officer may also deal with grievances, industrial relations, training and development, salary structure, as well as hygiene, safety and welfare. In some organisations house magazines, sports and social activities all come under the personnel department's responsibility.

Qualifications and Training

Applicants for membership of the Institute of Personnel and Development through the Institute's Professional Education Scheme should normally have three GCSEs or equivalent and two A levels or equivalent, or have two years' experience in a responsible personnel management position.

Personal Qualities

Personnel officers should have good administrative and organisational skills, be fair, logical and possess excellent interpersonal skills.

Starting Salary

A graduate's salary is between £12,000 and £15,000. An average salary is £18,000.

Further Information
The Institute of Personnel and Development, IPD House, 35 Camp Road, London SW19 4UX; 0181 971 9000

Pest Controller

Pest controllers control not only mice, rats, cockroaches and ants that may be damaging foodstuffs in a factory or hotel, or present in private homes, but also rabbits, moles, birds and foxes that attack farmers' crops. They work for local authorities and private firms. Service staff are employed to lay traps, set poison etc; there are also opportunities for graduates in research and management.

Qualifications and Training
Service staff should have GCSEs to include science subjects and English. Training is on the job and, in local government, there are courses available. Graduates should have a biology degree or a relevant science degree.

Personal Qualities
This is not a job for the squeamish but also not for the vicious. The work demands a mature outlook; an ability to get on with many kinds of people, and to work in varying conditions; and to be able to work on one's own. The ability to drive is useful.

Starting Salary
Salaries range from about £8000+ to £13,000+, the higher figure being for graduate entrants.

Further Information
Local authorities

Petrol Pump Attendant*, see *Garage Work

Pharmacist

The main work of pharmacists is the dispensing of doctors' prescriptions. There are three branches of the profession: community pharmacists, hospital pharmacists, and industrial and research pharmacists.

Community Pharmacist
They work in a shop, where as well as dispensing prescriptions – either those they have made up themselves or ready-made prescriptions – they explain the use of the drug to customers, keep a poisons register, and act as a link between the doctor and the pharmaceutical manufacturer, being prepared to discuss developments with both. In addition, they sell a wide range of non-pharmaceutical articles.

Hospital Pharmacist
They dispense drugs for hospital in- and out-patients. In addition, in some hospitals pharmacists manufacture their own products, take part in research work, and come into direct contact with in-patients by accompanying medical staff on their ward rounds.

Industrial and Research Pharmacist
They research diseases, develop new drugs and carry out clinical trials. Industrial pharmacists are also recruited to work in the areas of: manufacturing, regulatory and medical affairs, sales and marketing, computer science/information technology and others.

Qualifications and Training
Minimum qualifications are five GCSEs or equivalent to include English language and maths, and three A levels, in chemistry plus two subjects from a biological science, mathematics and physics. They lead to a three- or four-year degree course in pharmacy, plus one year's paid practical training before registration.

Personal Qualities
Meticulous attention to detail, a sense of responsibility and an ability to get on with people are required.

Starting Salary
Pre-registration year £7000–£9000 in London, £6000–£7500 elsewhere; qualified £15,000 (community), £12,350 (hospital), £15,500 (industry).

Further Information
The Association of the British Pharmaceutical Industry, 12 Whitehall, London SW1A 2DY; 0171 930 3477 (*write for free booklet offering guide to careers for graduates*)
Guild of Hospital Pharmacists, 50 Southwark Street, London SE1 1UN; 0171 378 7255
The National Pharmaceutical Association, Mallinson House, 38–42 St Peter's Street, St Albans, Hertfordshire AL1 3NP; 01727 832161

Pharmaceutical Society of Northern Ireland, 73 University Street, Belfast BT7 1HL; 01232 326927

Royal Pharmaceutical Society of Great Britain, 1 Lambeth High Street, London SE1 7JN; 0171 735 9141 (*Scottish Department*: 36 York Place, Edinburgh EH1 3HU)

'Entrance Requirements to Schools of Pharmacy' (The Royal Pharmaceutical Society of Great Britain)

'Pharmacy' (HMSO)

'Pharmacy: Effective Caring' (The Royal Pharmaceutical Society of Great Britain)

Pharmacy Technician

Pharmacy technicians help pharmacists in the dispensing of drugs, in the ordering and distribution of stock, in the manufacturing of medicines and quality control. Technicians may work in community pharmacies, in hospital pharmacies, health centres or in industry. They may manage staff and deal with patients, doctors and nurses. Technicians are an essential member of the team providing pharmaceutical care for the patient.

Qualifications and Training

For a place on the two-year part-time BTEC national certificate in pharmaceutical sciences, GCSEs in at least four subjects including at least two in chemistry, biology or mathematics are necessary. Students without these requirements may take the course over three years if they have relevant GCSEs at a reasonable standard. An alternative qualification to BTEC is a NVQ level 3 in pharmacy services.

In community pharmacy, students may train through an in-house training programme or the National Pharmaceutical Association distance learning programme and may gain the Society of Apothecaries dispensing technicians certificate.

In Scotland, students study for the SCOTVEC certificate in pharmaceutical sciences or the SNVQ level 3 in pharmacy services.

Personal Qualities

Pharmacy technicians should be accurate in their work, reliable, careful and have high standards of hygiene. They should also enjoy working with other people and in teams.

Starting Salary

At 16, a technician could expect about £6000–£7500 and over £10,000 when qualified.

Further Information

Education Officer, Association of Pharmacy Technicians, 7 Hampden Road, Wendover, Buckinghamshire HP22 6HU

The National Pharmaceutical Association, 40–42 St Peters Street, St Albans, Hertfordshire, AL1 3NP; 01727 832161

Royal Pharmaceutical Society of Great Britain, 1 Lambeth High Street, London SE1 7JN; 0171 735 9141

Your local hospital

Photographer *see Medical Illustrator*

Photography is an international means of communication, its great advantage over the written word being that it does not need to be translated for use in another country. The uses of photography range from commercial and press to medicine and crime detection. With the advent of microfilming, the storage and retrieval of information have been made much more convenient and involve the use of far less space.

Photography is also a popular hobby providing jobs for many in the photographic manufacturing, retailing, servicing and photo-finishing trades.

Commercial Photographer

This work includes advertising, fashion, industrial and general practice photography. Photographers in advertising and fashion are nearly always freelance, employed for a particular campaign or job. Industrial photographers may be freelance or employed by large organisations where they take photographs for brochures, catalogues, instruction manuals and in-house magazines. General practice photographers are mainly involved in portraiture and taking wedding photographs etc.

Photojournalism and Press Photographer

Press photographers work for newspapers, magazines, periodicals and technical journals. All these media, particularly the last three, employ freelance as well as in-house staff. Photojournalists are photographers who are able to tell a story with pictures. They are almost always freelance and the main market for their work is Sunday colour supplements.

Institutional and Specialist Photography

Scientific photographers are used to provide information essential for research in a scientific or engineering field. This work may include aerial photography as well as the use of techniques such as holography, photomicrography and macrophotography. The main employers are the Civil Service, private industries and universities. The main uses for photography in hospitals are to satisfy clinical, research, publication and teaching requirements. Clinical photography in particular demands the use of specialist techniques: photomicroscopy, macrophotography, endoscopic photography and the use of infra-red and ultra-violet light sources.

Institutions that require photographers include museums, trade associations, national parks departments, charities, advisory councils, education authorities and libraries.

Photographers are also employed to teach photography in colleges and in schools run by manufacturers and major retailers. There are opportunities to teach part-time photographic courses in many schools and some colleges.

There are also opportunities to be a photographer in the Army, Royal Navy and Royal Air Force but no one can join the Army or Royal Navy solely to be a photographer. The RAF does recruit directly into ground photography. As regards the police force, other than the City of London force, most photographers are civilian employees.

Qualifications and Training

Formal educational qualifications are not always required but, for a place on a course, four to five GCSEs or equivalent are usually necessary. See *Medical Illustrator* for the requirements for medical photography. To be a trainee press photographer, five GCSEs at grades A, B or C are necessary, or four GCSEs and one A level, or two GCSEs and two A levels. English language is necessary.

The Royal Navy requires a good general education to GCSE level with particular attention to maths and English. In the police force requirements vary; some ask for City and Guilds qualifications and some three GCSEs including English, maths and a science.

There are a number of HND and degree courses available and for entry to these five GCSEs plus two A levels or equivalent are necessary.

Training is often on the job in photography, in a junior position; for example, a messenger or general assistant in an advertising studio or as a trainee assistant photographer in the police force. Some employers provide courses and others allow time off for attendance at outside courses. NVQs in photography at levels 3 and 4 are available.

Personal Qualities

Photographers generally require a blend of artistic and scientific skills, the ability to deal with people and to put them at their ease, and good eyesight and colour vision. Medical and police photographers must have the ability to remain 'outside' their work and not be too squeamish.

Starting Salary

Salaries vary enormously but the following are intended to give some indication: for those starting in fashion and advertising the rates in a studio are £6000 or £25–£30 a day; experienced assistants can earn £100 a day. Social and wedding photographers with experience could expect about £10,000; newspaper trainees start at £7000 rising to £10,000 after a year. In London the rates are £18,000 with experience for a weekly publication and higher still for a national newspaper. Medical photographers begin at £6210, £8408 when trained.

Further Information

Association of Photographers Ltd (AFAEP), 9 Domingo Street, London EC1Y 0TA; 0171 608 1441

British Institute of Professional Photography, Fox Talbot House, Amwell End, Ware, Hertfordshire SG12 9HN; 01920 464011

The National Council for the Training of Journalists, Latton Bush Centre, Southern Way, Harlow, Essex CM18 7BL; 01279 430009

Local Army, Royal Navy, Royal Air Force and Police Careers Offices

Running Your Own Photographic Business, Kogan Page

Photographic Work

There are many varied activities of interest associated with the producation of photographs/images.

Wholesale Photofinishing Laboratories

Cater for the amateur photographic markets, large film volumes are handled amounting to many thousands per day. Highly sophisticated state of the art printing, processing, finishing, pricing and hands free dispatch equipment are used to ensure the very exacting service times are maintained. Most laboratories operate over a 24-hour cycle; skilled technicians and operators are a requirement of this sector of the industry.

Professional Laboratories/Imaging Centres

The professional laboratory/imaging centre can be divided into two major segments, social and commercial. The social laboratories harness all the skills of photographic processing technicians, covering a diversity of requirements from printing (hand and machine), processing (paper and film), colour negative/colour transparency, black and white, small prints to works of art adorning many stately homes. Weddings and portraiture are the life blood of a social laboratory. With the rapid advance of digital imaging, the commercial laboratories are having to face the challenge of a rapidly changing environment; a new breed of 'technocrats' are suddenly appearing, people with advanced computer skills and a creative talent to match. From dye-sublimation to ink-jet, from thumbnail images to giant murals, exhibitions, corporate organisations, PR agencies, a whole gamut of new and exciting markets awaits this sector of the business.

Manufacturing, Retailing and Service Trades

In the past the UK supported a host of camera manufacturers, today only highly specialised cameras are produced; however, there are large quantities of film, photographic and non-photographic papers and chemicals manufactured. Opportunities exist for technicians to research and develop new products; all aspects of the industry need support technicians, engineers and a whole plethora of sales personnel.

Qualifications and Training

The industry has its own training organisation, Photography and Photographic Processing Industry Training Organisation (PPPITO). NVQ and apprenticeship schemes are already well established for all aspects of the photographic, digital and allied services. There is an increasing requirement for personnel with degrees in the sciences. A new emerging workforce is beginning to appear with all the challenges associated with learning new skills and marrying them to the knowledge that has kept the industry to the forefront of new technology.

Personal Qualities

Staff are handling other people's memories which are often unique and carry commercial or sentimental value. All personnel must have a caring and responsible attitude to their work. Good colour vision is essential, especially for personnel engaged in colour coordination, equipment integration, etc. Photo scientists must have an interest in discovering environmental improvements, technological advancements, product improvements and increased efficiency.

Starting Salary

Laboratory technicians in photofinishing and pro-labs have a commencing salary of £5000–£8000. A technician would start at about the same as a non-graduate entry, rising to £12,500–£21,000, London rates being higher. Graduates in manufacturing and senior technical roles start at £12,000–£15,000 rising to £25,000–£30,000+ per annum.

Further Information

Professional Photographic Laboratories Association (PPLA), 35 Chine Walk, Ferndown, Dorset BH22 8PR; 01202 590 604; Fax: 01202 590 605

Physicist

Physics deals with the interrelation of matter and energy. Physicists are needed wherever the physical properties of materials have to be studied. They are employed in the fields of electronics, nuclear power, computing, aerospace, optics, telecommunications, engineering and instrument manufacture. In addition, hospitals employ medical physicists whose work includes support for medical use of radiation and design and implementation of new equipment for diagnosis and treatment of disease. Some physicists lecture in universities or teach in schools. Physics technicians assist fully qualified physicists.

Qualifications and Training

A qualified professional physicist needs a degree in physics. It is envisaged that this might be equivalent to NVQ level 4 in three subjects. College and university requirements are two A levels or three H grade passes to include physics, or a subject including physics, and a maths subject.

Junior technicians need a good education to GCSE level with particular attention to maths, a science and a subject showing the use of English in order to take a BTEC/SCOTVEC national certificate. There are special certificate courses for medical junior physics technicians. For senior technicians a BTEC/SCOTVEC HND award is available; the requirements are an A level (two H grades) in physics and GCSE maths, chemistry and English. A BTEC/SCOTVEC NC or ND award is acceptable in place of A/H levels. Training for technicians is generally on the job with time off to attend courses.

Personal Qualities

Physicists must be able to recognise a problem and plan an experiment or set of experiments to solve it. They should be imaginative, persevering, have good powers of concentration and adopt a sound, logical approach. Technicians should have the practical skills necessary to carry out experiments, be responsible, accurate and caring in their attitude to work.

Starting Salary

Trainee technicians start at £6500+, the majority of senior technicians earn from £12,000 to £18,000+ and qualified physicists' earnings are in the region of £13,000–£26,000+.

Further Information

The Institute of Physics and Engineering in Medicine, 4 Campleshon Road, York YO2 1PE; 01904 610821

The Institute of Physics, 47 Belgrave Square, London SW1X 8QX; 0171 235 6111

Physiotherapist

Chartered physiotherapists treat patients suffering from a wide variety of diseases, conditions or injuries by physical means. They help people who have had strokes to regain the use of lost functions, treat sports injuries and people with arthritis, and help children with cerebral palsy to learn to walk. The techniques used include massage and manipulation, exercise, electrotherapy and hydrotherapy. Most physiotherapists work in the health service but there are many opportunities now for employment in industry, sports clinics, schools and private practice.

Qualifications and Training

A minimum of five GCSEs and three A levels are normally required for a place on a three- or four-year course, leading to a degree. (Courses are in specialist schools and universities.) Many candidates offer three A levels but there are other routes such as BTEC science (health studies). Subjects at GCSE should ideally include English and two sciences and A levels should include a biological science.

Personal Qualities

Physiotherapists must be caring, patient, reasonably fit, good communicators and have the ability to inspire confidence in their patients.

Starting Salary

£12,500 rising to £27,000 for senior staff.

Further Information

The Chartered Society of Physiotherapy, 14 Bedford Row, London WC1R 4ED; 0171 306 6666

Careers in Nursing and Related Professions, Kogan Page

'Physiotherapist' (DH Leaflets Unit, PO Box 21, Stanmore, Middlesex HA7 1AY)

Piano Tuner

Piano tuners or technicians are able both to tune a piano evenly throughout the scale and to discover and put right any fault. They work with a kit of specialised tools, and are employed in piano factories and by piano dealers; some also work for themselves.

Qualifications and Training

Courses are available at five institutions: City of Leeds College of Music, London Guildhall University, Newark and Sherwood College, The Royal National College for the Blind, Hereford, and Stevenson College of Further Education, Edinburgh. Entry requirements are usually four GCSEs at grade C or above. The Piano Tuners' Association will accept a candidate for membership after five years from the start of training – at least two years training and at least two years working as a piano tuner.

Personal Qualities

Musical ability, while not essential, is an advantage. Patience and deftness are required, together with an aptitude to be able to use woodworking, home improvement DIY and/or car maintenance tools. As tuners are mostly self-employed, the ability to work alone, competence in managing a small business and self-motivation are also important.

Starting Salary

Salaries vary: £150–£170 a week when trained, lower without experience. Many piano tuners are self-employed and may earn up to £400 a week when established.

Further Information

Pianoforte Tuners' Association, c/o 10 Reculver Road, Herne Bay, Kent CT6 6LD; 01227 368808 (*send sae*)

Pilot,* see *Civil Aviation

Plasterer

Plasterers are among the most skilled of the building craftsmen. They not only wet plaster large wall areas but also may construct plaster fittings in a workshop and then fix them into place on a building site. Intricate details such as ceiling mouldings are also made wet by the plasterer or constructed in a workshop from fibrous plaster. Plasterers may also lay cement floors and carry out external finishes on houses. There are opportunities for work with building contractors and local authorities, and also for being self-employed.

Qualifications and Training

No formal educational requirements are necessary. Training is on the job as plasterer's mate, and by a three-year apprenticeship during which time it is possible to work towards NVQs awarded jointly by City and Guilds and the Construction Industry Training Board.

Personal Qualities

Plasterers must be physically strong and have the ability to work very quickly. Defects in a wall or ceiling surface are often very obvious so high standards and a responsible attitude to work are important.

Starting Salary

Recommended weekly rates are: £73.90 at 16; £103.46 at 17; £147.81 at 18; and, when qualified, the Craftsman rate is £178.62.

Further Information

Construction Industry Training Board, Bircham Newton, King's Lynn, Norfolk PE31 6RH; 01553 776677 (ext 2466)

Plumber

Plumbers fit and repair pipes connecting the cold and hot water supply, central heating or some domestic appliance such as a washing machine, and remove rain water and sewage. Plumbers work on roofs fitting flashings and are also responsible for putting up rainwater pipes and gutters. They may work on building sites employed by building contractors, property companies or local authorities and, also, many plumbers are self-employed, working mainly in private houses.

Qualifications and Training

No formal educational requirements are necessary. Training is on the job, and by a four-year apprenticeship during which time it is possible to work towards NVQs, levels 2 and 3. NVQs, levels 4 and 5, will be available in the future.

Personal Qualities
Plumbers must be agile, deft and able to work neatly, carefully and accurately. They must also be prepared to work outside and have a head for heights.

Starting Salary
Recommended weekly rates are: £73.90 at 16; £103.46 at 17; £147.81 at 18; and, when qualified, the Craftsman rate is £178.62.

Further Information
Construction Industry Training Board, Bircham Newton, King's Lynn, Norfolk PE31 6RH; 01553 776677 (ext 2466)
Institute of Plumbing, 64 Station Lane, Hornchurch, Essex RM12 6NB; 01708 472791

Podiatrist* see *Chiropodist

Police Officer

The police look after the community by keeping it a safe and ordered place to live in. They are responsible to the community they police and for doing their job properly. Their main objective is the prevention of crime and the detecting of wrongdoers but their work includes many other activities: controlling traffic, giving advice on road safety, advising on house security, dealing with missing persons and lost property.

There are many different specialities within the police service, although everyone joins as a constable. These include the Criminal Investigation Department (CID); traffic police; dog handlers; mounted police; river police; and crime prevention officers.

There are also special police forces in existence – the British Transport Police, the Ministry of Defence Police and (in London) the Parks Police. These special forces are separate from the other 43 forces in England and Wales, which are the general responsibility of the Home Secretary.

Qualifications and Training
There are no minimum formal educational requirements although applicants should have achieved a good all-round standard of education. All candidates sit an entrance test, made up of five separate tests to measure a different ability: to spell and construct sentences; to check information quickly and correctly; to solve numerical problems

accurately; to reason logically; and to observe scenes carefully and to recall the details accurately. Normal entry is at 18½ but it is possible (in a few forces) to join the police cadets from 16. Apart from learning about police life and experiencing police work, cadets have the opportunity to further their academic qualifications and to work in the community. Cadetship does not guarantee entry into the regular force. Many forces operate a voluntary cadet scheme, and YT schemes may also be in operation in many forces.

All recruits, whether they have been a cadet or not, serve a two-year probation period as police constables with training on residential courses included. After the two-year period there are opportunities for specialisation.

Graduates may apply to join the Accelerated Promotion Scheme for Graduates (APSG). After the initial two-year probationary period and after passing the sergeant's exam, these graduates will enter the Accelerated Promotion Course (APC). Officers who have joined the force under standard entry will have the opportunity to gain entry onto the APC if they have passed the sergeant's exam. Some officers who are already on the force may be sponsored at university.

Personal Qualities

Being a police officer is a varied job demanding many different qualities, but all officers must have self-discipline, be independent yet able to work in a team, adaptable, have a genuine concern for people, be completely fair and honest, with good powers of observation. In addition police officers must be prepared to work unsocial hours, have a disturbed family life and be witness to the seamy side of life.

The 43 forces in England and Wales, the eight Scottish forces and the one in Northern Ireland each have their own entrance requirements and it is advisable to check these before applying.

Starting Salary

Constables begin on £14,412 during initial training and then move to either £15,648 or £16,710 depending on age, skills and experience. Constables in London receive London weighting and a London allowance in addition.

Further Information

Local police forces

England and Wales

Police Recruiting Department, Room 514, Home Office, Queen Anne's Gate, London SW1H 9AT
(*Graduate entry: Room 553*)

Scotland
Police Division, Scottish Office Home Department, St Andrew's House, Edinburgh EH1 3DE

Careers in the Police Service, Kogan Page
'Police Officer' (Home Office)
'Police Officer – a Career for Graduates' (Home Office, Graduate Liaison Office, Room 553, Queen Anne's Gate, London SW1H 9AT)

Politics

Politics is a career for relatively few; there are 659 members of parliament and over 80 British members of the European parliament. MPs work long hours, often sitting in the House until the small hours. In addition, they spend one day a week in the constituency and specialise in a particular subject, such as health or education. Ministerial responsibilities impose many extra duties of national importance. All MPs must have another career to support them while they are seeking election and to fall back on if they lose their seats.

Another job in politics is that of constituency agent. They work for local branches of the party, organising the party and its publicity, and acting as a link between the MP and the party.

There are also opportunities for administrative and office staff in the central party offices. These central office staff, as well as general office duties, are responsible for writing speech material for party spokesmen and providing information to the national press.

Qualifications and Training

No formal educational requirements are necessary for political jobs. MPs are adopted by a constituency party because they are already well known to the party through their active voluntary work or, sometimes, because they have made a name for themselves in some other field.

Agents must be thoroughly versed in electoral law and party organisation, and are given training on courses – full time or by correspondence.

Head office staff are usually recruited from constituency agents and assistants.

Personal Qualities

It is necessary in politics to be hardworking, persevering, thick skinned and, for agents and administrative staff, to have excellent organisational powers. MPs should also have a certain personal charisma and be able to put their ideas across clearly and persuasively.

Starting Salary

MPs' salaries are £43,000, and ministers earn more. Cabinet ministers receive £87,851, ministers £74,985 and under-secretaries £67,483. The Prime Minister is entitled to £102,417 but the highest paid is the Lord Chancellor at £140,665.

Further Information

Local constituency parties

Polymer Science and Technology

Polymers is the name given to materials that are made up of large molecules of identical or similar units and united by chemical bonds. The main polymers are natural and synthetic rubbers, plastics and natural and synthetic fibres. The plastics industry makes products both for industrial and domestic use and is also involved in moulding, laminating and finishing products. The rubber industry produces tyres, hoses and footwear as well as numerous other products. Scientific staff work in research and development, and there are also opportunities for salespeople and technical advisers.

Qualifications and Training

NVQs are available for all the polymer processes, for example: injection moulding, blow moulding, extrusion, tyre manufacture, general rubber goods and retreading tyres. Technicians who wish to take the BTEC certificate in polymer technology need GCSE passes in English, maths and a science; for the SCOTVEC award the completion of four years' secondary education is required. The BTEC certificate course is available full and part time. On completion of the certificate it is possible to take the higher certificate on a part-time course. Professional qualifications are available through the Plastics and Rubber Institute at both technician and degree level (engineering technician, incorporated engineer, chartered engineer). In addition, the BTEC certificate can contribute as evidence towards the attainment of NVQ Level 3 and both the NVQ and BTEC form part of the modern apprenticeship scheme (for further information contact the BPTA at the address below).

To take a degree in polymer science and technology five GCSE passes or BTEC/SCOTVEC equivalents are necessary in chemistry, physics and maths, two A levels or three H grades. There are also higher degrees offered for students with less applicable first degrees.

Personal Qualities
An interest in solving practical problems, the ability to work as one of a team and high standards of professionalism are required. Technical staff also need practical skills necessary to carry out experiments.

Starting Salary
A trainee technician at 16 would earn about £8000, £9775–£11,000 when qualified, graduates £11,500–£14,000.

Further Information
The British Plastics Federation, Bath Place, Rivington Street, London EC2A 3JE; 0171 457 5000

British Polymer Training Association, Coppice House, Halesfield 7, Telford, Shropshire TF7 4NA; 01952 587020.

The British Rubber Manufacturers' Association, 90 Tottenham Court Road, London W1P 0PH; 0171 580 2794

Institute of Materials, 1 Carlton House Terrace, London SW1Y 5DB; 0171 839 4071

Post Office

The Post Office has changed out of all recognition. It now consists of three independent businesses. The Royal Mail delivers 60 million letters a day which involves an enormously complex distribution operation. Royal Mail Parcelforce is at the forefront of the UK's fiercely competitive parcel services market. Post Office Counters is Britain's largest retail network.

Opportunities for school-leavers include postal cadet, administration, secretarial, postman, postwoman, counter clerk, retail assistant, apprentice engineer. There are generally opportunities for graduates in marketing, personnel, finance, operations, planning, information technology and operational research.

Qualifications and Training
No formal educational qualifications are necessary for the jobs listed above for school-leavers but they must take an aptitude test. In the future NVQs will be available for a number of different tasks at a number of levels. Apprentice engineer entrants must have studied maths and science subjects to GCSE level. Graduate entrants should have studied a relevant degree. Useful subjects are: business studies, computing, maths, geography, transport and planning, mechanical and electrical engineering.

Personal Qualities
All employees who meet the public need to be able to communicate with people, and counter clerks and retail assistants, in particular, should be patient and prepared to help. Counter clerks also need numerical skills. Graduates should be numerate and possess good interpersonal and organisational skills.

Starting Salary
School-leavers £5620–£8830; graduates from £14,800, plus London and south-east allowances where appropriate.

Further Information
School-leavers: The Personnel Officer at the local Royal Mail, Royal Mail Parcelforce or Post Office Counters office (the address and telephone number are in the local telephone directory)
Graduates: The Assessment Consultancy, Freepost, Coton House, Rugby CV23 0BR

Potter

Employees in the pottery industry make ordinary domestic china, earthenware, vases and ornaments, fine bone china, ceramic tiles, sanitary ware, industrial and electrical porcelain and huge insulators used in generating electricity. Although the industry is mechanised there is still a predominant demand for skilled workers: hand painters, fettlers and spongers, casting, lithographing, binding and lining to name a few. Some potters work individually, hand throwing or casting their own pieces and selling them personally or through a shop or gallery.

Qualifications and Training
No formal educational requirements are needed for the industry; training is mainly on the job. Craftsmen potters sometimes become apprenticed to master potters but more commonly they take foundation courses followed by vocational or degree courses at an art school.

Personal Qualities
Potters need a good eye for shape and design, a steady hand and a delicate touch. Potters working for themselves must also be inventive and have business skills and marketing ability.

Starting Salary
Industry employees at 16 about £80 a week. Craftsmen set their own

rates and, if they are selling their work through a gallery, must pay the owner a percentage.

Further Information

Crafts Council, 44a Pentonville Road, London N1 9BY; 0171 278 7700 (*send sae*)

The Craft Potters' Association, 4 Marlborough Court, London W1V 1PJ; 0171 437 7605

Pre-school Leader

Pre-school leaders work in pre-schools where they provide an appropriate service for children, usually from two and a half upwards, by means of a range of educational play activities. Groups operate for a fixed time each day: some are morning only, some all day. Pre-school leaders are usually helped by paid assistants and by one or more parents on a voluntary basis. Groups may be funded by local authorities or by private concerns, but most are registered charities managed by parents and other interested adults from the local community.

Qualifications and Training

Training for a pre-school leader is by the 200-hour diploma in pre-school practice run by the Pre-school Learning Alliance, which also provides the underpinning knowledge and understanding for NVQ/SVQ in childcare and education, level 3. Shorter courses are available for assistants.

Personal Qualities

As well as having a genuine love of children, pre-school leaders should be creative and lively, good at working with an adult team and with some knowledge of child development.

Starting Salary

Salaries vary for playgroup leaders from one area of the country to another.

Further Information

Pre-School Learning Alliance, 69 Kings Cross Road, London WC1X 9LL; 0171 833 0991

Scottish Pre-School Play Association (SPPA), 14 Elliot Place, Glasgow G3 8EP; 0141 221 4148

Careers Working with Children and Young People, Kogan Page

Printing

The purpose of printing is communication, whether the printed matter be books, magazines, newspapers, security documents or bank cards. Printers are involved too in producing wallpaper, floor coverings and even advertising slogans on milk bottles. The printing industry covers a wide range of jobs in both factory and office.

Pre-press
Most setting is to computer floppy disk or compact disc. The operator is responsible for a keyboard, similar to that of a typewriter, which transfers typematter for output to paper or film.

Proof Reader
Proof readers check customers' proofs for spelling mistakes and incorrect typeface before returning them. When setting to disc, proof reading is done automatically.

Camera Operator/Scanner Operator
Camera operators photograph the original of a drawing or photograph and from this produce a negative or positive as required. In colour work a separate piece of film for each colour has to be produced. The operator requires considerable skill and judgement to do this accurately. Now the reproduction of colour photographs is largely done by electronic scanners and not so much skill is needed on the part of the operator.

Planner/Platemaker
If not completed through computer screen, make-up planning operators take the film and place the type and illustrations in the right place in the correct pages.

Machine Minder
They set up the machines for each job, feeding in paper and plates and adjusting the inks. They then check the printed material as it comes through, making sure that the quality is consistent.

Binding and Finishing
This involves trimming the paper, assembling it into book form and pasting or stitching sheets together. In the case of hardback books the hard cover is attached.

Office Jobs
Order clerks/account executives look after individual printing jobs;

they write instructions for each department and check the product's arrival into and departure from each section.

Estimators work out how much a job will cost. Cost clerks go through the costs item by item and discover where and why the money was spent. Sales staff find customers, and design staff are also needed.

Qualifications and Training

Academic qualifications are not mandatory for craft workers but the following subjects studied to GCSE level are preferred: English, maths, computer studies and science. Training is by a two-year training scheme with time off to attend courses.

Office staff have qualifications ranging from GCSEs to a degree. GCSEs are preferred for junior clerks and there are opportunities to gain further qualifications through BTEC/SCOTVEC or City and Guilds awards. To take the higher diploma in printing on a two- or three-year basis, four GCSEs to include English, maths and a science plus one A level are necessary, or a BTEC/SCOTVEC NC/ND in printing. There are in addition three print-related degree courses for which two A levels are necessary

NVQs at levels 2 and 3 are available both for print production and print administration.

Personal Qualities

The printing industry is changing rapidly; employees must be prepared to move with the times and retrain if necessary. A responsible attitude and a pride in what is being produced are necessary. Craft workers need good colour vision and manual dexterity.

Starting Salary

Salaries vary but at 18 all workers should earn £170+ a week.

Further Information

British Printing Industries Federation (BPIF), 11 Bedford Row, London WC1R 4DX; 0171 242 6904

Institute of Printing, 8 Lonsdale Gardens, Tunbridge Wells, Kent TN1 1NU; 01892 538118

Scottish Print Employers Federation, 48 Palmerston Place, Edinburgh EH12 5DE; 0131 220 4353

Daily Mail (job advertisements)

Prison Officer

Prison officers are employed in prisons, detention centres, young offender institutions and remand centres. The work involves supervising prisoners inside the place of detention, escorting them to courts and other prisons and, if relevant, teaching a skill or trade. Some specialist prison officers are employed as hospital officers, dog handlers, security experts and caterers.

Qualifications and Training
Five GCSEs including maths and English are required and applicants must pass an aptitude test and an interview. Training lasts for two weeks at a local prison then nine weeks at an officers' training school. In Scotland the training period is initially for one month followed by a six-week course. There is special training for caterers, dog handlers, physical education instructors and medical staff.

Personal Qualities
Officers must be fair, well balanced, have the ability to command respect and be able to submit written reports. The age span is between 20 and 49½. In Scotland the maximum age is 42.

Starting Salary
£14,600; additional sums are paid to officers working in London.

Further Information
Prison Officers' Association, 245 Church Street, London N9 9HW; 0181 803 0255
Prison Service HQ, Home Office, Cleland House, Page Street, London SW1P 4LN; 0171 217 3000
Scottish Prison Service, Carlton House, 5 Redheughs Rigg, Edinburgh EH12 9HW; 0131 556 8400
'HM Prison Service in England and Wales' (Home Office, Freepost, London SW1V 1YZ)
'HM Prisons in Scotland' (Scottish Prison Service)

Probation Officer *see Social Work*

Probation officers are attached to particular courts and may be asked by a court to provide a report on an offender. Offenders who are given probation by a court are placed under the care of a probation officer who sees them regularly and tries to help with any problems. Some officers are based in prisons and give advice to inmates. Others become involved with separation and divorce proceedings and give advice to the courts when they are concerned with the custody of children. In Scotland the functions of the probation officer are performed by social work departments in local authorities.

Qualifications and Training
The main professional qualification is the diploma in social work (DipSW) which can be studied for part time while working or full time via a college course. Entry requirements are five GCSEs plus two A levels or five SCEs including three at H level. Mature entrants may be accepted without these qualifications.

Personal Qualities
Probation officers should be strong characters, well balanced, have a flexible approach yet be able to work within the court system, and have a genuine interest in people of all types and a desire to help them.

Starting Salary
Students studying full time receive a grant of £3220 in London, £2525 elsewhere. Qualified staff under 30 start at £14,268 and those over 30 at £14,835.

Further Information
C6 Division, Home Office, Room 442, 50 Queen Anne's Gate, London SW1H 9AT; 0171 273 3000
Careers in Social Work, Kogan Page

Psychologist

Psychologists study the processes, motives, reactions and nature of the human mind. It is a profession with many different specialties, from clinical psychology concerned with human behavioural problems to market research where psychologists may be employed to discover why a consumer prefers one product to another. Psychologists work in the National Health Service, private hospitals, industry, for government and local authorities, in schools and privately as independent consultants and practitioners.

Clinical Psychologists
Clinical psychologists work in hospitals (including prison hospitals and military hospitals) and the community assessing patients who have psychological problems. They use interview techniques and specialist tests to diagnose behavioural problems and then use their detailed knowledge of learning patterns to help patients overcome problems such as addiction (to drink, gambling or petty theft, for instance), irrational fears (like claustrophobia, agoraphobia and so on). They also advise on rehabilitation for patients recovering from mental illness or those with permanent disabilities. A clinical psy-

chologist is not a qualified medical practitioner but works closely with psychiatric and other medical staff at all times. Most posts, particularly in teaching hospitals, give scope for individual research.

Educational Psychologist
The educational psychologist works with children and young people up to the age of 19. They may be suffering from physical or mental handicaps, have learning or communication problems or be encountering difficulties at home or school. The psychologist will work alongside parents and teachers to help the child to overcome problems.

Occupational Psychologists
Occupational psychologists study the needs and problems of people at work. They aim to increase understanding of how individuals and small groups fit within the organisational structure, as well as improve the effectiveness of working life and help people to find job satisfaction. Occupational psychologists give guidance on the choice of jobs, recruit people for the right job, devise training and retraining programmes as well as study ways of improving methods and conditions of work. They may also work with unemployed people.

Teaching and Research
Most teachers of psychology are employed by universities, polytechnics and colleges of further education. Some university posts also offer research facilities, and it is possible to undertake mainly or solely research work in the other branches of psychology, eg an educational psychologist may study how to teach concepts to blind children, and an occupational psychologist may research the relationship of stress to work conditions.

Government Work
There are opportunities for psychologists in the Civil Service in personnel research and selection; in the Department of Employment for occupational psychologists as practitioners, researchers and advisers; in the Ministry of Defence; and the prison service.

Medical Work
This is a relatively new area and involves the psychologist working alongside the remedial team. This work explores the interrelationship of psychology and medicine in terms of physical health and illness.

Ergonomist
Ergonomists study the relationship between man and machines. Their

work involves the study of people in their working environment and the equipment they use. Examples of ergonomists' work are: how heat affects work output, the advantage of two 15-minute breaks over one half-hour break, and noise control.

Qualifications and Training

Psychology can be studied as an art or a science and a mixture of art and science A levels is often useful; GCSE maths is usually required. Educational psychologists are required to have a degree in psychology plus a postgraduate certificate in education and two years' teaching experience before taking a postgraduate degree in educational psychology. (In Scotland a degree in psychology, a teaching qualification plus postgraduate work in the field are necessary.)

Teachers need a degree in psychology and, often, a higher qualification is required too. Teaching qualifications are necessary in order to teach in schools. Researchers too need a degree in psychology together with proven research experience. Government jobs necessitate a degree in psychology or a postgraduate diploma of at least two years' full-time study.

Psychologists working in medicine should have a science-oriented psychology degree. Ergonomists should be able to offer a psychology degree or an MSc in ergonomics.

Personal Qualities

All psychologists must have a strong interest in people, be curious as to why people act in a certain way, be able to set down clearly and logically the results of their investigations and be well balanced.

Starting Salary

Varies depending on the area of work, but from £9400 for an assistant psychologist and from £13,000 when trained. Occupational and educational psychologists should expect to earn £13,000–£30,000 when trained. The starting salary for an educational psychologist is £20,460.

Further Information

Association of Educational Psychologists, 3 Sunderland Road, Durham DH1 2LH; 0191 384 9512

The British Psychological Society, St Andrew's House, 48 Princess Road East, Leicester LE1 7DR; 0116 254 9568

'Careers in Psychology' (The British Psychological Society)

'Careers in Occupational Psychology' (British Psychological Society)

Psychotherapist

Psychotherapy involves treatment and preventive care for psychological disturbances of emotions, thought and behaviour. It concentrates on the whole individual, viewing symptoms as representing only a part of the whole being. Both adults and children are treated by psychotherapists, children for such problems as over-shyness, over-aggression and sleeping disorders. Adults' problems may be less easy to perceive but, for example, may be emotional, interfering with a person's work and home life.

Psychotherapists work in hospitals, in- and out-patient clinics, child guidance centres, special schools for disturbed children and in private practice.

Qualifications and Training

A psychology or related degree is required, followed by a post-graduate degree or diploma in clinical or educational psychology plus relevant experience. After completing the latter requirement, training then takes a further four years and involves academic study, workshop and supervised therapeutic treatment.

Personal Qualities

Psychotherapists must have a genuine interest in the problems of children and adults, and a desire to help. They must themselves be emotionally well balanced.

Starting Salary

£16,000–£20,000.

Further Information

The Association of Child Psychotherapists, 120 West Heath Road, London NW3 4S8; 0171 458 1609

The British Psychological Society, St Andrew's House, 48 Princess Road East, Leicester LE1 7DR; 0116 254 9568

Publican

The licensee of a pub may be a manager who is paid a salary, a lessee or tenant who rents the property from a brewer and keeps the profits, or a free trader who owns the premises. As well as the ever-popular traditional town and country pubs there is now a wide variety of pubs ranging from theme pubs, disco pubs, café bars and steak bars to pubs with gourmet restaurants and full entertainment facilities. Nearly all pubs serve food and an increasing number also offer accommodation. Many licensees operate as a husband and wife team.

Qualifications and Training

No formal academic qualifications are necessary but increasingly those with NVQs or SVQs (offered by the British Institute of Innkeeping), diploma or degree qualifications, especially in hotel, catering and licensed trade management, are sought.

Brewery companies will put their managers through a comprehensive training programme. Licensees could well be running businesses grossing more than £½ million a year. They must know how to market their services and devise new ideas to attract customers. They must also have a good knowledge of subjects such as bookkeeping, licensing laws, hygiene, staff motivation, customer care and cellar management. Other training courses are available from a variety of commercial training organisations and colleges of further education.

Personal Qualities

Publicans should be ambitious and willing to take responsibility. They must like people and the idea of looking after customers.

Starting Salary

Managers who are single earn from £12,000 with participation in bonus schemes – £20,000 in London. Accommodation, lighting and heating are normally provided. Bar and cellar catering staff aged 21 or over can earn around £3.00 an hour.

Further Information

Retail Department, Brewers and Licensed Retailers Association, 42 Portman Square, London W1H 0BB; 0171 486 4831

British Institute of Innkeeping, Wessex House, 80 Park Street, Camberley, Surrey GU15 3PT; 01276 684449

Hotel and Catering Training Company, International House, 3 High Street, London W5 5DB; 0181 579 2400

Hotel and Catering International Management Association (HCIMA), 191 Trinity Road, London SW17 7HN; 0171 672 4251

Kogan Page Guide to Careers in the Catering, Travel and Leisure Industries, Kogan Page

The Publican's Handbook, Kogan Page

Public Relations Officer

The chief aim of the public relations officer is to ensure that the correct information about his employer, client or product is made known to the right people. This is done by a variety of means including press releases, press conferences, television and brochures. The two main branches of public relations work are corporate PR and product promotion. Corporate PR work is concerned with effectively putting across an organisation's policy and activities to a variety of people: government, employers and shareholders. The kind of organisation requiring this approach might be a government department, a charity, a company or local authority. Product promotion is concerned with giving information about a product; it is closely allied with marketing and advertising and, in fact, public relations work in this field often backs up an advertising campaign. PROs are employed by organisations or work in PR consultancy agencies.

Qualifications and Training

Qualifications vary from a certificate/diploma in public relations to a degree. Fourteen establishments offering a degree or MA in public relations are recognised by the Institute of Public Relations.

Entry requirements for a certificate course are five GCSEs plus a year's experience or five GCSEs plus two A levels or BTEC/SCOTVEC/NC/ND equivalents. Candidates for a degree course need five GCSEs and two A levels or equivalents.

Personal Qualities

Public relations officers must understand people and what motivates them and be able to get on well with a variety of people. They must be imaginative, creative with regard to ideas and writing skills, reliable and good managers.

Starting Salary

Trainees in PR earn £8000–£10,000, but later rewards can be high.

Further Information

Communication, Advertising and Marketing Foundation Ltd, Abford House, 15 Wilton Road, London SW1V 1NJ; 0171 828 7506

The Institute of Public Relations, The Old Trading House, 15 Northburgh Street, London ECIV 0PR; 0171 253 5151

Careers in Marketing, Advertising and Public Relations, Kogan Page

Publishing

Publishing is concerned with choosing, planning, editing, designing and producing books and periodicals, but not newspapers. The books may be hardback or paperback, fiction or non-fiction or specialist books such as school or university textbooks or books aimed at a specific trade or profession – for example, legal books. Periodicals include weekly magazines, learned journals, trade publications and staff magazines. Book publishing is divided into three main categories: editorial, production and design, and marketing (including sales and publicity).

Some would argue that it is all 'marketing' and all the functions work towards satisfying the customer.

Editorial

Editors tend to separate into commissioning editors who are responsible for initiating new ideas, finding authors and assessing and sponsoring unsolicited manuscripts; and desk editors who prepare manuscripts and put them into house style, rewriting parts if necessary, and correcting proofs. In a small house these functions are often combined. Editors in small houses are also sometimes concerned with selling rights to a foreign publishing house and taking in books from abroad.

Production and Design

The production department is responsible for buying paper, dealing with typesetters, printers and binders and seeing that schedules are kept. The design or art department is responsible for the overall appearance of the book including choosing the typeface and designing the jacket. In a small house these functions may be combined, with freelance artists engaged for jacket design.

Marketing

The department must ensure that the book is ordered by bookshops and that information reaches potential buyers. Representatives are employed who visit bookshops, library suppliers and educational establishments. Adverts are placed in relevant daily and trade publications, mailings are sent to specific groups of people, review copies of new books are despatched and publicity tries to obtain interviews for authors in the press and on radio and television.

Magazine Publishing

The functions of the above departments are similar, with the following variations. Commissioning editors tend to commission articles rather than books. The design of a magazine once established must be followed. Often much more colour work is involved in magazine than in book production. The advertising for the sale of popular magazines is more aggressive than for the sale of books.

Picture Research
This may be a separate department in a large house or one dealing with highly illustrated books, a function performed as necessary by the editorial department, or by a freelance. Picture researchers are responsible for finding pictures to illustrate a book or magazine. Sometimes they must search for very specific material to illustrate certain subject matter, sometimes pictures generally pertaining to a topic are required.

Packagers
They sell complete books to publishers, often supplying publishers at home and abroad simultaneously. The publishers are then responsible for marketing and selling the book.

Qualifications and Training

There are no formal educational requirements necessary for editors but many do have a degree; this is particularly necessary in a house dealing with a very small, specialised area only. Oxford Brookes University, West Herts College, The Robert Gordon University, Loughborough University, Thames Valley University and Napier University offer first degree courses in publishing. Secretarial qualifications are also useful.

Production staff generally first take a printing course, or a degree as above. The London College of Printing and Distributive Trades offers a BA in publishing, also a diploma course in publishing production, entry requirements being three GCSEs or two years' appropriate experience. Various diploma courses are available and the Book House Training Centre runs a variety of short courses. Women in Publishing also run a training programme. Postgraduate courses are also available at many of the universities above.

Most artists and designers have taken appropriate courses. The LCPDT course in graphic origination and reproduction requires five GCSEs or two years' experience. Sales and marketing staff do not always have academic qualifications but it is usual and many have degrees. Sales representatives need a good standard of general education.

NVQs are available in ten occupational areas of publishing. Details are available from the Book House Training Centre, the Open University Validation Services, or the Periodical Training Council.

Personal Qualities

Attributes vary depending on department, but all staff should have a feeling for books or language combined with a keen business sense. In addition commissioning editors need imagination and creativity and desk editors an eye for detail. Design staff must have good colour vision. Picture researchers must have excellent visual memories.

Starting Salary

Editorial assistants start from £8500 to £13,000, commissioning editors £16,000–£26,000; picture researchers £9500–£13,000; production salaries start at £9000–£12,000 for qualified workers; art department salaries range from £9000 to £11,000; sales, marketing and publicity start at £9000–£12,000, and sales representatives £13,000–£18,000 plus a car.

Further Information

Book House Training Centre, 45 East Hill, London SW18 2QZ; 0181 874 2718

Open University Validation Services, 344–354 Gray's Inn Road, London WC1X 8BP; 0171 278 4411

Periodicals Training Council, Imperial House, 15–19 Kingsway, London WC2B 6UN; 0171 836 8798

Publishers Association, 1 Kingsway, London WC2 6XF; 0171 580 6321

Publishing Qualifications Board, 344–354 Gray's Inn Road, London WC1X 8BP; 0171 278 4411

Women in Publishing, c/o J Whitaker & Sons Ltd, 12 Dyott Street, London WC1A 1DF; 0171 836 8911

The Kogan Page Guide to Working in the Media, Allan Shepherd

Careers in Publishing and Bookselling, and *Careers Using English*, Kogan Page

Purchasing Officer

Purchasing officers are responsible for the buying in of raw materials needed for manufacture, ready-made components and finished goods and services. They must be aware of price, quantities to be supplied and delivery dates. In addition they must be familiar with new developments in their purchasing field and any new technology. Purchasing officers may or may not be involved in drawing up specifications. When a product is decided upon, the purchasing officer must approach a number of suppliers for quotations, select one and negotiate terms.

Qualifications and Training

Entry is possible at various stages: with five GCSEs, with A levels or BTEC/SCOTVEC NC/ND in business studies, and with a degree. Training is largely on the job and some employers have special training schemes. Qualifications are also offered by the Chartered Institute of Purchasing and Supply (CIPS).

To take the CIPS examinations five GCSE passes plus an A level are necessary. BTEC qualifications are also acceptable. Applicants without these qualifications may be accepted provided they are 23, have suitable experience and have their employer's support.

At supervisory level, the Institute offers an open access certificate programme.

Personal Qualities

Officers must be prepared to take responsibility, be able to get on with people easily, be firm and persuasive. They must be prepared to undertake a lot of travel and work under considerable stress.

Starting Salary

£13,500–£15,000.

Further Information

The Chartered Institute of Purchasing and Supply, Easton House, Easton-on-the-Hill, Stamford, Lincolnshire PE9 3NZ; 01780 56777

Quantity Surveying, **see** *Surveyor/Surveying Technician*

Quarrying

The quarrying industry is concerned with extracting from the ground materials such as limestone, granite, slate, chalk, gravel, clay and sandstone. Some quarries also produce materials, for example, making lime, making ready-mixed concrete and coating stone needed for road building. The industry employs people at operative, craft, technician and management levels.

Qualifications and Training

Operatives need no formal qualifications although N/SVQs are available in mobile plant and process operations and will soon be available in drilling and shotfiring operations. Applicants can also enter an apprenticeship scheme to qualify for a N/SVQ in engineering maintenance. Those entering the industry with A levels or a BTEC national diploma certificate may enter the three-year sandwich degree course in quarrying and road surfacing at Doncaster College. Technicians, supervisors and management trainees with other qualifications can prepare for the HNC-level Institute of Quarrying professional examination by way of the Doncaster assisted private study course. Passes in the degree or the professional examination, with appropriate experience, lead to corporate membership of the Institute of Quarrying.

Personal Qualities

Operative and craft employees must have good physical ability and possess the necessary mechanical skills to operate quarrying machinery such as loaders and dumptrucks. Supervisors must have the usual organisational skills combined with a knowledge of the technology and of the materials involved.

Starting Salary
About £100 a week at 16 for an apprentice trainee.

Further Information
Institute of Quarrying, 7 Regent Street, Nottingham NG1 5BS; 0115 9411315

Quarry Products Training Council, Sterling House, 20 Station Road, Gerrards Cross, Buckinghamshire SL9 8HT; 01753 891808

R

Radio, see *Broadcasting*

Radiographer

Radiography is a caring profession which calls for considerable technological expertise. There are two branches: diagnostic radiography and therapeutic radiography.

Diagnostic radiographers are responsible for producing high quality images on film and other recording materials which help doctors to diagnose disease and the extent of injuries. Therapeutic radiographers help to treat patients, many of whom have cancer, using x-rays, ionising radiation and sometimes drugs.

Qualifications and Training

All radiography qualifying courses are now at degree level, and most are honours degrees.

It normally takes three years to qualify (except in Northern Ireland where the course is a four-year honours degree course).

Even though the course will normally be in a university or higher education institution affiliated to a university, half the course will be spent on clinical education with hospital departments associated with the university.

On graduation entrants are eligible for State Registration by the Radiographers Board of the Council for Professions Supplementary to Medicine which is an essential requirement for employment in the National Health Service. The requirements for entry to radiography courses are two A levels and three GCSEs at grade C or above although other combinations of A and AS levels and GCSEs are acceptable.

BTEC national certificates and diplomas in relevant studies are also acceptable.

Entry is also possible through validated access courses and applications from mature candidates are especially welcomed by many radiography education centres.

These are the minimum entry requirements and radiography education centres may ask for additional or more specific qualifications than the minimum.

Personal Qualities

As well as having an interest in science, you should be a caring and compassionate person, sufficiently level-headed not to get upset when dealing with sick people. You should be patient and calm when faced with people who may be frightened or difficult. Your health must be good and you have to be reasonably strong, because you may have to help lift people and move heavy equipment. In addition radiographers should be good humoured, be able to work well in a team and assume responsibility.

Starting Salary

£12,634.

Further Information

College of Radiographers, 2 Carriage Row, 183 Eversholt Street, London NW1 1BU; 0171 391 4500; Fax: 0171 391 4504

Careers in Nursing and Related Professions, Kogan Page

Radiotherapist*, see *Radiographer

Railway Work

British Rail/Railtrack employs a vast number of people: drivers, guards, signalmen, general railmen, clerical workers, technicians, craftsmen and managers. The latter are responsible for the day-to-day running of the railways or in charge of departments such as planning, engineering, marketing and accounts.

Qualifications and Training

Train drivers do not require formal educational qualifications but are expected to have studied English, maths and a science. Training is on the job. Guards, signalmen and general railmen are also trained on the job and do not need academic qualifications. Clerical staff should hold four GCSEs or else pass an entrance exam. Technicians need four GCSEs including maths, English and a science. They undertake four years' training involving attendance at day and block release courses leading to a BTEC qualification. Technician trainees without suitable GCSEs who have studied the relevant subjects may also be accepted but will follow City and Guilds rather than BTEC courses. City and Guilds courses are also taken by craft trainees who are recruited to take care of track repair and maintenance rather than civil, mechanical and electrical engineering tasks performed by technicians. NVQs levels 1 to 4 are being developed.

Managers are recruited with five GCSEs and two A levels, or with a degree. Trainees with A levels may be sponsored for a degree course on a sandwich basis; or they may be trained on the job with some time spent in colleges of further education. Training for graduate trainees varies depending on the nature of their work and lasts two years.

Personal Qualities
All rail staff must have a strong interest in providing an efficient service and in promoting and caring for passengers' needs. In addition drivers need perfect vision without glasses. Managers need qualities appropriate to their departments plus managerial and administrative skills.

Starting Salary
Operatives' salaries range from £160 a week to £225+, with drivers' commanding the higher amounts. Senior technical officers earn £11,000+ to £14,500, signal and telecommunications staff £9000–£24,000, Clerical Officers £10,000+ to £13,500.

Further Information
Local station managers

Receptionist

Receptionists work in hotels, large organisations and private firms, sometimes combining the job with that of telephonist. In hotels, they welcome the guests, make bookings and prepare the final account. They also deal with reservation correspondence and act as a general information office. In small hotels this can be handled by one person but in most, and especially the larger, hotels, they work in a team headed by the reception manager.

In large official organisations, such as a town hall, or in firms with many staff, they direct visitors to the correct department. In small firms the job is often combined with answering the phone, typing and franking the mail.

Qualifications and Training
Formal educational qualifications are not necessary, but proficiency

in English and simple maths is, and languages are an advantage. Training is mostly on the job and there are local authority courses available leading to Royal Society of Arts examinations. Receptionists in catering may work towards NVQs or SVQs, levels 1, 2 and 3.

Personal Qualities
Receptionists should be friendly and pleasant and have a neat appearance. They also need stamina, as they are expected to work on shifts and during evenings and weekends. They should have a real liking for people and a good memory for faces. It helps to have a methodical approach and an aptitude for accounting machines/computers.

Starting Salary
From £7000 to £12,500+, more in London.

Further Information
Hotel and Catering Training Company, Careers Information Services, International House, High Street, London W5 5DB; 0181 579 2400
Hotel and Catering International Management Association, 191 Trinity Road, London SW17 7HN; 0181 672 4251
Springboard Careers Advice Centre, 1 Denmark Street, London WC2H 8LP; 0171 497 8654

Recording Engineer, **see** ***Broadcasting, Engineering***

Recreational Manager, **see** ***Leisure and Amenity Management, Sport and Recreation Facility Management***

Refrigeration Engineer, **see** ***Engineering***

Recruitment Consultant

The aim of recruitment/employment consultants is to fit people to jobs. Agencies deal with all types of staff from office and secretarial to highly complex and specialist technical roles. The work involves interviewing prospective job candidates, keeping records of their details and matching them to employers' requirements. Much of the work involves selling to potential users.

Qualifications and Training
Many recruitment consultants have come into the industry after some

experience of another job; for example, sales, personnel, office work. They are trained either in house or on courses run by the Institute of Employment Consultants. The IEC offers two levels of qualification; the Foundation Award, suitable for those in their first year in the industry, and the Certificate in Recruitment Practice, for those with more than one year's experience in the industry. Both qualifications can be studied for by distance learning, in addition to which the Certificate can be studied at evening class.

Personal Qualities

Recruitment consultants must be able to get on with all kinds of people, have good communication skills, work quickly and calmly under pressure and be organised.

Starting Salary

Varies greatly for trainees, but with experience consultants can earn a salary of £25,000+ with commission.

Further Information

Institute of Employment Consultants, 6 Guildford Road, Woking, Surrey GU22 7PX; 01483 766442

Registrar

Registrars are involved in registering births, deaths and marriages. They also supply copy certificates to members of the public. Registrars of marriage officiate at Registry Office marriages, and also marriages at churches where the incumbent is only able to perform the spiritual functions but not to legalise a marriage. Registrars must be knowledgeable in all aspects of the law relating to birth, death and marriage.

Qualifications and Training

No formal educational requirements other than a good general education are necessary. Training is on the job.

Personal Qualities

Registrars must be able to get on with people, giving advice calmly and sympathetically and be even tempered. They should be able to do their job well in situations of excitement, emotion and distress. Good handwriting is important, and the ability to drive is an advantage. Entrants must be prepared for Saturday work.

Starting Salary
£10,500+.

Further Information
Office of Population Censuses and Surveys, St Catherine's House, 10 Kingsway, London WC2B 6JP; 0171 242 0262
Local authorities

Removals

Removals is an industry where people matter. In a modern society the remover plays a key role in the chain of events leading up to a family's departure from one home and arrival in another – which can be around the corner or the other side of the world. It is the remover's job to see that all the customer's belongings are professionally packed and transported to their destination. The jobs available will depend very much on the employer company, which could range from a small firm with up to a dozen or so vans, to a huge multinational. Each will offer particular benefits which should be considered. A person may start his or her career by working on a removal van as a porter and finish as managing director of a large company, or running his or her own removals business. Throughout the career there are ample opportunities for training at all grades, including training to gain an LGV driving licence.

Qualifications and Training
No formal education requirements for operatives, but management entrants should be at least 18 years old and have a minimum of six GCSE grades, preferably including English, maths and geography. Training is provided by BARTS, the training company of the British Association of Removers, and ranges from packing to a certificate recognised by the Department of Transport, which will allow the person to operate a transport company.

Personal Qualities
Removers should be fit and strong. They must be honest and have a sense of responsibility towards other people's possessions.

Starting Salary
£150–£230 a week, young entrants about £70.

Removals Estimator
Estimators are the technical salespeople in a removals company. They visit customers' homes and estimate the amount of packing space needed, the time it will take and the price. They should have a good standard of education with good passes preferably in English, maths, geography and modern languages, hold a full car driving licence and be able to express themselves clearly and persuasively. Training is on the job and some estimators attend a qualification course.

Further Information

British Association of Removers (Training Services) Limited, 3 Churchill Court, 58 Station Road, North Harrow, Middlesex HA2 7SA; 0181 861 3331

The Movers Institute (*address as above*)

Local Jobcentres and Careers Offices

Reporter*, see *Broadcasting, Journalist

Representative – Selling

A sales representative usually works for a manufacturer, wholesale distributor or service industry. He or she persuades potential customers to buy the firm's products and also looks after the needs of existing customers. The representative is usually assigned an area to cover and travels regularly around it on the firm's behalf. It is possible to be a representative for any number of products: soap powder, double glazing, books, machine tools, beauty products and thousands of others.

Qualifications and Training

Requirements for potential trainees vary, but most firms would look for two or three GCSEs grades A, B, C or equivalent. Training periods vary from one firm to another. Representatives may study for examinations set by such bodies as the Chartered Institute of Marketing, the Institute of Sales and Marketing Management which offer joint ISMM/City and Guilds courses in local colleges of further education and correspondence courses, or the Managing and Marketing Sales Association. Diplomas and certificates are also issued by various trade associations representing particular types of product. Technical sales representatives usually have a degree or equivalent in the relevant subject.

Personal Qualities
An outgoing, friendly personality, a manner that inspires confidence and the ability to speak forcefully and persuasively, plus persistence and stamina are all important.

Starting Salary
£13,000–£18,000 and car.

Further Information
The College of Sales and Marketing, Education Division, The Institute of Sales and Marketing Management (ISMM), National Westminster House, 31 Upper George Street, Luton, Bedfordshire LU1 2RD; 01582 411130

Making it in Sales: A Career Guide for Women, Kogan Page

Residential Care

Some children and adults with special needs require more support than their families can provide, even with the help of domiciliary and day care services; they need to live in residential homes or hostels or in sheltered housing or some other form of group care.

Residential care is provided by the statutory services, national voluntary societies, local organisations and private individuals.

Some residents go out to work each day and some need to live in the home or hostel only for a relatively short period. For those who are too young, too old or too frail to fend for themselves and who need control or guidance, help has to be provided in a way which offers the benefits of communal living without infringing on the need for independence and privacy.

In some cases senior members of staff live in or on the site. When this is a condition of service they may be offered self-contained accommodation, but they are not usually expected to be on call all the time without breaks and holidays. Residential work sometimes offers opportunities for joint appointments of married couples. Many staff posts in residential homes are non-residential or require the postholder to live in on a shift basis.

The work may involve: teaching clients how to undertake basic life tasks, such as cooking, filling in forms, the use of the telephone or shopping. It can range from accepting responsibility for celebrating events, such as a birthday or an examination success, to encouraging creativity. Many natural opportunities arise for on-the-spot counselling, often around ordinary day-to-day events.

Children and Young People

Residential establishments for children include reception centres where children are assessed and plans made for their future; small family-type homes accommodating just a few children of different ages; larger homes, some catering for groups of children with special needs and nurseries for babies and young children. Children may need permanent care, but more often it is required temporarily while their parents are unable to look after them. Children in homes may display behaviour problems because they have been separated from their parents or familiar surroundings, or because of their early experience of neglect, rejection, insecurity or abuse. They need skilled care and treatment.

In addition, there are special boarding schools and homes for children who have a visual or hearing impairment, an emotional or physical handicap or a learning difficulty.

Special provisions for young people in trouble or in need of care include community homes and hostels, and probation homes and hostels. Some hostels cater for people who have left school, are in employment and need somewhere to live.

Adults

Residential homes and hostels for adults include provision for people who have a visual or hearing impairment, a physical handicap or learning difficulty, are mentally ill, or have social handicaps which make a more normal pattern of life difficult to maintain.

There are also a number of hostels and 'half-way houses' where, for instance, ex-prisoners or people with an alcohol problem can live until they are sufficiently adjusted to be able to return to a more normal life.

Hostel accommodation and rehabilitation centres are provided for homeless families and for parents who need to be helped to learn how to give their families satisfactory care. Some single mothers need residential care in mother-and-baby homes where they can live both before and after their children are born, or hostels where their babies can be looked after when they go to work.

The largest category of all residential homes in the UK is for older people who have no families or whose relatives are unable to look after them, even with the help available from the social services in the community. Some cater for people with special problems, such as blindness, deafness or mental infirmity, but most homes for older people do not specialise in this way.

Provision is also made for more active older people to be catered for in sheltered housing schemes which are, in effect, groups of small houses, flats or bungalows where the residents can live independently with some communal facilities and help with emergencies from a resident warden.

Qualifications and Training

The main professional qualification is the diploma in social work (DipSW) which can be studied for part time while working or full time via a college course. Entry requirements are five GCSEs including two at A level or five SCEs and three H levels. Mature entrants may be accepted without these qualifications. It is also possible to work towards NVQs, levels 2 and 3, in social care.

Personal Qualities

Residential care workers should realise that the comfort and happiness of residents depend upon the understanding and sensitivity of the staff. Care staff should be able to get on with people, work in a team and be prepared to acquire new knowledge and skills.

Starting Salary

Salaries range from £6000+ for staff under 18, and £8000+ for those over 18, to approximately £13,000–£21,000 for officers in charge (depending on number of residents). Qualified social workers start at £13,581–£19,818.

Further Information

England: CCETSW Information Service, Derbyshire House, St Chad's Street, London WC1H 8AD; 0171 278 2455

Northern Ireland: CCETSW Information Service, 6 Malone Road, Belfast BT9 5BN; 01232 665390

Scotland: CCETSW Information Service, 78–80 George Street, Edinburgh EH2 3BU; 0131 220 0093

Wales: CCETSW Information Service, South Gate House, Wood Street, Cardiff CF1 1EW; 01222 226257

Careers Working with Children and Young People, Kogan Page

'Work with Children and Young People', CCETSW information sheet

'Working with People with Handicaps', CCETSW information sheet

'Working with Older People', CCETSW information sheet

Resort Representative*, see *Courier (Travel)

Retailing

The retailing industry covers a range of businesses: department stores, supermarkets, cash-and-carry and discount warehouses, mail order firms, local shops, and some manufacturing companies which sell direct to the public. Work opportunities include shop assistants, warehousemen, cashiers, managers – store or department – and buyers; large concerns will also have administrators, personnel officers and transport departments. In some shops the owner or manager must have special training, in a profession such as pharmacy, or in a trade such as butchery. Most people in the retail trade have to work Saturdays and, increasingly, at least one late night a week, but there is often a rota system to make the working week more flexible. Sunday trading is becoming more common, and stores need full staffing. In large stores, bank holiday working is often recompensed by time off plus extra payment.

Qualifications and Training

Sales staff generally do not need academic qualifications and training is on the job. Entrants may work towards NVQs, levels 1 to 4. However, to be taken on as a junior trainee or trainee supervisor, three to four GCSEs or equivalent are required. Trainee managers and buyers need two A levels and some have degrees. Junior and management trainees are trained by their firms and there are also BTEC/ SCOTVEC courses available involving day and evening study and correspondence options. Trainees without A levels may qualify for management traineeship after gaining experience and studying further.

Personal Qualities

Employees in retailing should enjoy meeting and helping people and have a pleasant manner. Those involved with handling money and checking stock should be numerate and methodical. The majority of applicants in retailing must be prepared to spend a great part of the day on their feet, and at times to have little to do.

Starting Salary

On average, sales assistants earn £8300–£8500.

Riding Instructor

Riding instructors teach people, individuals or groups, how to ride. They may also accompany riders who hire horses by the hour and be required to help train horses and look after them, cleaning tack and stables. The work includes teaching in riding schools and clubs and in summer camps, training competition riders and, occasionally, sitting as a judge or examiner.

Qualifications and Training

To take the British Horse Society's assistant instructor certificate, candidates must be members of the Society and, if under 18, have four GCSEs, one of which should be in English. On completion of stages 1, 2 and 3, the preliminary teaching test, a full first aid at work certificate and 500 hours of teaching experience, they are awarded the assistant instructor's certificate.

There are two methods of training: at a school, paying fees for instruction, board and lodging – the courses can be as short as three months or as long as a year, depending on the type of course; or as a working pupil at a riding school, doing stable work while receiving some instruction. This takes one year, the last three months being a concentrated course of instruction. Pupils pay for their keep, and the instruction is given in return for their work.

After being awarded the assistant instructor's certificate, candidates may take the intermediate instructor's exams after reaching 20. At 22 intermediate instructors may go on to take the British Horse Society instructor's certificate. The Fellowship may be taken from 25 years.

Personal Qualities

Patience and authority, but above all a love of horses, are indispensable for this work. A riding instructor must enjoy being out of doors and get on well with people, especially children.

Starting Salary

£6000–£8000 for an assistant instructor as a rough guide; the amount will vary depending on whether instruction is being provided, accommodation and stabling for the instructor's own horse, and the instructor's age and experience.

Further Information

The British Horse Society, British Equestrian Centre, Stoneleigh, Kenilworth, Warwickshire CV8 2LR; 01203 696697

National Rivers Authority* see *The Environment Agency

Road Haulage *see Lorry Driver, Vehicle Technician, Freight Forwarding*

Moving goods internationally can be very complicated, so a company with goods to dispatch can employ the services of a freight forwarding firm to make the arrangements for them. They will select the means of transport most suited to their requirement of cost, date of delivery and nature of the goods. Freight forwarders will be responsible for the documentation, for legal and insurance requirements and for the clearance of cargo through customs.

Qualifications and Training

For driving, no formal educational qualifications are required, but drivers are tested for road sense by the licensing authorities. A variety of training schemes is available; length of training varies according to type of vehicle driven.

Mechanics are usually expected to have GSCEs or equivalent in maths and a science and their apprenticeship averages four years.

Trainee managers need to show a good basic educational background and will train for a varying period depending on their type of work.

To take the Chartered Institute of Transport's qualifying examinations five GCSEs and one or two A levels are necessary, or equivalents.

Personal Qualities

Drivers need to have a robust physique, stamina, initiative, practical intelligence, and a liking for an active, roving life. They must be responsible, safety-conscious, able to keep to schedules and to understand something of vehicle mechanics.

Mechanical staff need the usual technical abilities, plus physical fitness, a sense of responsibility and an affinity for motor vehicles.

For managerial and clerical staff the qualifications are more general, but an interest in road transport is obviously paramount. Possession of the Royal Society of Arts certificate of professional competence (CPC) is very worthwhile.

Starting Salary

Drivers earn from £150–£250 a week; mechanics £65–£70 at 16, £150–£230 when qualified. Managers' salaries are variable and negotiable.

Further Information

The Chartered Institute of Transport, 80 Portland Place, London W1N 4DP; 0171 636 9952

Freight Transport Association, Hermes House, St John's Road, Tunbridge Wells, Kent TN4 9UZ; 01892 526171

Institute of Road Transport Engineers, 22 Greencoat Place, London SW1P 1PR; 0171 630 1111

Institute of Transport Administration, 32 Palmerston Road, Southampton SO1 1LL; 01703 631380

Road Haulage and Distribution Training Council, Suite C, Shenley Hall, Rectory Lane, Shenley, Radlett, Hertfordshire WD7 9AN; 01923 858461

Road Haulage Association, Roadway House, 35 Monument Hill, Weybridge, Surrey KT13 8RN; 01932 841515

RTITB Services Centre, York House, Empire Way, Wembley, Middlesex HA9 0RT; 0181 902 8880

Road Transport *see Road Haulage*

This industry includes road haulage, plus passenger transport and commercial companies that have their own transport and delivery facilities. The commercial companies need to plan the flow of materials or parts for manufacturing and the subsequent delivery of their products to their customers. Similarly retail organisations need transport to bring merchandise to their outlets. Passenger transport covers bus and coach services. The work divides basically into loading, moving and unloading, and a wide range of operative and administrative staff is involved in these operations: drivers, warehousemen, depot managers, mechanics, clerical staff, transport planners and many others. There is a variety of public-sector and private-sector employers.

Qualifications and Training

Jobs range from those that demand formal qualifications to those that require a degree. Training varies similarly. However, there are a number of relevant courses: NVQs in road passenger and road freight transport for operative staffs; the BTEC/SCOTVEC national certificate, entry requirements four GCSEs or equivalent to include English and maths; the Chartered Institute of Transport qualifying examination course, entry requirements five GCSEs and one or two A levels, or equivalents. A degree in transport or business subjects may lead to full or partial exemption from the qualifying exam.

Personal Qualities

Similar personal qualities are necessary as apply to road haulage.

Starting Salary

Drivers earn from £150–£250 a week, mechanics £65–£70 at 16 to around £150–£230 when qualified; clerks £6000–£7000 a year at 16, £10,000+ with experience; warehousemen £8000+, transport managers £12,000–£16,000+.

Further Information
See addresses under *Road Haulage*.

Roofer

This title covers a variety of jobs concerned with erecting a roof: laying down roofing felt, nailing down wooden battens to support tiles, tiling and slating. Other specialities include built-up felt roofing when layers of felt are alternated with tar, then finished off with slabs of concrete or other materials; and roof sheeting, when large sheets of waterproof material are attached to roof frames. Some roof work includes working from scaffolding.

Qualifications and Training
Formal educational requirements are not necessary. Apprenticeship lasts for three years; training is on the job and at training centres, leading to NVQs, levels 2 and 3, awarded jointly by City and Guilds and the Construction Industry Training Board.

Personal Qualities
A head for heights is essential, plus an ability to work out of doors in all weather conditions.

Starting Salary
Recommended weekly rates are: £73.90 at 16; £103.46 at 17; £147.81 at 18; and, when qualified, the Craftsman rate is £178.62.

Further Information
Construction Industry Training Board, Bircham Newton, King's Lynn, Norfolk PE31 6RH; 01553 776677 (ext 2466)

Royal Air Force

The RAF consists of a small flying force (almost exclusively officers) supported by a large number of ground workers including engineers, mechanics, caterers, air traffic controllers, medical personnel and many more categories. Altogether it embraces over 18 officer branches and 40 different non-commissioned trades. It integrated with the Women's Royal Air Force in 1994.

Qualifications and Training

Officers
Candidates for permanent commissions must be between 17½ and 39 (24 for pilot) years old and have at least five GCSEs/Standard grades at grade C/level 3 or above including English and maths, and two A levels at grade C or three Highers. Training for a pilot is about three years. Other officers train for varying periods depending on the job. The RAF offer students sponsorship while still qualifying – ranging from a bursary at £1500 per year to a salary paid up to £26,000 for a three-year degree.

Non-commissioned Personnel
Candidates must be between 16½ and 39. Entry at the lowest level requires no formal qualification. Other levels vary in their requirements – for example, technician candidates need GCSEs/SCEs at grade C/level 3 or above in maths and physics or their equivalent. Length of training varies with trade.

Personal Qualities
Air force personnel must enjoy teamwork and a disciplined regime. They need physical fitness, dedication, commitment, initiative and a sense of responsibility.

Starting Salary
The following are intended to give an indication of salary: officer cadets £10,165, pilot officers £14,486, flying officers £19,147. Under 16 entry receive £5653, £6862 at 17. Those over 17 receive £9077. In addition to basic salaries, there are many extra allowances; for example, travel, accommodation and overseas service.

Further Information
Local RAF Careers Information Offices

Royal Marines

The Royal Marines is an arm of the Royal Navy whose personnel are trained for amphibious assaults and for commando operations on land. It has a well-deserved reputation for toughness, and training is arduous.

Qualifications and Training

Officers

Full career entry is between 17½ and 22, and at least two GCE A levels are required. Graduates can enter up to the age of 25. Basic training varies from 15 months to three years depending on the intended length of service and level of entry. Undergraduates may be recruited on a university cadetship scheme whereby they are sponsored throughout their time at university.

Other Ranks

Entry for most categories is between 17½ and 28. Recruits are given 14 weeks' initial training, plus a period of more advanced training, depending on category for length.

Personal Qualities

The same basic qualities are needed as for the other services: discipline, dedication, fitness, initiative and an ability to work with others, plus an appetite for operating in tough conditions.

Starting Salary

Officers' salaries start from £9774–£13,932; ratings' salaries start from £717 a month. Extra allowances are made for such items as education and family separation etc.

Further Information

Local Royal Navy Careers Information Offices

Directorate of Naval Recruiting, Victory Building, HM Naval Base, Portsmouth PO1 3S

Officers Enquiry Section (*address above*)

Royal Navy

Navy personnel work in the nation's combat fleet and at its land bases. Like the other services, the Navy uses many trades and skills. It is the smallest of the three armed forces.

Qualifications and Training

Officers

Entry is on various levels, each of which has different age limits and requirements. For the Naval College, entrants must be between 17 and 23 and have five acceptable GCSE grades including English language and maths, and two A levels. Length of training varies likewise according to level of entry, intended length of service and other factors. Undergraduates may take advantage of the cadetship scheme whereby the Navy sponsors them throughout their time at university.

Ratings

For most categories the age of entry is 16–33 and most candidates do not have to possess formal qualifications but only pass a selection test. The majority have six weeks of initial training, followed by specialised training, varying in length according to category.

Personal Qualities

For most Navy personnel a liking for the sea is important. Other requirements are the same as for the other services: discipline, dedication, fitness, initiative and an ability to work with others.

Starting Salary

Officers' salaries start from £9774–£13,932; ratings' salaries from £717 a month at 18. Extra allowances are payable for accommodation, removal etc.

Further Information

See addresses under *Royal Marines*.

RSPCA Inspector

Inspectors for the Royal Society for the Prevention of Cruelty to Animals deal with complaints from the general public about the alleged ill-treatment of animals, and also perform more routine tasks. Inspectors have no power to take an animal from its owner unless the owner legally signs it over. They may caution people and, in some circumstances, the organisation will ensure that cases go before the courts. Inspectors also visit boarding kennels, pet shops and riding schools. They can be involved in physical rescues, often working unsociable hours and driving considerable distances.

Qualifications and Training

A good general education is necessary, personal attributes being more important than formal qualifications. However, GCSEs or equivalent in English and a science are an advantage. Training is by a six-month training course at the RSPCA Training School. Candidates must have the academic capability to deal with the study of animal law in depth and dexterity to deal with ropes, boats and ladders in rescue situations.

Personal Qualities
As well as having compassion for animals, inspectors must be firm, authoritative, tactful, persuasive and have good communication skills.

Starting Salary
In the region of £9800 plus an accommodation allowance.

Further Information
Chief Superintendent, Training School, RSPCA Headquarters, Causeway, Horsham, West Sussex RH12 1HG; 01403 264181
Careers Working with Animals, Kogan Page

S

Saddler

Saddle-making is still carried out by hand, so craftsmen of considerable experience are needed. They usually work in one of the many small companies which specialise in saddlery and harness-making, and other leather goods such as satchels and wallets. Saddlers' shops stock all these items and may also stock suitcases and sports goods, and offer a repair service.

Qualifications and Training

The Society of Master Saddlers administers a four-year apprenticeship indenture scheme leading to certification by the Worshipful Company of Saddlers. Saddlery courses of varying lengths are available at the Cordwainers College in Hackney and the Walsall College of Arts and Technology. Cordwainers College offers two courses in saddlery: a diploma in saddlery studies and an HND in saddlery technology. Both courses cover many aspects of running a small business, and both last for two years.

NVQs in both the manufacturing and rural saddlery sectors are being developed; a level 2 qualification is now available.

Personal Qualities

Painstaking attention to detail and pride in craftsmanship are needed. Owners of saddlers' shops often have a strong interest in horses too.

Starting Salary

£70–£200+ with experience.

Further Information

Cordwainers College, Mare Street, London E8 3RE; 0181 985 0273

The Saddlers Company, Saddlers Hall, 40 Gutter Lane, London EC2V 6BR; 0171 726 8661

Walsall College of Arts and Technology, Leather Department, Broadway Training, 54–57 Wisemore, Walsall WS2 8EQ; 01922 657000

Salesperson,* see *Representative – Selling, Retailing

Sales Representative,* see *Representative – Selling

Sawyer,* see *Furniture and Furnishing

Secretary *see Personal Assistant*

A secretary probably works for several people and is a member of a management team, or may be employed by an agency as a temporary secretary (ie working at a different organisation every few weeks). The work is extremely varied, but secretaries must have accurate skills (ie shorthand or audio typewriting, word processing and computer skills). He or she may act as: administrator, information centre, organiser of the boss(es)' day, progress chaser, arranger of travel and meetings, receptionist, communicator (oral and written) internally and externally. A secretary may be asked to assume responsibility without direct supervision and take decisions within the scope of assigned authority.

Bilingual Secretary
He or she is usually fluent in a second or third language and may work in commerce, overseas or as an EU employee.

Farm Secretary
In addition to accurate skills (including the use of computers), the work involves helping the employer to complete forms, keep records and accounts, calculate farm employees' wages etc. A farm secretary may work for one employer, be freelance or be sent out by an agency to smaller farms.

Legal Secretary
Accurate skills have always been paramount for legal paperwork, but word processors have made the job much easier. Legal secretaries are employed by barristers and solicitors (in professional practice and in large commercial organisations).

Medical Secretary
Medical secretaries are good administrators, keep records, handle correspondence and filing. They work in hospitals, for individual doctors/consultants and in health centres.

Qualifications and Training

NVQs in administration are available, levels 2 and 3. GCSEs are usually required to obtain a place on a full-time secretarial course. A good knowledge of English and spelling is essential. Additional qualifications are needed to specialise as a legal, medical or farm secretary.

Personal Qualities

Good secretaries are judged by what they do, but qualities such as self-motivation, discretion, tact, loyalty, personality, flexibility, communication skills and smart appearance are expected.

Starting Salary

About £10,000 without experience in London, senior secretaries in London earn from £14,000–£23,000.

Further Information

The Association of Legal Secretaries, The Mill, Clymping Street, Clymping, Littlehampton, West Sussex BN17 5RN; 01903 714276

Association of Medical Secretaries, Practice Administrators and Receptionists, Tavistock House North, Tavistock Square, London WC1H 9LN; 0171 387 6005

Institute of Linguists, 24a Highbury Grove, London N5 2EA; 0171 359 7445

Institute of Qualified Private Secretaries, First Floor, 6 Bridge Avenue, Maidenhead FL6 1RR; 01628 25007 (625007 in 1998)

Security Work

There are many aspects of security work which include patrolling, guarding, operating delivery services for documents and valuables, advice on burglary prevention and installation of security systems. There is also work in other areas such as preventing industrial espionage, the personal protection of public figures and the supplying of store detectives. The industry has two main sections – 'in house', where major manufacturers and distributors have their own security force dealing with the protection of their property and assets, and 'contract guarding'. This includes guards, patrolmen, drivers of 'cash-in-transit' vans etc.

Qualifications and Training

Experience and skills such as those acquired in the armed forces or the police are useful. Otherwise there are no specific entry requirements and no formal training, although many larger companies give some training in the equipment used, legal responsibilities and relations between the company, the police and the public. However, the introduction of NVQs (level 2) means that there are recognised training standards which provide an effective career structure for employees.

Personal Qualities

It is essential to have an impeccable background for security work plus a fair amount of strength and common sense, initiative and reliability. Entrants must also be prepared for night work

Starting Salary

There is a great variety in payment which may range from £3.50 an hour to £5 an hour for guards.

Further Information

British Security Industry Association Limited, Security House, Barbourne Road, Worcester WR1 1RS; 01905 21464

Inspectorate of the Security Industry, Security House, Barbourne Road, Worcester WR1 1RS; 01905 617499

International Institute of Security, IPSA House, 3 Dendy Road, Paignton, Devon TQ4 5BD; 01803 554849

International Professional Security Association, IPSA House, 3 Dendy Road, Paignton, Devon TQ4 5DB; 01803 554849

Security Industry Training Organisation, Security House, Barbourne Road, Worcester WR1 1RS; 01905 20004

Service Engineer,* see *Electrician

Service Mechanic

Mechanics are needed to service and repair a range of business machines such as typewriters and photocopiers, as well as domestic machines such as washing machines and televisions. Service mechanics are employed by machine manufacturers; although some work may be done in the company's workshop, more frequently the mechanic will visit offices or private homes.

It is also necessary to service office information technology equipment and systems. This work is not done by 'mechanics' as there is no mechanical element involved in the equipment.

Qualifications and Training
These vary, but formal academic qualifications are not necessary. Some employers require City and Guilds certificates in mechanical, electrical or electronic engineering. Training is then given in the company workshop. Some employers (for example, sewing machine manufacturers) train completely on the job without requiring prior qualifications.

Personal Qualities
Service mechanics spend a great deal of their time in other people's homes; for this reason a polite and friendly manner plus the ability to work quickly and neatly are useful. A driving licence is an advantage.

Starting Salary
£65–£70 a week at 16, and £160+ when trained.

Further Information
Local Jobcentres and Careers Offices

Sheet Metal Worker

Sheet metal workers, known too as platers and boilermakers, are engaged in shaping, cutting and joining together pieces of metal.

Sheet metal workers work with thin metal sheet up to 3mm thick and use a wide range of hand and power tools to manipulate it. They make such items as aircraft sections and car prototypes.

Boilermakers work with thick metal plates from 3mm thick upwards. As well as hand and power tools, heavy presses are needed to bend the plate. Products include ship and submarine parts and industrial boilers.

Qualifications and Training
No formal educational qualifications are required but mathematical ability is necessary. It is possible to work without a formal apprenticeship. However, if one is entered into an apprenticeship training takes four years, during which time courses are available leading to NVQs sponsored by City and Guilds and the Engineering Industry Training Board.

Personal Qualities
Sheet metal workers must be good at working with their hands, able to read technical drawings, strong, able to work in a noisy atmosphere, and as one of a team.

Starting Salary
About £85 a week at 16, when trained £230.

Further Information
Engineering Careers Information Service, 54 Clarendon Road, Watford, Hertfordshire WD1 1LB; 01923 238441
Local Jobcentres and Careers Offices

Shipbroker

Shipbrokers act as go-betweens for shipowners, looking for cargoes to fill their vessels, and charterers, seeking to ship their dry cargo and tanker requirements. Sale and purchase of vessels is also an important service offered to their clients. Brokers are paid commissions on the contracts arranged. The Baltic Exchange in London is the centre of the chartering market which covers the whole world and keeps a register of those seeking employment in this field. Additionally there are shipbrokers/ship's agents in ports who make arrangements when a ship calls for customs clearance, loading and discharging cargoes, crew requirements etc. Such port agents which attend to cargo liners may also be involved in marketing and documenting cargo. In order to maintain contact with the international scene, shipbrokers tend to work long hours and to travel abroad frequently.

Qualifications and Training
There are no specific academic qualifications needed for shipbroking beyond a good general educational background. However, members of a firm who wish to make a career in the shipping business usually study for the examination leading to membership of the Institute of Chartered Shipbrokers. Such study can be part time or by correspondence course and covers not only shipping practice but more general studies in commerce, law and geography. The Institute also offers a Foundation Diploma in shipping for those just beginning in the business.

Personal Qualities
A good business sense, the ability to learn through practical experience, willingness to work long and irregular hours and to travel are all necessary.

Starting Salary
Earnings vary greatly.

Further Information

The Baltic Exchange, 14–20 St Mary Axe, London EC3A 8BH; 0171 623 5501

The Institute of Chartered Shipbrokers, 3 St Helen's Place, London EC3A 6EJ; 0171 628 5559

Shipbuilding

The shipbuilding industry employs a high proportion of craftsmen to carry out the many processes in constructing and fitting out a ship. The jobs available tend to fall into one of four main groups: metal-using (platers or shipwrights, welders, caulkers, burners, drillers, riveters, boilermen and blacksmiths); outfitting (electricians, pipe-workers, joiners, sheet-metal workers, ship riggers and woodcutting machinists); engineering (fitters, turners, machinists and wood-working shipwrights); and non-craft manual work (crane drivers, plater's helpers, outfitting workers and stagers). There are a number of commercial shipbuilding companies involved in constructing both merchant and naval vessels.

Qualifications and Training

A period of apprenticeship is served by anyone training in the above shipbuilding crafts. Some of the larger employers demand GCSEs or equivalents for entry into an apprenticeship but academic qualifications are not always necessary. The first year of an apprenticeship is often spent at a special training centre, further training leads to an NVQ/SVQ award.

Personal Qualities

Manual dexterity and some physical strength are required in most shipbuilding work. Entrants should also be prepared to work out of doors for much of the time.

Starting Salary

£29.50 at 16; £35 at 17 rising to £160 during the apprenticeship.

Further Information

Engineering and Marine Training Authority, Vector House, 41 Clarendon Road, Watford, Hertfordshire WD1 1HS; 01923 238441; Fax: 01923 256069

Shop Assistant*, see *Retailing

Shopfitter, see *Carpenter and Bench Joiner*

Signwriter

Signwriters design and hand-paint company names and logos on to shop fronts and the sides of vans and lorries; they may also paint estate agents' signboards and a wide variety of other temporary signs and notices. Some signwriters are in business on their own, others work for commercial signwriting companies.

Qualifications and Training

Some commercial signwriting firms may take on trainees who also take an evening course such as that run by City and Guilds. An art school course in graphic design will normally include some typography and signwriting in the syllabus and will provide a wider training; academic qualifications are not always necessary for entry to art school for those with exceptional talent.

Personal Qualities

Artistic talent combined with an interest in lettering is a prerequisite for this job.

Starting Salary

Low initially; when trained £160+ a week.

Further Information

Local Jobcentres and Careers Offices

Social Work

Social workers are employed in a number of settings: in area offices, in day centres, in offices near the courts, in residential hostels, hospitals, health centres or group practices, child guidance clinics, day or boarding schools or prisons. Social workers employ three main methods of working: case work, group work and youth and community work.

Case work is the main method used by local authority social service departments. Each social worker has a case load of 20 cases upwards and gives a personal service to each of his or her clients. Group work is increasingly in use to tackle a variety of problems. The social worker arranges for groups of people with common problems to meet together and discuss ways of solving them. Youth and community workers are employed in a particular neighbourhood and connect the residents there with the services available to them. Community work can vary tremendously, depending on the type of area and the individual worker. Community workers also play an important part in trying to keep local race relations harmonious. (*See* Community Work, page 83.)

Psychiatric Social Worker

Psychiatric social workers deal with people who are seriously depressed or suffering from some form of mental illness. They work to resolve or alleviate personal, emotional or environmental problems and thus help patients to recover. They often work in psychiatric hospitals or in special units such as clinics for the treatment of drug, solvent or alcohol abuse or in general medical practices or health centres as part of the primary healthcare team.

Medical Social Worker

Medical social workers may be employed in a hospital or by the local authority's social services department, to help with problems that arise as a result of illness or disability. These include ensuring that children whose mother is in hospital receive necessary care; helping patients and family with aftercare in the case of a disability, with a particular condition such as diabetes or kidney failure; or with the emotional adjustment to the possibility of death. The help may be of a practical nature, or it may mean giving counselling or information about where further help and benefits can be obtained.

Qualifications and Training

The main professional qualification is the diploma in social work (DipSW) which can be studied for part time while working full time via a college course. Entry requirements are five GCSEs including two at A level or five SCEs including three at H level. Mature entrants may be accepted without these qualifications.

Personal Qualities

The desire to help people is of paramount importance; sympathy, tolerance, a sense of humour and perseverance are also assets to the social worker. It is important that candidates should be able to get on with people from all backgrounds.

Starting Salary

£13,581–£19,818.

Further Information

England: CCETSW Information Service, Derbyshire House, St Chad's Street, London WC1H 8AD; 0171 278 2455

Northern Ireland: CCETSW Information Service, 6 Malone Road, Belfast BT9 5BN; 01232 665390

Scotland: CCETSW Information Service, 78–80 George Street, Edinburgh EH2 3BU; 0131 220 0093

Wales: CCETSW Information Service, South Gate House, Wood Street, Cardiff CF1 1EW; 01222 226257

Careers in Social Work, Kogan Page

Solicitor

The role of the solicitor is to provide his or her clients with skilled legal representation and advice. The clients can be individual people or companies or any type of organisation or group. A solicitor can work on all kinds of legal matters from buying a home to defending people accused of murder; from selling a corporation to drafting a complicated will or trust. Solicitors may also represent their clients in all courts but often a solicitor will brief a barrister to represent the client and act as liaison between them. While some solicitors may deal with a variety of legal problems, others specialise in a particular area such as shipping, planning and construction, financial services or social security. Specialisation within the profession is increasing.

The majority of solicitors work in private practice with firms made up of several partners. Many others work as employed solicitors in commerce, industry, local and central government, and other organisations. Some solicitors are employed in the Army Legal Services giving advice on all aspects of service and civil law which may affect the Army.

Qualifications and Training

The Law Society governs the training of solicitors, which takes place in two stages – the academic and the professional. Most, but not all, entrants to the profession are graduates. Training begins for non-law graduates by taking the Law Society's common professional examination (CPE); those with the qualifying law degrees are exempt from this. The next stage, the vocational stage, is taken by means of the legal practice course which is undertaken at one of the many colleges or universities running the course.

It is a one-year full-time or two-year part-time course. The trainee solicitor then has to undertake a two-year training contract with an authorised firm or organisation. During the course of this, a 20-day professional skills course is undertaken, usually on a modular basis.

Personal Qualities

A high level of academic achievement, integrity, good communication skills, patience, discretion, a good command of language, and problem-solving skills are all required.

Starting Salary

Salaries vary but trainees can receive up to about £20,000 in the City of London and newly qualified solicitors can earn considerably more than this. Those working for provincial solicitors and for small firms may find the salaries slightly lower. The Law Society lays down minimum salaries below which trainees cannot be paid. On average qualified solicitors earn £28,000–£30,000.

Further Information

The Law Society Information Services, Ipsley Court, Berrington Close, Redditch, Worcestershire B98 0TD; 01527 504400

The Law Society of Scotland, 26 Drumsheugh Gardens, Edinburgh EH3 7YR; 0131 226 7411

Directorate of Army Legal Services (ALS 1), Ministry of Defence, AGC Centre, Worthy Down, Winchester SO21 2RG

Careers in the Law, Kogan Page

Speech and Language Therapist

Speech and language therapists (SLTs) identify, assess and treat people who have communication disorders. A large proportion of these will be children but SLTs also help adults who may have speech problems caused by disease, accident or psychological trauma. Some SLTs may specialise in a particular patient group, for example, in the areas of severe learning difficulties, hearing impairment or neurological disorders, while others choose more general, broad-based practice. The National Health Service is the largest employer of SLTs, using them in community clinics, hospitals, special schools and homes for the mentally or physically disabled. Some of the larger voluntary organisations also employ SLTs. Often the SLT works closely in a team which may include members of the medical, teaching, therapeutic, psychological and other caring professions.

Qualifications and Training

Speech and language therapy is a degree entry profession. Courses leading to professional qualifications are offered at 15 universities and colleges of higher education throughout the United Kingdom, with three- and four-year courses providing both honours and ordinary degree qualifications. In addition, there are a number of two-year postgraduate diploma and masters courses available to candidates with relevant degrees.

Entry qualifications for courses vary from one institution to another, but the minimum is five GCSEs and two A levels or seven SCE passes with three at Higher grade. A good balance of language and science is expected. Other equivalent qualifications are considered on merit.

All courses will consider applications from mature students (ie over 21) who are encouraged to apply in the normal way.

Students who successfully pass all academic and clinical components of an accredited course are eligible to obtain a certificate to practise and to enter the professional register of the Royal College of Speech and Language Therapists as full professional members.

Personal Qualities

It is essential that speech therapists themselves should have clear speech, with a good ear. In addition, they must have a real interest in people as individuals, as well as an enquiring mind, initiative, patience, imagination and a willingness to take responsibility.

Starting Salary

£12,500 upwards.

Further Information

Royal College of Speech and Language Therapists, 7 Bath Place, Rivington Street, London EC2A 3DR; 0171 613 3855

'Speech Therapist' (Health Service Careers, PO Box 204, London SE5 7ES)

Sport and Recreation Facility Management *see Leisure and Amenity Management*

Sport and recreation facility managers are responsible for the efficient running of leisure centres, swimming pools, sports halls and associated facilities. Managers usually start their careers as recreation assistants and progress through supervisory and assistant manager positions and by on-the-job training and professional development.

Qualifications and Training

The Institute of Sport and Recreation Management (ISRM) offers a comprehensive programme of training and qualifications designed to cover all aspects of sport and recreation facility management and operation ranging from recreation assistant, NVQ level 2 and supervisor, NVQ level 3, to management, NVQ levels 4 and 5.

Personal Qualities
A liking for people, a strong interest in sport and organising skills are essential. Swimming and lifesaving ability are essential for swimming pool work.

Starting Salary
Recreation assistants 18 years old around £155 a week; managers' salaries are variable depending upon level of responsibilities, type of facility, location, qualifications and experience.

Further Information
Institute of Sport and Recreation Management, Giffard House, 36–38 Sherrard Street, Melton Mowbray, Leicestershire LE13 1XJ; 01664 65531

Sportsperson *see Coach, Jockey, Leisure and Amenity Management*

There are opportunities in sport as a professional or a coach.

Professional Sportsperson
Not all sports allow players to be professionals, and there are others, such as snooker, where there is room for only a very few professionals. Sports attracting professionals in relatively large numbers are: football, cricket, golf, horse racing, rugby league and tennis.

Sports people's careers are generally short but, if during their careers they have made a name for themselves, there may be opportunities in journalism, broadcasting or consultancy work.

Qualifications and Training
Professional sportspeople naturally need to be very good at their sport. Those in team games generally begin by playing for their school, town or county side. It is in this way, in the case of football, for example, that a young player may be noticed by professional selectors. It is not necessary to join one's local football league club; apprentices are taken on from all over the country. Because a club apprentice has no guarantee that he will ever play for the first side, some clubs encourage apprentices and allow them time off to obtain academic qualifications.

Coaches must gain recognised coaching qualifications which are awarded by the governing bodies of the various sports and acquired either at evening class or weekend school.

Personal Qualities

As well as talent, professional sportspeople must possess dedication, perseverance, commitment and a degree of ruthlessness. Coaches and teachers too need perseverance but also patience, tact and the ability to inspire children or adults of very different abilities, often in less than ideal situations.

Starting Salary

Salaries for professionals are often low initially; however, the rewards for top performers may be very high. Coaches' salaries vary according to whether the work is full or part time, type of work and number of hours.

Further Information

Institute of Professional Sport, Francis House, Francis Street, London SW1P 1DE; 0171 630 7486

The English Sports Council, 16 Upper Woburn Place, London WC1H 0QP; 0171 388 1500

The Scottish Sports Council, Caledonia House, South Gyle, Edinburgh EH12 9DQ; 0131 317 7200

The Sports Council for Wales, Sophia Gardens, Cardiff CF1 9SW; 01222 397571

Careers in Sport, Kogan Page

Careers in Sport Compendium, The English Sports Council

Stage Manager*, see *Theatre

Statistician

Statisticians are concerned with the collection, analysis and interpretation of numerical data. They work in both central and local government, commerce and industry, universities and other research and teaching institutions.

Qualifications and Training

Most statisticians begin their careers by gaining a degree in statistics, or a mathematics degree with a specialisation in statistics, or a postgraduate diploma in statistics. Alternatives are an examination administered by the Royal Statistical Society, for which a three-year course of study is necessary, or the relevant BTEC/SCOTVEC certificate or diploma at a very high grade.

Personal Qualities

Skill at mathematics, a logical mind and the ability to select and interpret essential facts and figures are required, and also the ability to communicate the results.

Starting Salary

£11,000+.

Further Information

Royal Statistical Society, 12 Errol Street, London EC1Y 8LX; 0171 638 8998

'Careers in Statistics' (The Royal Statistical Society)

Steel Erector*, see *Building

Steeplejack

Steeplejacks are the mavericks of the building industry, able to tackle any job at any height in any trade. While working high up, safety chairs and harnesses are used and sometimes safety nets and rescue lines. Steeplejacks are mostly employed on repair and maintenance work: painting, pointing brick and masonry. Basic electrical skills are needed on some jobs.

Some firms of steeplejacks specialise; for example, in power station chimneys, demolition work, restoration work, erecting and maintaining lightning conductors.

Qualifications and Training

The Construction Industry Training Board offers a course for those aged 16 and over. The course provides some work experience and is an entry to the industry's own apprenticeship scheme. NVQs are available at levels 1, 2 and 3.

Personal Qualities

A head for heights is most important, plus the ability to work quickly, neatly and carefully, and being prepared to work on one's own for longish periods.

Starting Salary

Recommended weekly rates are: £73.90 at 16; £103.46 at 17; £147.81 at 18; and, when qualified, the Craftsman rate is £178.62.

Further Information

Construction Industry Training Board, Bircham Newton, King's Lynn, Norfolk PE31 6RH; 01553 776677 (ext 2466)

National Federation of Master Steeplejacks and Lightning Conductor Engineers, 4D St Mary's Place, The Lace Market, Nottingham NG1 1PH; 0115 955 8818

Stockbroker

A stockbroker works for one of the broking companies which is a member of the Stock Exchange. Stockbrokers buy and sell securities on the Stock Exchange on behalf of investors, who may be individuals but are increasingly institutions such as banks, insurance companies, pension funds or unit trusts.

Traditionally securities were traded face to face on a market floor. Now much trade is carried out by stockbrokers from their own dealing rooms.

Qualifications and Training

School-leavers aged 16 to 18 with good GCSEs can join stockbroking firms as clerical staff. Graduates may also join as trainee brokers; recruitment at all levels is mainly by recommendation and personal introduction. All entrants to this profession can eventually become members of the Stock Exchange provided they are over 21 years old, have had at least three years' experience and have passed the Stock Exchange examination. They must be proposed and seconded by members and pay a large entry fee, which their employers may help them with.

Personal Qualities

It is necessary to be able to think and calculate quickly and have a good memory.

Starting Salary

Young clerks begin at £8000–£9000; brokers' salaries depend on the amount of business carried out but £45,000+ is fairly average, and a top stockbroker may earn £275,000+.

Further Information

The Securities Institute, Centurion House, 24 Monument Street, London EC3R 8AJ; 0171 626 3191

Stonemason

Stonemasons repair and restore stonework on old buildings and also provide stonework for new buildings, anything from walls, cladding and paving, to arches, staircases and fireplaces. The two kinds of masonry work are banking and fixing. Banker masons prepare the rough stone ready for use in a building and fixers assemble the stone where needed. In large firms the jobs are separate but in smaller firms a mason may do both.

There are many different jobs for stonemasons: some specialise in monumental work – making and carving grave stones; others specialise in particular types of stone – for example, granite, marble, limestone.

Qualifications and Training

Formal academic qualifications are not required. Training is by a three-year apprenticeship supplemented by study through day or block release leading to NVQs, levels 2 and 3, awarded jointly by City and Guilds and the Construction Industry Training Board.

The Building Crafts College also offers a one-year full time City and Guilds course in Advanced Stonemasonry – this covers basic traditional stonemasonry up to City and Guilds Craft level (NVQ 3) and additionally stone carving, letter cutting and conservation and restoration techniques.

Personal Qualities

Manual skills are all-important in stonemasonry; candidates must be strong, prepared to work out of doors and possess great patience and accuracy.

Starting Salary

Recommended weekly rates are: £73.90 at 16; £103.46 at 17; £147.81 at 18; and, when qualified, the Craftsman rate is £178.62.

Further Information

Building Crafts College, 153 Great Titchfield Street, London W1P 7FR; 0171 636 0480

College of Masons (General Secretary: R Francis), 42 Magdalen Road, London SW18 3NP; 0181 874 8363

Construction Industry Training Board, Bircham Newton, King's Lynn, Norfolk PE31 6RH; 01553 776677 (ext 2466)

Stores Supervisor*, see *Purchasing Officer

Structural Engineering*, see *Engineering

Studio Manager*, see *Broadcasting

Sub-editor*, see *Journalist

Surveyor/Surveying Technician

Surveying covers a wide variety of work within the one profession and there are a number of professional bodies offering qualifications in these different areas, which are set out below. There are also technician qualifications. Surveying technicians work in all the same fields as surveyors but without being professionally qualified.

General Practice

This includes auctioneering, estate agency, valuation and estate management. People working in this area are responsible for the selling or letting, surveying, valuation and management of both urban and rural property. Qualifications in general practice are offered by the Royal Institution of Chartered Surveyors (RICS), the Incorporated Society of Valuers and Auctioneers (ISVA), the Association of Building Engineers (ABE), the Institute of Revenues, Rating and Valuation (IRRV) and the Architects' and Surveyors' Institute. Technician qualifications are also offered by the Society of Surveying Technicians (SST).

Aerial Surveying

A specialisation of land surveying (see below), this involves photogrammetry – the use of aerial photographs as a basis for calculations.

Rural Practice

This is often combined with land agency and concerns the use and development of agricultural land. The qualifying bodies in this area are RICS, ISVA, the Architects' and Surveyors' Institute (ASI) and the SST.

Archaeological Surveying
This relatively new specialisation involves working on an archaeological dig, making plans, maps and cross-sections of the excavations. It thus involves the skill of a cartographer as well as that of a land surveyor. The Architects' and Surveyors' Institute has members in this discipline.

Building Surveying
The structural surveying of properties and reporting on their condition and valuation is carried out by building surveyors/building engineers. They advise on necessary repairs and maintenance and prepare plans and specifications for alterations and improvements. Local and central government employ a large proportion of qualified building surveyors, although many are in private practice. Qualifications in this area are available from RICS, ISVA, ABE, ASI and the SST.

Hydrographic Surveying
The hydrographer surveys and charts underwater areas, such as ports and harbours and offshore areas where drilling for oil takes place. Hydrographic surveying qualifications are offered by RICS, ASI and the SST.

Land Surveying
The land surveyor measures and charts the earth's physical features so that maps can be drawn. The scale of the work can range from a one-house building site to a whole region of Africa and there are opportunities in public services (the Ordnance Survey and the Ministry of Defence, for example) as well as in private practice or large commercial organisations. The RICS, ASI and the SST all offer qualifications in land surveying.

Minerals Surveying
Minerals surveyors assist in the design, development and surveying of quarries and underground mines, ensuring safety for the workers as well as optimum profitability for the company extracting the minerals. They also value mineral workings for rating and taxation and therefore need to be all-rounders with a knowledge of geology, the management of mineral workings, taxation and planning legislation. This area of surveying is unique in having its qualifications and duties laid down by law. Mineral surveyors must hold the surveyor's certificate granted on behalf of the Secretary of State for Industry by the Mining Qualifications Board. They must be at least 21 and have at least four years' practical experience (including 2000 hours underground) in order to sit the examination for this certificate. Further qualifications are provided by the RICS, ASI and the SST.

Quantity Surveying
In private practice, quantity surveyors work with an architect to draw up design specifications in line with the client's budget; when the finished design is agreed, the quantity surveyor draws up a bill of quantities, detailing the materials and labour that will be needed. Building contractors work on this bill of quantities in preparing their tender for the job; they will use their own quantity surveyors to estimate their costs. The monitoring of costs as the work progresses and is completed is also carried out by quantity surveyors. If they train for this work while employed by construction contractors, they usually take the qualification of the RICS. Professional qualifications are also offered by the IAAS and ASI. Technician qualifications are offered by SST.

Qualifications and Training

There are several professional bodies offering a range of qualifications in the many different areas of surveying. Minimum entry requirements are generally five GCSE or equivalent passes plus two A levels or three H grades. English and maths passes are required. For graduates there are two components to qualifying as a chartered surveyor. First you must successfully complete a RICS accredited degree or diploma and second a period of practical training known as the Assessment of Professional Competence (APC). Postgraduate conversion courses are also available; full-time one year and part-time two years. Four GCSEs grade A–C or equivalent including English and maths are the entry to technician qualification. Surveying technicians begin by working as trainees in a professional surveyor's office, taking BTEC or SCOTVEC certificates and higher certificates which are being replaced gradually by NVQs and GNVQs.

Personal Qualities

Logical and orderly thinking, ability in figure work and detailed drawings are called for in this precision work. Communication skills and business acumen are essential. Good oral and written English is an asset and some areas may require specialised mathematical ability.

Starting Salary

Trainees at 18 £8000–£9000; graduates with relevant degrees £11,000–£13,800, the higher amounts being paid in London; newly qualified £13,000–£19,000.

Further Information

Architects and Surveyors Institute, St Mary's House, 15 St Mary Street, Chippenham, Wiltshire SN15 3WD; 01249 444505

The Association of Building Engineers (ABE), Jubilee House, Billing Brook Road, Weston Favell, Northampton NN3 8NW; 01604 404121

ISVA (The Incorporated Society of Valuers and Auctioneers), 3 Cadogan Gate, London SW1X 0AS; 0171 235 2282

The Institute of Revenues, Rating and Valuation (IRRV), 41 Doughty Street, London WC1N 2LF; 0171 831 3505

The Royal Institution of Chartered Surveyors (RICS), 12 Great George Street, London SW1P 3AD; 0171 222 7000

The Royal Institution of Chartered Surveyors in Scotland, 9 Manor Place, Edinburgh EH3 7DN; 0131 225 7078

Society of Surveying Technicians, Surveyor Court, Westwood Way, Coventry, West Midlands CV4 8JE

Tax Consultant

Tax consultants/advisers work for private firms or independently, offering assistance to other firms/individuals who need guiding through the complications of the tax laws. A tax consultant would be able to advise his client on how to plan and present his taxable income so that he legally pays the least tax possible.

Tax technicians work for firms of accountants, solicitors, in clearing banks and for consultancy firms who offer a complete tax service to their clients. However, the largest area of work involves corporate tax in organisations which have their own tax department to prepare corporate tax and VAT returns on behalf of the company.

Qualifications and Training

Many tax consultants qualify first as accountants, but a growing number begin with A levels as tax trainees.

The Chartered Institute of Taxation offers a qualifying examination for candidates already qualified as accountants or lawyers. The Association of Taxation Technicians is a starting point for all other tax trainees and offers an examination. This may be sufficient in itself for those candidates who do not expect to give detailed planning advice in their careers, or provide a stepping stone to the Institute's exam.

Personal Qualities

Tax advisers/technicians must be prepared to keep on learning, be able to keep up to date with numerous tax changes each Budget, have an analytical mind, be able to apply lateral thinking and have good communication skills.

Starting Salary

The starting salary is similar to others in finance and the eventual rewards are high.

Further Information

Association of Taxation Technicians, 12 Upper Belgrave Square, London SW1X 8BB; 0171 235 2544
The Chartered Institute of Taxation (*address as above*); 0171 235 9381

Tax Inspector

Tax inspectors work for the Tax Inspectorate of the Inland Revenue, the branch of the Civil Service concerned with assessing income tax, corporation tax and capital gains tax. Inspectors are responsible for particular tax districts (there are about 750 of these) and are often in charge of a substantial number of junior staff (known as revenue officers). They assess the tax liability of individuals and companies, examine appeals against such assessments and (if there is cause) examine possible cases of tax evasion or fraud.

Qualifications and Training

Many tax inspectors work their way up by internal promotion from the lower grades. It is possible to enter as a revenue officer with five GCSEs or equivalent. Training on the job may then lead to internal examinations and promotion to revenue executive, and thence to inspector. Inspectors must qualify in tax law, accountancy and management by means of courses which generally last some three years (and include part-time and private study). Honours graduates with degrees of sufficiently good standard may apply to join via the direct entry scheme and shorten the training time.

Personal Qualities

Tax inspectors must be highly responsible and very discreet. (In fact, they must sign a declaration under the Official Secrets Act saying that they will not discuss their work.) A mathematical mind and an ability to communicate clearly and pleasantly (face to face and on the telephone) are also necessary.

Starting Salary

A newly qualified graduate tax inspector earns from about £12,000–£24,000 in the provinces; salaries in London are higher.

Further Information

Inland Revenue, Somerset House, Strand, London WC2R 1LB; 0171 438 6622

Taxi Driver *see Minicab Driver*

A 'taxi' is a traditional hackney carriage (like the famous black London taxis). The hackney carriage driver is allowed to 'ply for hire', ie drive around the streets looking for passengers, and can be flagged down by a 'fare' (as the passengers are called). They may also operate from taxi ranks (known as 'standing for hire') in the streets. A private hire vehicle, on the other hand, has to be booked over the telephone or in person at the office from which it operates. Drivers therefore spend a good proportion of their time waiting around for passengers. Hours for both types of driver are generally long and anti-social (since there is a good deal of evening or night work as well as weekend and public holiday work involved). Drivers may be owner-drivers (owning their own vehicles and working as and when they please) or may work for a company.

Qualifications and Training

Taxi drivers must be at least 21 years of age to be granted a licence, although in practice, because of insurance requirements, most are over 25. A valid Group A driving licence and relevant driving experience are also necessary. Hackney carriage drivers are legally bound to take the shortest or quickest route to a passenger's destination. Trainee drivers usually have to pass special tests, known as Knowledge Tests to prove that they know their way about sufficiently well. These tests are generally oral, the most demanding being the Knowledge of London Test required before drivers may operate in the capital. This usually takes some 18 months to two years to complete. There are specialised training schools available, and there are also special training schemes for the disabled and for people who have been in the forces. In London, too, an additional driving test must be passed before a licence is granted.

Personal Qualities

Driving in traffic demands a calm, unflappable personality, with lots of patience; drivers also need good memories. In addition a taxi driver must be 'of good character' as a licence will not be granted to anyone who has committed certain offences.

Starting Salary

Almost all taxi drivers are self-employed and have to pay tax and national insurance out of their earnings. Owner-drivers generally earn more than drivers employed by a company (who are often on a fixed rate), although they must also finance the repairs and servicing costs incurred by their own vehicles.

Further Information
Local taxi companies
Licensed Taxi Drivers Association, 9–11 Woodfield Road, London W9 2BA; 0171 286 1046

Teacher

Teaching offers a wide variety of openings working with children and young people of all ages and backgrounds. Teachers do not merely stand in front of a chalkboard and teach facts to their particular class, nor does a teacher's day end when the final bell rings. They are expected to take a full and active part in their pupils' development as well as covering the relevant academic courses for routine examinations. They will also have the opportunity to devise projects, extra-curricular activities, special outings and so on. A good deal of time out of school hours is spent marking work and preparing lessons, and keeping up with new developments in specific subjects or in education as a whole (and this applies to the relatively long holidays, too). The work, naturally enough, varies with the age group being taught. Nursery teachers take the under-fives, infant teachers the five to seven year olds. Secondary education starts at 11 and continues (in some cases) to 18 or 19. In addition, teachers are needed in sixth form colleges and the numerous further and higher education establishments. Teachers at primary, and junior level (8 to 11), generally teach a variety of basic subjects and specialist subject teachers are not introduced until secondary level, although specialist music or sports teachers may be brought in at an earlier age.

Teaching has undergone radical changes in recent years and nowadays a large part of secondary education in comprehensive schools is directed at mixed ability classes, which makes great demands on the teacher concerned. The majority of pupils attend state schools (maintained schools, as they are known), although there are also a limited number of openings in private education. There are also opportunities for teachers in special schools: for the handicapped (either boarding or day establishments), for disturbed children (in community homes or approved schools), for those with learning difficulties (such as deafness, or dyslexia) and in children's hospitals where long-term patients are expected to take lessons. Such schools often make even greater emotional demands on their staff than normal.

Anyone wishing to teach in a state-maintained school in England and Wales must normally hold Qualified Teacher Status (QTS), obtained by completing an approved course of initial teacher training (ITT).

The two main routes to achieve QTS are: (a) the Bachelor of Education (BEd) degree (some institutions offer a BA or BSc degree with QTS) – usually four years; (b) a subject degree appropriate for the national curriculum subject to be taught followed by a postgraduate certificate in education (PGCE) – three years plus one year. Most BEd courses are for primary teaching, and most PGCE courses for secondary teaching.

All applications for either route regardless of subject or teaching level must have attained the standard equivalent to at least grade C in both GCSE English language and maths. (GCSE science is also required from those born after 1 September 1979 entering teacher training courses after 1 September 1998.)

Entry requirements for BEd courses are five different subjects at GCSE grades A to C, two of which must be at A level or equivalent.

Other types of courses have been developed with the more mature entrant in mind: the two-year BEd, designed for those who already have appropriate technical and professional qualifications (eg HND); the two-year part-time PGCE for those with other commitments; and the two-year full-time conversion PGCE for those wishing to teach a subject which is not the main subject of their first degree. These courses are not available for all subjects or at all locations.

Other developments include the introduction of postgraduate school-centred courses and the Open University distance learning PGCE: both these routes require an appropriate degree.

In Scotland would-be teachers may obtain a teaching qualification (in primary education): (a) a university degree course followed by a one-year course at a teacher education institution (TEI); (b) a four-year course at a TEI leading to the award of a BEd. The teaching qualification in secondary education may be obtained by means of: (a) a relevant university degree followed by a one-year TEI course; (b) a four-year BEd degree in music, technology or physical education.

Personal Qualities

Teachers do not merely need good academic ability; they must be able to communicate their knowledge clearly and in an interesting fashion. They must also be able to establish a good relationship with their pupils and be prepared to take on considerable responsibility. Infinite patience and a sense of humour are great assets.

Starting Salary

All qualified teachers in state maintained schools are paid on an 18-point pay scale ranging from £12,711–£34,044. Salaries are scaled according to qualifications, experience, responsibilities and excellence. Those with a first or second class honours degree can expect a starting salary of at least £14,280. Extra allowances are paid for working in London.

Further Information

England and Wales: Teacher Training Agency, Communication Centre, PO Box 3210, Chelmsford, Essex CM1 3WA; 01245 454454

Northern Ireland: Department of Education, Rathgael House, Balloo Road, Bangor, Co Down BT19 7PR; 01247 279000

Scotland: Advisory Service on Entry to Teaching, 5 Royal Terrace, Edinburgh EH7 5AF; 0131 556 0072

Careers in Teaching, Kogan Page

Technical Illustrator

The job involves the drawing of technical subjects, free-hand and in accurate detail. The sort of things illustrated are car engines, the insides of machinery and other scientific, mechanical and technical equipment.

Qualifications and Training

Four GGSEs are preferred. Art is not essential but some artistic ability is necessary. Training is on the job and by attendance at courses. Many courses require the student to have completed a foundation course in art and design. Some firms may offer apprenticeships. City and Guilds qualifications are relevant. There is a BTEC HND course in design (technical illustration), two years, full time, and a BTEC HND course (also two years, full time) in design (illustration).

Personal Qualities

Accuracy, neatness, good concentration and the ability to work on one's own are required.

Starting Salary

Low to begin with, but with experience a salary of £14,500 upwards may be earned.

Further Information

Local Jobcentres and Careers Offices

Technical Writer*, see *Writer

Telecommunications

British Telecom operates the telephone and other telecommunications services, inland and abroad. It carries television signals from the studio to the broadcasting transmitters and provides circuits between local radio stations and transmitters. Satellite services are provided with other parts of the world. Services for private industry include: telex and fax, data processing and video conferencing to name only a few.

Mercury Communications now joins British Telecom in providing telephone and related services.

Opportunities for school and college leavers in telecommunications are minimal at present; any external recruitment is likely to be for very specialised posts requiring professionally qualified people to fill them.

Qualifications and Training

Telephonists need no formal educational qualifications and are trained on the job. Clerical assistants need GCSEs to include English and maths but those without GCSEs may take a written test instead. Draughtsmen should hold approved GCSEs or equivalent. Trainee technicians should have studied maths and science subjects to GCSE level or equivalent. Management entrants need two A levels (three H grade) and three GCSEs to include English. There are training facilities for graduates and, in some cases, for those with A levels at British Telecom's management college, college of engineering studies and computer school.

Personal Qualities

All staff who deal with the public need to be able to communicate clearly. Other staff require qualities pertaining to their particular job, eg management entrants need organisational and administrative skills.

Starting Salary

Salaries vary considerably but are commensurate with similar work in other fields.

Further Information

BT Head Office, 81 Newgate Street, London EC1A 7AJ; 0171 356 5000

Mercury Communications Ltd, Head Office: New Mercury House, 26 Red Lion Square, London WC1R 4HQ; 0171 528 2000

The Personnel Departments of local telephone area offices

Telephonist *see Receptionist, Telecommunications*

Telephonists are needed in virtually every commercial organisation. The job entails taking calls on a small switchboard with only a few extensions to working in a large organisation with literally hundreds of telephones in constant use. In addition, of course, there are telephonists who work for British Telecom, routeing the operator calls, the enquiries, the complaints and so on, as well as coping with the numerous emergency 999 calls received daily.

In the business world the telephonist plays an important role; she/he is the first person in the firm to whom a prospective client may speak and first impressions of how a business is run are crucial.

The telephonist may frequently be asked to put through overseas calls for busy managerial staff and may be responsible for making sure that the telephone books and relevant number lists (including those needed in an emergency) are available when needed. In some firms the telephonist manages a switchboard and also acts as a receptionist in the front office.

Qualifications and Training

Some telephonists employed in commerce have been British Telecom trained. No rigid academic qualifications are demanded; candidates must pass specific aptitude tests before they are accepted. Other telephonists may be trained on the job by their firms.

Personal Qualities

Good hearing and a clear speaking voice are important. Patience and an even temper are essential to cope with difficult or confused callers.

Starting Salary

BT salaries range from £5000+ at 16 to about £10,000.

Further Information

The Personnel Department of local telephone area offices
Local Jobcentres and Careers Offices

Television*, see *Broadcasting

Thatcher

Thatchers are self-employed craftsmen who thatch houses, pubs, barns and summerhouses with long straw, Devon wheat straw or Norfolk reed. A thatched roof gives good insulation against heat and cold and lasts 10 to 50 years. A roof is thatched by taking off the old thatch and then pegging down layers of new straw or reed. A four-bedroom house, for example, would take a master thatcher and two apprentices about eight weeks to complete.

Qualifications and Training

Academic qualifications are not essential. Thatching can be learned on the job as an apprentice to a master thatcher. Training takes four to five years and may be supervised by a local government training officer or by the Rural Development Commission which also provides a series of short courses to supplement training.

Personal Qualities

Thatchers need to be robust, good with their hands and not mind bad weather or heights. They also need common sense, the ability to take decisions and deal with customers.

Starting Salary

About £65–£75 a week as an apprentice, thereafter depending on amount of work and individual charges.

Further Information

National Council of Master Thatchers Association, Thatcher's Rest, Levens Green, Great Munden, Nr Ware, Hertfordshire, SG11 1HD

National Society of Master Thatchers, 20 The Laurels, Tetsworth, Thame, Oxfordshire OX9 7BH; 01844 281568

Training and Productivity Section, Rural Development Commission, 141 Castle Street, Salisbury, Wiltshire SP1 3TP; 01722 336255

The Thatcher's Craft, Rural Development Commission

Theatre *see Actor*

Theatre comprises much more than the actors and directors who receive publicity. Many other people are involved in a theatrical production. Lighting and sound effects are created and handled by electricians; scenery and props are built, arranged and moved by technicians; the practical aspects of the production are organised and run by the stage manager and his or her assistants. The designer creates the sets; the wardrobe mistress makes the costumes and the director or producer is responsible for the production as a whole. Other staff include publicity officer, house manager and box office staff.

Producer

The producer chooses the play, rents the theatre, engages the director and actors and is responsible for paying the bills. He/she has to raise the money for the production.

Qualifications and Training

None; but university-based drama experience is useful. Producers sometimes take assistants.

Personal Qualities

Tact, persuasiveness, sound business sense, flair for organisation and knowledge of what 'sells' in the theatre are all necessary.

Director

The director is in charge of the actors, dancers, designers, singers and technicians. He/she must work within the managerial brief and, in consultation with the producer and playwright, be responsible for casting. The director's main work is in taking rehearsals and in turning the play into a theatrical production. The casting director auditions actors and arranges financial details with the actors and their agents.

Qualifications and Training

A thorough grounding in dramatic arts is essential. A degree in drama is useful. There are a few trainee director posts, mostly under the auspices of the Arts Council. Directors will have had extensive experience of the theatre, probably as stage managers or actors. Some directors come to the theatre from film or television, which also offer training.

Personal Qualities

Directors need creativity, strong character, the ability to direct and weld together a team of people and a strong sense of the theatre. The casting director needs tact and the ability to cope with crises.

Designer

The designer is responsible for sets and costumes and works closely with the director. He/she produces drawings of sets and costumes for the scenery and costume departments to work from, also scale models of the sets.

Qualifications and Training
Most designers will complete a full-time art and design course.

Personal Qualities
The designer needs a thorough knowledge of period settings and costumes, and what looks effective on stage, also a sense of style, an ability to work within a budget and adapt to a variety of stage shapes.

Stage Manager
The stage manager is responsible for the smooth running of rehearsals and productions. It is his/her job to ensure that properties and costumes are ready when required, that actors know when they are needed, to supervise lighting, scene-making and scene changes and to be responsible for effects, music, curtain calls and prompting. A stage manager will often have assistants (ASMs) and scene shifters. Stage managers may sometimes become producers or directors.

Qualifications and Training
A full-time stage management course is provided at drama school for one to two years.

Personal Qualities
Managers need organising ability, tact, calmness in a crisis, a good memory, an eye for detail, a practical approach and an interest in the literary and technical aspects of theatrical production.

Lighting Designer
The theatre electrician may be in sole charge of the lighting or, in a large company with sophisticated equipment, be part of a team headed by an expert who will design a lighting plan. Appropriate electrician qualifications are needed.

Production Staff
A large theatre may have a series of production workshops; smaller theatres may combine several jobs in one.

Armoury: the armoury is responsible for making armour or weapons, for special effects like gunfire and shells, and for decorative metalwork. The members of the team are experts, eg gunsmith.

Metal workshop: here the heavy metalwork is designed and manufactured, eg for steel supports and complex trees. A welding qualification is useful.

Carpenters' workshop: technical drawing and carpentry skills come in useful for building sets. RADA offers a course for theatre carpentry.

Paint workshop: this is where the sets are painted. Knowing how to create the right textures and effects is part of the scene painter's skill.

Property-making shop: properties are often bought but in many productions the props have to be specially made, eg a throne or special upholstery. An enthusiasm for research and an eye for detail are needed.

Wardrobe and wigs: although costumes and wigs may be hired, many are made by the wardrobe department. A good knowledge of period fashion and skills in dressmaking and tailoring are needed. Casual help is also needed when there is much sewing for a new production. Special hats are usually produced by a freelance milliner. Accessory making is another specialist job, as is wig- and beard-making for which a City and Guilds certificate is a useful qualification. The wardrobe department is also responsible for looking after costumes and repairing and cleaning them.

Qualifications and Training

NVQs are available at levels 1, 2 and 3 for theatre technicians.

Box Office

The box office is in charge of ticket sales. The manager is responsible for promotion and marketing, for hiring his or her staff and for checking the takings. Experience of accounts or general management is useful. This office makes a good starting place for anyone interested in arts administration.

Press Office

This department deals with all publicity. It liaises with the press, arranges for photosessions and interviews, produces posters, advertisements and mails leaflets and programmes. An arts graduate with secretarial training may find work here. Tact, self-confidence and a pleasant voice are useful qualities.

Theatrical Agent

Agents try to find work for the actors and actresses on their books. Experience and good contacts are essential. Payment is usually 10 to 15 per cent of the client's fee.

Starting Salary

Salaries in the theatre are not high. Design staff, when qualified, should receive £10,000+, production staff too when trained. Office staff receive £130+ a week.

Further Information

Royal Academy of Dramatic Art (RADA), 62 Gower Street, London WC1E 6ED; 0171 636 7076

Careers in the Theatre, Kogan Page

Theatrical Agent*, see *Theatre

Therapist*, see *Art Therapist, Dental Therapist (Dentistry), Drama Therapist, Music Therapist, Occupational Therapist, Physiotherapist, Speech and Language Therapist

Toolmaker

Toolmakers work in engineering making a wide range of jigs, used to guide cutting tools and to hold the work in position; fixtures, to hold metal for bending or welding or to hold parts together; press tools in different shapes and sizes for cutting parts; mould tools to make items such as fridge interiors; and measuring gauges. Toolmaker machinists make the tools, often specialising in just one kind. Toolmaker fitters work on large structures that are constructed from many parts. They check all the parts, number them and then fit them together.

Qualifications and Training

Formal educational requirements are not essential but GCSE grade E (or equivalent) in English, maths and a science are recommended, particularly for those who want to take the BTEC certificate course. BTEC higher certificate courses are available for those with a certificate or with education to A level standard in maths and a science. Training is on the job by three-year apprenticeship; time off is allowed for course attendance leading to City and Guilds or BTEC qualifications.

Personal Qualities

Toolmakers must be deft and accurate in their work. Toolmaker fitters must be capable of reading technical drawings.

Starting Salary

About £75–£80 a week at 16, and over £200 when trained.

Further Information

Engineering Careers Information Service, 41 Clarendon Road, Watford, Hertfordshire WD1 1LB; 01923 238441

Local Jobcentres and Careers Offices

Tourist Information Officer

They work for national or regional boards with the aim of trying to attract visitors to Britain or to a particular region. They provide information, often in the form of brochures, and are responsible for placing advertisements. They keep a watchful eye on standards and visit hotels, tourist attractions, transport and travel organisations. They are also involved in research work, assessing future trends and needs.

Qualifications and Training

Qualifications vary; some entrants begin as clerks and work their way up to higher positions. Clerks should have a good general education, preferably with GCSEs or equivalent.

NVQ qualifications are available, awarded by the Association of British Travel Agents (ABTA), National Training Board (NTB) and City and Guilds (C & G).

There are college courses available leading to BTEC NC or ND awards. To take a BTEC HND course in business studies with a major option in travel and tourism, three GCSEs and one A level or equivalents are necessary.

Degrees in travel and tourism are available, and also one-year full-time postgraduate courses leading to an MSc or diploma in tourism.

Personal Qualities

Tourist information officers must enjoy working with the general public, and adopt a responsible and helpful attitude in the giving of information. A friendly personality and good administrative skills are useful.

Starting Salary

£5000+ at 16 with GCSEs, managers' salaries from £10,000 upwards.

Further Information

The Travel Training Company, The Cornerstone, The Broadway, Woking, Surrey GU21 5AR; 01483 727321 (*send sae*)

Institute of Travel and Tourism, 113 Victoria Street, St Albans, Hertfordshire AL1 3TJ; 01727 854395

National and local tourist boards

Careers in the Travel Industry, Kogan Page

Tour Operator

Tour operators arrange holidays for travellers in this country and abroad. Some operators deal mainly with traditional package holidays based at one or two resorts, others are involved with specialist holidays such as trekking or adventure. Holidays are sold to the public directly or by means of a travel agent. Operators may provide couriers and representatives to look after holidaymakers and deal with any problems. Many of the staff are office based, dealing with bookings, accounts and administration, but there are opportunities for some employees to go abroad. They may check areas where new holidays are proposed or visit hotels and resorts already in use.

Qualifications and Training

NVQs are available, awarded by the Association of British Travel Agents' National Training Board (ABTA–NTB) and City and Guilds (C&G).

Personal Qualities

Tour operators must be good at dealing with people, have imagination, administrative and organisational skills. Foreign languages are an asset.

Starting Salary

Salaries vary according to job and position; a junior clerk would begin at £5000+ and a graduate at £10,000+.

Further Information

Institute of Travel and Tourism, 113 Victoria Street, St Albans, Hertfordshire AL1 3TJ; 01727 854395

Careers in the Travel Industry, Kogan Page

Town and Country Planner

Town and country planners are concerned with reconciling the needs of the population for buildings, shopping centres, schools, leisure centres etc with the necessity of preserving and enhancing the natural and built environment. Planners are involved in collecting information about the present use of land, the position of roads and other features, as well as drawing up plans for new schemes. Planners in development control ensure that buildings or developments intended for a particular area are suitable and do not conflict with existing buildings or the surrounding environment. Planners work for local and central government, environmental charities and to a lesser, but increasing, extent in private practice. There are also varied opportunities for planning support staff.

Qualifications and Training

To enter a degree or diploma course in town planning, five GCSE passes and two A levels are desirable. Useful subjects are maths, English language, geography and history or a foreign language. Those with accredited degrees or diplomas in town planning are exempt from the examinations of the Royal Town Planning Institute. Planning courses are available at undergraduate and postgraduate levels, full time and part time and on a distance learning basis.

Technicians need four GCSEs or equivalent to include maths, English and preferably the subjects mentioned above. A number of colleges offer courses for technicians on a part-time or block release basis. Qualifications gained are the BTEC certificate, higher certificate or higher diploma in administration or the SCOTVEC certificate or higher certificate in planning. N/SVQs are being developed for support staff.

Personal Qualities

Town planners and support staff need to have a knowledge of many subjects: economics, sociology, architecture and geography. Planners must be able to work as a team and cooperate with experts in other subjects. They must have imagination and an interest in and understanding of both people and the environment.

Starting Salary

Qualified planners about £11,000–£13,000, support staff £7000–£9000 upwards depending upon qualifications.

Further Information

The Royal Town Planning Institute, 26 Portland Place, London W1N 4BE; 0171 636 9107

Society of Town Planning Technicians (*address as above*)

Trading Standards Officer

These officers are employed within local government with the responsibility to enforce a very wide range of legislation aimed at protecting the consumer and honest trader. Laws relate to such diverse subjects as metrology, food and consumer product safety, credit, descriptions of goods and services, prices, animal health and welfare. While most operations are carried out by random inspectional work, officers are also required to investigate complaints and where appropriate it may be necessary to pursue matters to Court.

Qualifications and Training

The principal qualification is the diploma in trading standards (DTS) which may be obtained via a block release course or with an additional examination added to specified honours degree courses in consumer protection. Entrants to the former course will require five GCSE/SCE passes, (two at A level or three at H level), to include English, mathematics and physics (with certain alternatives). Training will take three years and will include on-the-job experience. A further qualification which pays specific attention to specialised working practices is the diploma in consumer affairs (DCA). This examination demands an entrance of five GCSEs to include English and the normal training programme takes two years.

Personal Qualities

Officers will need to be able to apply their training and knowledge in a fair, open and common-sense manner. An ability to communicate clearly; to appreciate the demands of business; to ensure consumers are not deprived of their legal rights, are all component parts of the duties. The wide variety of interests provided by the job is frequently quoted as a main attraction.

Starting Salary

Trainees may expect to earn up to £9000 per annum and on full qualification this can rise to £14,000.

Further Information

Institute of Trading Standards Administration, 3–5 Hadleigh Business Centre, 351 London Road, Hadleigh, Essex SS7 2BT; 01702 559922

Local Government Opportunities, The LGMB, Layden House, 76–86 Turnmill Street, London EC1M 5QU; 0171 296 6600 (*for exam details*)

Traffic Warden

Traffic wardens are civilians who work in conjunction with local police forces. They check parking meters and penalise those parking on double yellow lines or other illegal places. They may also be required to do school crossing patrols or traffic control duty, as well as receiving vehicles towed into the police pound, and looking out for out-of-date car licences.

Qualifications and Training
No formal educational requirements are necessary; training is on the job.

Personal Qualities
Traffic wardens must be responsible, self-confident, good communicators and must possess good health and eyesight.

Starting Salary
This varies according to area, ranging from about £10,500; wardens in inner London receive more.

Further Information
Local police forces

Metropolitan Police Service, Recruitment & Selection Centre, 26 Aybrook Street, London W1M 3JL; 0171 224 7232

Training Officer

Training officers work in medium-sized firms and organisations, national and local government, emergency services and countless voluntary organisations. They are responsible for identifying training requirements, designing training programmes, delivering training to individuals or groups and evaluating the success of training.

Qualifications and Training
There are a lot of short courses for those interested in training but, for those interested in making training a career, a professional qualification is advisable. The Institute of Personnel and Development (IPD) offers a certificate in training practice for those new to or with limited experience in training and gives associate membership (AssocIPD) of the IPD. The IPD also offers higher level qualifications at licentiate and graduate membership levels. N/SVQs in training and development at levels 3, 4 and a level 5 are available. Candidates who successfully complete an N/SVQ level 3 in training and development can apply for associate membership with the IPD and those who complete level 4 can apply for licentiate membership. Those who complete level 5 can apply for graduate membership.

Personal Qualities
Training officers should have good communication, presentation, diagnostic, organisational and negotiation skills. They need to be able to set realistic targets, meet deadlines and plan ahead.

Starting Salary
Trainees about £12,500; when qualified over £20,000.

Further Information
The Institute of Personnel and Development, IPD House, Camp Road, London SW19 4UX; 0181 971 9000; Fax: 0181 263 3333 *(IPD qualifications and membership information as well as a career pack)*
Course information – Professional Education Department; 0181 263 3307

Translator

Translators either work freelance from home or as staff translators. They should only translate from another language into their mother tongue. The work varies from the translation of whole books for publishing houses, to business letters and documents. Translators, particularly those who specialise in literary work, must be able to express themselves well. In areas where the subject matter of the text is specialised, for example computing, mathematics, or sports such as mountaineering, expert knowledge is required of the translator. Broad-based general knowledge is always an advantage. Translators may be responsible for finding their own work and/or may be registered with translation companies or agencies.

Qualifications and Training
Proficiency in a language other than one's own is necessary, plus the ability to write well in one's native language. An understanding of the culture of the country/ies of the language is important. The ability to use a word processor or personal computer is essential, as is access to a fax machine. Most translators today have a postgraduate qualification in translation or the Institute of Linguists diploma in translation.

Personal Qualities
Translators must be meticulous, conscientious, creative and persistent. They must be prepared to do some research if necessary.

Starting Salary
Translators are usually paid per 1000 words. Average freelance rates

into/from English: French, Spanish, Italian £58/£56; German, Dutch, Greek, Portuguese and Scandinavian Languages £55/£65; Russian and other Slavonic Languages £62/£69; Others £67; Japanese £100/£100; Chinese, £140/£150.

Staff translators earn on average from £15,500 to £24,000 pa (depending on experience and location).

Further Information

The Institute of Linguists, 24a Highbury Grove, London N5 2EA; 0171 359 7445

Institute of Translating and Interpreting, 377 City Road, London EC1V 1NA; 0171 713 7600

The Translators Association, 84 Drayton Gardens, London SW10 9SB; 0171 373 6642 (*for published literary translators*)

Careers Using Languages, Kogan Page

Transport Engineering*, see *Engineering

Travel Agent

Travel agents sell tickets for travel by air, land and sea on behalf of transport organisations. They make hotel bookings for individual travellers, business people or holidaymakers. Some travel companies deal only with business travel and are involved too in arranging conferences and trade fairs. However, the area in which the travel agent is largely known is the selling of package holidays on behalf of tour operators. Many travel agents will also advise travellers on matters such as visas, foreign currency and necessary injections.

Qualifications and Training

NVQ qualifications are available, awarded by the Association of British Travel Agents' National Training Board (ABTA–NTB) and City and Guilds (C&G).

Personal Qualities

Travel agents must enjoy dealing with the general public, have a responsible attitude regarding the accuracy of information given and good administrative skills.

Starting Salary

Varies according to job; clerks earn £5000+, managers £10,000+.

Further Information

ABTA, The Travel Training Company, The Cornerstone, The Broadway, Woking, Surrey GU21 5AR; 01483 727321

Institute of Travel and Tourism, 113 Victoria Street, St Albans, Hertfordshire AL1 3TJ; 01727 854395

Careers in the Travel Industry, Kogan Page

Trichologist

Trichologists treat hair and scalp disorders, the most common being hair loss. Electrical and heat treatments are used, massage and special lotions and ointments. Trichologists practise on their own behalf; some of their patients are referred to them from doctors but trichology is not available on the National Health Service.

Qualifications and Training

Basic academic qualifications are necessary. Training may be by a three-year pupillage with a practising trichologist. The necessary theoretical instruction is available at technical colleges, evening classes or by correspondence. It is also necessary to have some practical experience of working in a recognised clinic.

Personal Qualities

Trichologists must understand the necessary biological principles, have a knowledge of nutrition, plus an interest in helping people. They must have high standards of personal hygiene.

Starting Salary

Dependent upon number of patients, hours worked and fees charged.

Further Information

Institute of Trichologists, 20–22 Queensberry Place, London SW7 2DZ; 0171 491 7253

Truck Driver,* see *Lorry Driver

Undertaker, see *Funeral Director*

Underwriter, see *Insurance*

Upholsterer *see Furniture and Furnishing*

Upholsterers measure up, prepare and fit the fabric components in all kinds of furniture. It is highly skilled work and includes not only the visible top coverings (which can vary from velvet to leather) but also the preparation and supports below, such as padding, stuffing, springing or webbing. Large furniture manufacturers employ upholsterers in their factories and there are also a fair number of smaller, often family-run, businesses which specialise in certain types of upholstery work. The job may entail anything from providing modern chairs, sofas and so on for large hotel chains to the restoration of unique pieces of antique furniture (in private homes or museums).

Qualifications and Training

No specific academic qualifications are required. Training combines on-the-job apprentice work with day release courses, leading to the City and Guilds diploma.

Personal Qualities

Upholsterers need to have nimble fingers and infinite patience and must enjoy working on individual projects.

Starting Salary

A 16-year-old trainee can expect to earn around £75 a week. A trained upholsterer would receive about £175.

Further Information

Local Jobcentres and Careers Offices

London Guildhall University, Old Castle Street, London E1 7NT; 0171 320 1000

V

Valuer *see Auctioneer, Surveyor/Surveying Technician*

Valuers are employed by a wide variety of firms to assess the worth of goods and property (including land, buildings, fine arts, chattels, machinery and livestock). They may work for building societies, estate agents, insurance companies, property companies or any commercial, financial or industrial organisation that has to know true commercial values for selling, renting, investment or taxation purposes. Some valuers are also surveyors, auctioneers or land agents.

Qualifications and Training

Professional qualifications are awarded by the Institute of Revenues, Rating and Valuation (IRRV) and the Incorporated Society of Valuers and Auctioneers (ISVA). The IRRV demands a minimum of one A level and four GCSEs (or two A levels and at least two GCSEs) including English and maths. The ISVA asks for five GCSE passes at A, B or C, including English and maths, three of which must have been gained at the same time. Training combines practical work with appropriate studies in a variety of available part-time, full-time and sandwich courses. There is also a correspondence course for the ISVA examinations.

Personal Qualities

A valuer needs discretion combined with aptitude to understand the various economic factors involved in commerce.

Starting Salary

Trainees £8000–£13,000 depending on age and qualifications, higher salaries being paid in London; £13,000–£19,000 when qualified.

Further Information

ISVA (The Incorporated Society of Valuers and Auctioneers), 3 Cadogan Gate, London SW1X 0AS; 0171 235 2282

The Institute of Revenues, Rating and Valuation, 41 Doughty Street, London WC1N 2LF; 0171 831 3505.

Vehicle Technician *see Garage Work, Road Transport*

Apart from working in garages, maintaining and repairing cars belonging to the general public, technicians are also employed to maintain heavy goods vehicles, buses and coaches owned by large road transport operators, motorcycles, agricultural machinery or 'performance' cars. The areas of work are varied, and also include the maintenance of aero engines and a number of jobs in industry, involved with machinery of all kinds.

Industry
Categories include: metal-working machine tools, industrial pumps, valves and compressors, textile machinery, construction and earth-moving equipment, office machinery, refrigeration machinery, industrial plant and steelwork. The machinery is designed by the mechanical engineer, and maintained by the technician.

Agriculture
As farming becomes increasingly mechanised, technicians are more in demand for the maintenance of such equipment as tractors, crop harvesters of all kinds, seed drills, even automated revolving milk parlours.

Qualifications and Training

16–17 year olds may embark upon a training scheme whereby different skills are learnt and tested. NVQs are now available for a range of vehicle technician occupations. There is a BTEC national certificate in mechanical engineering, and City and Guilds offer a course in three parts for mechanical engineering technicians.

Candidates for the BTEC HND course in mechanical and production engineering should be 18 and hold either the BTEC certificate or an A level in maths, chemistry or physics. Courses are for two years full time, or three years sandwich.

Personal Qualities

Mechanical aptitude, the ability to diagnose faults with the aid of a workshop manual and to work responsibly without supervision and undertake routine tasks.

Starting Salary

£65–£70 a week at the start of training (Stage 1), £130+ at Stage 3.

Further Information

Bus and Coach Training Ltd, Regency House, 43 High Street, Rickmansworth, Hertfordshire WD3 1ET; 01923 896607

The Institution of Mechanical Engineers, 1 Birdcage Walk, London SW1H 9JJ; 0171 222 7899
RTITB Services Ltd, York House, Empire Way, Wembley, Middlesex HA9 0RT; 0181 902 8880

Veterinary Nurse

They assist vets during operations and X-rays, sterilise instruments, look after animals recovering from surgery and keep the animals and their cages clean. In addition, a veterinary nurse will often act as receptionist, secretary and office clerk. As well as working for a private vet, there are opportunities to work for animal welfare organisations such as the RSPCA and the PDSA.

Qualifications and Training
Four GCSEs/SCE Standard grade passes at grades A, B or C are necessary, subjects to include English language and either a physical or biological science or maths. Training with an approved veterinary practice takes two years, and students must pass the Part 1 and 2 examinations before entry to the list of veterinary nurses. Day release, block release and evening courses are available to provide the necessary theory.

Personal Qualities
A love of animals is of course essential, plus patience, a calm manner and good health.

Starting Salary
£3000 for students; £5000–£9000 when qualified.

Further Information
British Veterinary Nursing Association (BVNA), Unit D12 Seedbed Centre, Coldharbour Road, Harlow, Essex CM19 5AF; 01279 450567
The Royal College of Veterinary Surgeons, Belgravia House, 62–64 Horseferry Road, London SW1P 2AF; 0171 222 2001
Careers Working with Animals, Kogan Page

Veterinary Surgeon

Most vets work in private practice, usually starting out as veterinary assistants and working their way up into a partnership or into their own business. Some specialise in small animal treatment (including pets such as dogs, cats, cage birds and so on), others work with particular kinds of animals (such as farm animals, race horses or the more exotic zoo animals). Other vets go into research or industry. The Ministry of Agriculture, for instance, employs a substantial number to work on disease control (monitoring such epidemics as foot and mouth or swine vesicular disease for instance). Others are employed by animal welfare organisations, such as the PDSA, in animal hospitals. Vets are also needed in the food processing industries where their job is concerned with checking that conditions are humane and hygienic.

Qualifications and Training

A veterinary surgeon must hold a degree from one of the six veterinary schools in the UK. The six universities offering the course set their own entrance requirements but all demand an extremely high standard with good A levels. Chemistry is essential, other subjects are: physics, maths, biology or zoology. The course lasts five years (six at Cambridge) and covers a formidable amount of academic and practical work, comparable to that involved in training to be a doctor.

Personal Qualities

Vets need sympathy combined with detachment, endless patience and physical fitness (particularly if dealing with larger animals). They must also be self-reliant and prepared to work anti-social hours. Some business sense and the ability to keep accounts are also important.

Starting Salary

Assistants (less than five years qualified) in general practice start at £14,000–£15,000, more than five years qualified £18,000–£25,000 (with a car and accommodation generally provided), partners earn £32,000–£37,000; government vets start at £20,000+.

Further Information

The British Veterinary Association, 7 Mansfield Street, London W1M 0AT; 0171 636 6541

The Royal College of Veterinary Surgeons, Belgravia House, 62–64 Horseferry Road, London SW1P 2AF; 0171 222 2001

A Career as a Veterinary Surgeon (The Royal College of Veterinary Surgeons, *£4.00 including postage and packing*)

Vision Mixer*, see *Broadcasting

Waiting, see *Catering and Accommodation Management, Hotel Work*

Warden, see *Caretaker, Leisure and Amenity Management, National Trust Work*

Watch and Clock Maker/Repairer

Watch and clock makers make timepieces by hand, sometimes to a design of their own.

Repairers receive watches and clocks from customers for servicing and repair. They must be able to examine a timepiece thoroughly for worn-out parts, clean and regulate a watch or clock, and repair or replace faulty parts. The work involves the use of precision tools and electronic equipment. Restoration is carried out on antique clocks and watches.

Qualifications and Training

A good general education is advisable, to include English, maths and physics. Preferably training is by five-year apprenticeship, some of which may be spent on full- or part-time courses, leading to the examinations of the British Horological Institute (BHI). These courses are held at a number of colleges. It is also possible to study for the BHI examinations by correspondence course. NVQs will be available in the future.

Personal Qualities

Applicants must have good eyesight, have the physical skill and patience to do the intricate work required, and be able to work on their own.

Starting Salary

About £60 a week at 16, and £110+ when qualified.

Further Information

The British Horological Institute, Upton Hall, Upton, Newark, Nottinghamshire NG23 5TE; 01636 813795

Water Engineering*, see *Engineering

Welder

Welders join pieces of metal together by applying intense heat and melting the edges so that two pieces become one. The sorts of things welded are: metal sections of aeroplanes, ships, oil rigs and power turbines. Welders work in light and heavy engineering firms, in foundry work and in shipbuilding.

Qualifications and Training

Formal academic qualifications are not necessary but GCSEs in English, maths and a science are preferred, and it is necessary to take the BTEC certificate. Training is on the job by three-year apprenticeship with time off allowed to attend courses leading to NVQs awarded jointly by City and Guilds, BTEC, the Engineering Training Authority (ENTRA) and the Marine and Engineering Training Association (META).

Welders engaged in very important work such as for the Ministry of Defence are required to take quality tests every six months.

Personal Qualities

A welder must have a steady hand and excellent powers of concentration. Workers must be careful and follow safety instructions as the work is potentially dangerous.

Starting Salary

About £80 a week at 16, £260 with experience.

Further Information

Engineering Training Authority (ENTRA), 41 Clarendon Road, Watford, Hertfordshire WD1 1LB; 01923 238441

The Marine and Engineering Training Association (META), Rycote Place, 30–38 Cambridge Street, Aylesbury, Buckinghamshire HP20 1RS; 01296 434943

Welding Institute, Abington Hall, Abington, Cambridge CB1 6AL; 01223 891162

Wholesaling

Wholesalers buy in goods from manufacturers then sell them to a number of smaller customers (or retailers). The advantage to the manufacturer is that he has only to deliver to a few specific points. Wholesalers tend to specialise in particular types of goods such as books, garden equipment and costume jewellery.

There is a variety of staff employed in wholesaling: clerks, accounts staff, buyers, managers, storekeepers and drivers.

Qualifications and Training

These vary depending on the type of job. Many of the managerial positions are filled by people who have worked their way up. Entrants may work towards NVQs, levels 1 and 2.

Personal Qualities

Staff employed in wholesaling must be speedy, efficient and reliable.

Starting Salary

Salaries are commensurate with those paid for similar work in other industries, eg £5000+ for a junior clerk, and about £11,000 for managerial staff. London salaries are generally considerably higher.

Further Information

Local Jobcentres and Careers Offices

Window Dresser

Window display covers window arrangements as well as displays inside a big store, eg an arrangement in the ladies' fashion department. Display managers and buyers have considerable authority in deciding what is to be displayed.

Junior window dressers start by assisting seniors and will probably be assigned periodically to different kinds of merchandise, eg household goods and china as well as clothes. Freelances may also be employed part time to dress windows. In small specialist shops, members of staff will probably be responsible for all the window displays.

Qualifications and Training

Three GCSEs (grades A, B or C), including English and art, are necessary for a two-year full-time course leading to the British Display

Society's advanced diploma; or a one-year full-time course may be taken, leading to the general certificate. There are BTEC awards in vocational art and design. Some companies have their own training schemes which are intended to supplement the college training but not to replace it. A degree in art and design is valuable for the top jobs.

Personal Qualities

Dressers must have an interest in art and fashion and skill in handling materials; they should have an appreciation of colour, design and texture. They must have an understanding of sales techniques, be resourceful and have the ability to produce scale drawings.

Starting Salary

£7500–£9000 with training.

Further Information

Local Jobcentres and Careers Offices

Wine Trade

The wine trade has grown beyond the small merchant or importer and most opportunities are with the large companies which import, retail and deal with the licensed trade, hotels and catering, off-licences, supermarkets and multiple stores. There are posts in marketing, advertising, packaging, promotion, market research, buying and quality control.

Qualifications and Training

Opportunities exist at GCSE, A and degree level for entry into the wine trade. The Wine and Spirit Education Trust (a registered educational charity set up by the drinks industry) offers courses and qualifications.

Personal Qualities

These depend on the area entered, but a love and knowledge of wine are obviously important, plus relevant knowledge about the chief wine growing areas – type of soil, climate etc.

Starting Salary

Dependent upon position and experience, but commensurate with salaries in other industries for a similar job, such as in advertising or quality control.

Further Information

Wine and Spirit Education Trust, Five Kings House, 1 Queen Street Place, London EC4R 3AJ; 0171 236 3551; Fax: 0171 329 8712

Harpers Wine & Spirit Gazette, Harling House, 47 Great Suffolk Street, London SE1 1RQ (*job advertisements*)

Work Study Practitioner *see Organisation and Methods Work*

The practitioner is involved in the detailed study of work practices in order to measure and improve the way work is carried out and to advise on the most efficient use of resources. Practitioners provide data to aid management in its planning, staffing and control functions. They may work in industrial, commercial, government or public-sector organisations.

Qualifications and Training

Practical on-the-job experience is combined with study for the examinations of the Institute of Management Services. A BTEC national award in business studies or alternatively A levels or good GCSEs are needed.

The City and Guilds sets examinations for a certificate in work study and several colleges offer this course, either part time or full time.

The Institute of Administrative Management offers a certificate and diploma in administrative management with sections covering organisation and methods. Many practitioners have degrees or higher technical qualifications.

Personal Qualities

Practitioners must be tactful, self-confident and able to withstand criticism. They should be able to communicate, be numerate and have clear-thinking, analytical minds.

Starting Salary

£12,000 upwards, depending on educational qualifications and previous experience.

Further Information

The Institute of Administrative Management, 40 Chatsworth Parade, Petts Wood, Orpington, Kent BR5 1RW; 01689 875555

Institute of Management Consultants, 32–33 Hatton Garden, London EC1N 8DL; 0171 242 2140

The Institute of Management Services, 1 Cecil Court, London Road, Enfield, Middlesex EN2 6DD; 0181 366 1261

Writer *see Journalist*

Some authors do exist solely on the proceeds of their writing, but for many it is a part-time occupation, additional to a full-time job. The field of creative writing is probably the most difficult in which to succeed. It is also the area which contains some of the best-known writers, the authors of popular fiction best sellers.

It is probably slightly easier to make a living by non-fiction writing: writing on a specialist subject, textbook writing and technical writing.

There are a few posts as writer in residence, where writers work for regional authorities developing writing projects with people living in that region.

Journalists have been dealt with elsewhere. There are opportunities, however, of a journalistic nature for non-journalists. Writers may contribute to specialist journals or submit short stories to magazines interested in fiction.

Qualifications and Training

Generally writers are born, not made. However, it is possible to take courses in both creative and technical writing.

Personal Qualities

Writers must be self-disciplined, able to work on their own, highly motivated and persevering.

Starting Salary

Earnings vary enormously, but the majority of writers do not support themselves by their writing alone. Writers in residence can expect about £10,000–£12,000.

Further Information

Institute of Scientific and Technical Communicators, Kings Court, 2–16 Goodge Street, London W1P 1FF; 0171 436 4425

Society of Authors, 84 Drayton Gardens, London SW10 9SB; 0171 373 6642

Youth and Community Worker *see Social Work*

Youth and community workers work in a range of settings including youth clubs, schools, colleges, community centres and specialist agencies such as those offering information, advice and counselling. Some workers also work in mobile centres and with young people on the streets and in cafés. The majority of youth and community workers are either part time or unpaid.

The aim of youth workers is the informal education and social development of those with whom they work and is accomplished through work with individuals, work with and in groups, and with communities.

In Scotland, youth and community work is combined with adult education under the generic term 'community education'.

Qualifications and Training

Various routes to a recognised qualification, including an NVQ award, exist. These include full- and part-time courses of study, postgraduate courses, and employment-based apprenticeship schemes. (Courses are available at a number of educational institutions and details of these can be obtained from the National Youth Agency. Details of training and employment in Scotland can be obtained from the Scottish Community Education Council.)

Applicants are normally at least 21 years old, although some institutions set higher and lower age limits, and applicants are usually expected to have substantial experience of work with young people or adults. This can be paid or unpaid. Mature entrants may be accepted without formal academic qualifications.

Personal Qualities

An interest in and understanding of the issues that affect people's lives, plus patience, stamina and a sense of humour are all qualities demanded of youth and community workers.

Starting Salary

Ranges from £11,500+ to £21,500+.

Further Information

The National Youth Agency Guide to Initial Training Courses in Youth and Community Work (National Youth Agency, *£3.95*)

NYA Guide to Becoming a Youth Worker (National Youth Agency, *£1*)

What is the Youth Service? (National Youth Agency, *£1*)

The National Youth Agency, 17–23 Albion Street, Leicester LE1 6GD; 0116 285 6789

Scottish Community Education Council, Rosebery House, 9 Haymarket Terrace, Edinburgh EH12 5EZ; 0131 313 2488

Z

Zoo Keeper

Keepers look after animals in zoos, mucking out their living quarters, preparing their food and feeding them. They work long hours – from 8am to as late as 7pm – much of the time outdoors and the work is often physically demanding.

Qualifications and Training

No specific school-leaving qualifications are asked for and training is on the job and by a correspondence course followed by a City and Guilds qualification. So far the NVQ qualifications in animal care have not been adopted by zoos. Unfortunately, applications for such jobs far exceed the number of places available, and zoos prefer people to enquire only when a vacancy is advertised.

Personal Qualities

Affection and respect for animals, combined with an unsentimental approach, are essential.

Starting Salary

Applicants should apply to individual zoos. Salaries range from about £5000+ to £12,000+.

Further Information

The Association of British Wild Animal Keepers, 12 Tackley Road, Eastville, Bristol BS5 6UQ (*sae required*)

Careers Working with Animals, Kogan Page

Zoologist

Most zoologists work in either research or teaching; a very small number find jobs in industry, mainly in pharmaceutical and animal food-stuff companies. Research zoologists will probably work in one of the many government-backed centres on a variety of projects including animal behaviour, pest control and the population ecology of birds.

Qualifications and Training
A degree in zoology, available at most universities, is needed for a career as a zoologist. Postgraduate training in specialisations such as entomology or nematology is also available.

Personal Qualities
Zoologists should have a scientific mind and a bent for research.

Starting Salary
£12,000 upwards.

Further Information
Careers in Biology (The Institute of Biology, 20–22 Queensberry Place, London SW7 2DZ; *send £3.90*)

Useful Addresses

Business and Technology Education Council (BTEC), Central House, Upper Woburn Place, London WC1H 0HE; 0171 413 8400

City and Guilds of London Institute, 1 Giltspur Street, London EC1A 9DD; 0171 294 2468

Department for Education, Sanctuary Buildings, Great Smith Street, London SW1P 3BT; 0171 925 5000

Further Education Information Officer, (*address as above*)

The London Chamber of Commerce and Industry Examinations Board (LCCIEB), Marlowe House, Station Road, Sidcup, Kent DA15 7BJ; 0181 302 0261

The National Council for Vocational Qualifications, 222 Euston Road, London NW1 2BZ; 0171 387 9898

Northern Ireland Department of Education, Rathgael House, Balloo Road, Bangor, Co Down BT19 7PR; 01247 279000

Pitman Examinations Institute, 1 Giltspur Street, London EC1; 0541 561 061

RSA Examinations Board, Westwood Way, Coventry CV4 8HS; 01203 470033

Scottish Education Department, 43 Jeffrey Street, Edinburgh EH1 1DN; 0131 556 8400

Scottish Home and Health Department (*address as above*)

Scottish Vocational Education Council (*SCOTVEC*), 24 Douglas Street, Glasgow G2 7NQ; 0141 248 7900

Index